Praise for Design Patterns in Ruby

"*Design Patterns in Ruby* documents smart ways to resolve many problems that Ruby developers commonly encounter. Russ Olsen has done a great job of selecting classic patterns and augmenting these with newer patterns that have special relevance for Ruby. He clearly explains each idea, making a wealth of experience available to Ruby developers for their own daily work."

—Steve Metsker, Managing Consultant with Dominion Digital, Inc.

"This book provides a great demonstration of the key 'Gang of Four' design patterns without resorting to overly technical explanations. Written in a precise, yet almost informal style, this book covers enough ground that even those without prior exposure to design patterns will soon feel confident applying them using Ruby. Olsen has done a great job to make a book about a classically 'dry' subject into such an engaging and even occasionally humorous read."

—Peter Cooper

"This book renewed my interest in understanding patterns after a decade of good intentions. Russ picked the most useful patterns for Ruby and introduced them in a straightforward and logical manner, going beyond the GoF's patterns. This book has improved my use of Ruby, and encouraged me to blow off the dust covering the GoF book."

—Mike Stok

"*Design Patterns in Ruby* is a great way for programmers from statically typed object-oriented languages to learn how design patterns appear in a more dynamic, flexible language like Ruby."

—Rob Sanheim, Ruby Ninja, Relevance

DESIGN PATTERNS IN RUBY

Addison-Wesley Professional Ruby Series

Obie Fernandez, Series Editor

The Addison-Wesley Professional Ruby Series provides readers with practical, people-oriented, and in-depth information about applying the Ruby platform to create dynamic technology solutions. The series is based on the premise that the need for expert reference books, written by experienced practitioners, will never be satisfied solely by blogs and the Internet.

Books currently in the series

RailsSpace: Building a Social Networking Website with Ruby on Rails™
Michael Hartl, Aurelius Prochazka • 0321480791 • ©2008

The Ruby Way: Solutions and Techniques in Ruby Programming, Second Edition
Hal Fulton • 0672328844 • ©2007

Professional Ruby Collection: Mongrel, Rails Plugins, Rails Routing, Refactoring to REST, and Rubyisms CD1
James Adam, David A. Black, Trotter Cashion, Jacob Harris, Matt Pelletier, Zed Shaw
0132417995 • ©2007

The Rails Way
Obie Fernandez • 0321445619 • ©2008

Mongrel: Developing, Extending and Deploying Your Ruby Applications   *Coming Spring 2008*
Zed Shaw • 0321503090 • ©2008

Short Cuts

Rails Routing
David A. Black • 0321509242 • ©2007

Rails Refactoring to Resources: Using CRUD and REST in Your Rails Application
Trotter Cashion • 0321501748 • ©2007

Mongrel: Serving, Deploying and Extending Your Ruby Applications
Matt Pelletier and Zed Shaw • 0321483502 • ©2007

Rails Plugins: Extending Rails Beyond the Core
James Adam • 0321483510 • ©2007

Rubyism in Rails
Jacob Harris • 0321474074 • ©2007

Troubleshooting Ruby Processes: Leveraging System Tools when the Usual Ruby Tricks Stop Working
Philippe Hanrigou • 0321544684 • ©2008

Writing Efficient Ruby Code
Dr. Stefan Kaes • 0321540034 • ©2008

Video

RailsSpace Ruby on Rails Tutorial (Video LiveLessons)
Aurelius Prochazka • 0321517067 • ©2008

www.awprofessional.com/ruby

DESIGN PATTERNS IN RUBY

Russ Olsen

✦✦ Addison-Wesley

Upper Saddle River, NJ • Boston • Indianapolis • San Francisco
New York • Toronto • Montreal • London • Munich • Paris • Madrid
Capetown • Sydney • Tokyo • Singapore • Mexico City

Many of the designations used by manufacturers and sellers to distinguish their products are claimed as trademarks. Where those designations appear in this book, and the publisher was aware of a trademark claim, the designations have been printed with initial capital letters or in all capitals.

The author and publisher have taken care in the preparation of this book, but make no expressed or implied warranty of any kind and assume no responsibility for errors or omissions. No liability is assumed for incidental or consequential damages in connection with or arising out of the use of the information or programs contained herein.

The publisher offers excellent discounts on this book when ordered in quantity for bulk purchases or special sales, which may include electronic versions and/or custom covers and content particular to your business, training goals, marketing focus, and branding interests. For more information, please contact:

U.S. Corporate and Government Sales
(800) 382-3419
corpsales@pearsontechgroup.com

For sales outside the United States please contact:

International Sales
international@pearsoned.com

 This Book Is Safari Enabled

The Safari® Enabled icon on the cover of your favorite technology book means the book is available through Safari Bookshelf. When you buy this book, you get free access to the online edition for 45 days.

Safari Bookshelf is an electronic reference library that lets you easily search thousands of technical books, find code samples, download chapters, and access technical information whenever and wherever you need it.

To gain 45-day Safari Enabled access to this book:

- Go to http://www.awprofessional.com/safarienabled
- Complete the brief registration form
- Enter the coupon code CPJF-9RBK-LP1S-JCK1-NLRA

If you have difficulty registering on Safari Bookshelf or accessing the online edition, please e-mail customer-service@safaribooksonline.com.

Visit us on the Web: www.awprofessional.com

Library of Congress Cataloging-in-Publication Data

Olsen, Russ.
    Design patterns in Ruby/Russ Olsen.
        p. cm.
    Includes index.
    ISBN 978-0-321-49045-2 (hbk. : alk. paper)
    1. Ruby on rails (Electronic resource)   2. Software patterns.   I. Title.

    QA76.64.O456 2007
    005.1'17—dc22

                                            2007039642

ISBN-13: 978-0-321-29045-2
ISBN-10:   0-321-49045-2

Text printed in the United States on recycled paper at Courier in Westford, Massachusetts.
First printing, December 2007

Editor-in-Chief: Karen Gettman
Acquisitions Editor: Chris Guzikowski
Managing Editor: John Fuller

Project Editor: Lara Wysong
Copy Editor: Jill Hobbs
Indexer: Ted Laux

Proofreader: Deborah Prato
Composition: International Typesetting and Composition

For Karen,
who makes it all possible,

and Jackson,
who makes it all worthwhile.

Contents

Foreword   xvii

Preface   xix

Acknowledgments   xxv

About the Author   xxvii

PART I: Patterns and Ruby   1

Chapter 1: Building Better Programs with Patterns   3

The Gang of Four   4

Patterns for Patterns   4

    Separate Out the Things That Change from Those That Stay the Same   5

    Program to an Interface, Not an Implementation   5

    Prefer Composition over Inheritance   7

    Delegate, Delegate, Delegate   12

    You Ain't Gonna Need It   13

Fourteen Out of Twenty-Three   15

Patterns in Ruby?   17

Chapter 2: Getting Started with Ruby   19

Interactive Ruby   20

Saying Hello World   20

Variables   23

Fixnums and Bignums   24

Floats   26

There Are No Primitives Here   26
But Sometimes There Is No Object   27
Truth, Lies, and nil   28
Decisions, Decisions   30
Loops   32
More about Strings   34
Symbols   37
Arrays   38
Hashes   40
Regular Expressions   40
A Class of Your Own   41
Getting at the Instance Variables   43
An Object Asks: Who Am I?   46
Inheritance, Subclasses, and Superclasses   46
Argument Options   47
Modules   49
Exceptions   52
Threads   53
Managing Separate Source Files   54
Wrapping Up   55

PART II: Patterns in Ruby   57

Chapter 3: Varying the Algorithm with the Template Method   59
Keeping Up with What Life Throws at You   60
Separate the Things That Stay the Same   61
Discovering the Template Method Pattern   65
Hook Methods   66
But Where Are All the Declarations?   68
Types, Safety, and Flexibility   69
Unit Tests Are Not Optional   71
Using and Abusing the Template Method Pattern   73
Templates in the Wild   74
Wrapping Up   75

Chapter 4: Replacing the Algorithm with the Strategy   77
Delegate, Delegate, and Delegate Again   78
Sharing Data between the Context and the Strategy   80

Duck Typing Yet Again   82
Procs and Blocks   84
Quick-and-Dirty Strategies   88
Using and Abusing the Strategy Pattern   90
The Strategy Pattern in the Wild   90
Wrapping Up   92

Chapter 5: Keeping Up with the Times with the Observer   95
Staying Informed   95
A Better Way to Stay Informed   97
Factoring Out the Observable Support   100
Code Blocks as Observers   104
Variations on the Observer Pattern   105
Using and Abusing the Observer Pattern   106
Observers in the Wild   108
Wrapping Up   109

**Chapter 6: Assembling the Whole from the Parts
           with the Composite   111**
The Whole and the Parts   112
Creating Composites   114
Sprucing Up the Composite with Operators   118
An Array as a Composite?   119
An Inconvenient Difference   120
Pointers This Way and That   120
Using and Abusing the Composite Pattern   122
Composites in the Wild   123
Wrapping Up   125

Chapter 7: Reaching into a Collection with the Iterator   127
External Iterators   127
Internal Iterators   130
Internal Iterators versus External Iterators   131
The Inimitable Enumerable   133
Using and Abusing the Iterator Pattern   134
Iterators in the Wild   136
Wrapping Up   140

Chapter 8: Getting Things Done with Commands   143

An Explosion of Subclasses   144
An Easier Way   145
Code Blocks as Commands   147
Commands That Record   148
Being Undone by a Command   151
Queuing Up Commands   154
Using and Abusing the Command Pattern   154
The Command Pattern in the Wild   155
    ActiveRecord Migrations   155
    Madeleine   156
Wrapping Up   160

Chapter 9: Filling in the Gaps with the Adapter   163

Software Adapters   164
The Near Misses   167
An Adaptive Alternative?   168
Modifying a Single Instance   170
Adapt or Modify?   172
Using and Abusing the Adapter Pattern   173
Adapters in the Wild   173
Wrapping Up   174

Chapter 10: Getting in Front of Your Object with a Proxy   175

Proxies to the Rescue   176
The Protection Proxy   178
Remote Proxies   179
Virtual Proxies Make You Lazy   180
Eliminating That Proxy Drudgery   182
    Message Passing and Methods   183
    The method_missing Method   184
    Sending Messages   185
    Proxies without the Tears   185
Using and Abusing Proxies   189
Proxies in the Wild   190
Wrapping Up   192

Chapter 11: Improving Your Objects with a Decorator   193

Decorators: The Cure for Ugly Code   193
Formal Decoration   200
Easing the Delegation Blues   200
Dynamic Alternatives to the Decorator Pattern   201
   Wrapping Methods   202
   Decorating with Modules   202
Using and Abusing the Decorator Pattern   204
Decorators in the Wild   205
Wrapping Up   206

Chapter 12: Making Sure There Is Only One with the Singleton   207

One Object, Global Access   207
Class Variables and Methods   208
   Class Variables   208
   Class Methods   209
A First Try at a Ruby Singleton   211
   Managing the Single Instance   212
   Making Sure There Is Only One   213
The Singleton Module   214
Lazy and Eager Singletons   214
Alternatives to the Classic Singleton   215
   Global Variables as Singletons   215
   Classes as Singletons   216
   Modules as Singletons   218
A Safety Harness or a Straitjacket?   219
Using and Abusing the Singleton Pattern   220
   They Are Really Just Global Variables, Right?   220
   Just How Many of These Singletons Do You Have?   221
   Singletons on a Need-to-Know Basis   221
   Curing the Testing Blues   223
Singletons in the Wild   224
Wrapping Up   225

Chapter 13: Picking the Right Class with a Factory   227

A Different Kind of Duck Typing   228
The Template Method Strikes Again   231

Parameterized Factory Methods   233
Classes Are Just Objects, Too   236
Bad News: Your Program Hits the Big Time   237
Bundles of Object Creation   239
Classes Are Just Objects (Again)   241
Leveraging the Name   242
Using and Abusing the Factory Patterns   244
Factory Patterns in the Wild   244
Wrapping Up   246

Chapter 14: Easier Object Construction with the Builder   249
Building Computers   250
Polymorphic Builders   253
Builders Can Ensure Sane Objects   256
Reusable Builders   257
Better Builders with Magic Methods   258
Using and Abusing the Builder Pattern   259
Builders in the Wild   259
Wrapping Up   260

Chapter 15: Assembling Your System with the Interpreter   263
The Right Language for the Job   264
Building an Interpreter   264
A File-Finding Interpreter   267
    Finding All the Files   267
    Finding Files by Name   268
    Big Files and Writable Files   269
    More Complex Searches with Not, And, and Or   270
Creating the AST   272
    A Simple Parser   272
    A Parser-less Interpreter?   274
    Let XML or YAML Do the Parsing?   276
    Racc for More Complex Parsers   277
    Let Ruby Do the Parsing?   277
Using and Abusing the Interpreter Pattern   277
Interpreters in the Wild   278
Wrapping Up   279

PART III: Patterns for Ruby   281

Chapter 16: Opening Up Your System with Domain-Specific Languages   283

The Domain of Specific Languages   283

A File Backup DSL   284

It's a Data File—No, It's a Program!   285

Building PackRat   287

Pulling Our DSL Together   288

Taking Stock of PackRat   289

Improving PackRat   290

Using and Abusing Internal DSLs   293

Internal DSLs in the Wild   294

Wrapping Up   295

Chapter 17: Creating Custom Objects with Meta-programming   297

Custom-Tailored Objects, Method by Method   298

Custom Objects, Module by Module   300

Conjuring Up Brand-New Methods   301

An Object's Gaze Turns Inward   306

Using and Abusing Meta-programming   306

Meta-programming in the Wild   308

Wrapping Up   311

Chapter 18: Convention Over Configuration   313

A Good User Interface—for Developers   315

Anticipate Needs   315

Let Them Say It Once   316

Provide a Template   316

A Message Gateway   317

Picking an Adapter   319

Loading the Classes   320

Adding Some Security   323

Getting the User Started   325

Taking Stock of the Message Gateway   326

Using and Abusing the Convention Over Configuration Pattern   327

Convention Over Configuration in the Wild   328

Wrapping Up   328

Chapter 19: Conclusion   331

Appendix A: Getting Hold of Ruby   333

Installing Ruby on Microsoft Windows   333
Installing Ruby on Linux and Other UNIX-Style Systems   333
Mac OS X   334

Appendix B: Digging Deeper   335

Design Patterns   335
Ruby   336
Regular Expressions   337
Blogs and Web Sites   337

Index   339

Foreword

Design Patterns: Elements of Reusable Object-Oriented Software, affectionately known by many as the "Gang of Four book" (GoF) is the first reference work on the topic to be published in a mainstream book. It has sold over half a million copies since 1995 and undoubtedly influenced the thoughts and code of millions of programmers worldwide. I still vividly remember buying my first copy of the book in the late nineties. Due in part to the enthusiasm with which it was recommended to me by my peers, I treated it as part of my coming-of-age as a programmer. I tore through the book in a few days, eagerly thinking up practical applications for each pattern.

It's commonly agreed that the most useful thing about patterns is the way in which they form a vocabulary for articulating design decisions during the normal course of development conversations among programmers. This is especially true during pair-programming, a cornerstone of Extreme Programming and other Agile processes, where design is an ongoing and shared activity. It's fantastically convenient to be able to say to your pair, "I think we need a strategy here" or "Let's add this functionality as an observer."

Knowledge of design patterns has even become an easy way to screen programming job candidates in some shops, where it's common to hear:

"What's your favorite pattern?"

"Um . . . factory?"

"Thanks for coming, there's the door."

Then again, the whole notion of having a *favorite* pattern is kind of strange isn't it? Our favorite pattern should be the one that applies to a given circumstance. One of the classic mistakes made by inexperienced programmers just beginning to learn about patterns is to choose to implement a pattern as an end of its own, rather than as a means. Why do people get wrapped up in implementing patterns "just for fun" anyway?

At least in the statically typed world, there are a fair amount of technical challenges to tackle when you implement design patterns. At best, you use some ninja techniques that really show your coding prowess. Worst case scenario you end up with a bunch of boilerplate gunk. It makes the topic of design patterns a fun one, at least for programming geeks like me.

Are the GoF design patterns difficult to implement in Ruby? Not really. For starters, the absence of static typing lowers the code overhead involved in our programs overall. The Ruby standard library also makes some of the most common patterns available as one-line includes, and others are essentially built into the Ruby language itself. For instance, a Command object in the GoF sense is essentially a wrapper around some code that knows how to do one specific thing, to run a particular bit of code at some time. Of course, that is also a fairly accurate description of a Ruby code block object or a Proc.

Russ has been working with Ruby since 2002 and he knows that most experienced Rubyists already have a good grasp of design patterns and how to apply them. Thus his main challenge, as far as I can tell, was to write this book in such a way that it would be relevant and essential for professional Ruby programmers, yet still benefit newcomers to our beloved language. I think he has succeeded, and you will, too. Take the Command object example again: In its simple form it may be implemented with simply a block, but add state and a bit of behavior to it and now the implementation is not so simple anymore. Russ gives us proven advice that is specific to Ruby and instantly useful.

This book also has the added benefit of including new design patterns specific to Ruby that Russ has identified and explained in detail, including one of my favorite ones: Internal Domain Specific Languages. I believe that his treatment of the subject, as an evolution of the Interpreter pattern, is the first significant reference work in publication on the topic.

Finally, I think this book will hugely benefit those that are just beginning their professional careers in Ruby or migrating from languages such as PHP, where there isn't as much of a cultural emphasis on OO design and patterns. In the process of describing design patterns, Russ has captured the essence of solving many of the common programming hurdles that we face in day-to-day programming of significant Ruby programs—priceless information for newbies. So much so that I'm sure that this book will be a staple of my gift-list for new programmer colleagues and friends.

—Obie Fernandez, Professional Ruby Series Editor

Preface

A former colleague of mine used to say that thick books about design patterns were evidence of an inadequate programming language. What he meant was that, because design patterns are the common idioms of code, a good programming language should make them very easy to implement. An ideal language would so thoroughly integrate the patterns that they would almost disappear from sight.

To take an extreme example, in the late 1980s I worked on a project that produced object-oriented code in C. Yes, C, not C++. We pulled off this feat by having each "object" (actually a C structure) point to a table of function pointers. We operated on our "objects" by chasing the pointer to the table and calling functions out of the table, thereby simulating a method call on an object. It was awkward and messy, but it worked. Had we thought of it, we might have called this technique the "object-oriented" pattern. Of course, with the advent of C++ and then Java, our object-oriented pattern disappeared, absorbed so thoroughly into the language that it vanished from sight. Today, we don't usually think of object orientation as a pattern—it is too easy.

But many things are still not easy enough. The justly famous Gang of Four book (*Design Patterns: Elements of Reusable Object-Oriented Software* by Gamma, Helm, Johnson, and Vlissides) is required reading for every software engineer today. But actually implementing many of the patterns described in *Design Patterns* with the languages in widespread use today (Java and C++ and perhaps C#) looks and feels a lot like my 1980s-vintage handcrafted object system. Too painful. Too verbose. Too prone to bugs.

The Ruby programming language takes us a step closer to my old friend's ideal, a language that makes implementing patterns so easy that sometimes they fade into the background. Building patterns in Ruby is easier for a number of reasons:

- Ruby is dynamically typed. By dispensing with static typing, Ruby dramatically reduces the code overhead of building most programs, including those that implement patterns.

- Ruby has code closures. It allows us to pass around chunks of code and associated scope without having to laboriously construct entire classes and objects that do nothing else.

- Ruby classes are real objects. Because a class in Ruby is just another object, we can do any of the usual runtime things to a Ruby class that we can do to any other object: We can create totally new classes. We can modify existing classes by adding or deleting methods. We can even clone a class and change the copy, leaving the original alone.

- Ruby has an elegant system of code reuse. In addition to supporting garden-variety inheritance, Ruby allows us to define mixins, which are a simple but flexible way to write code that can be shared among several classes.

All of this makes code in Ruby compressible. In Ruby, as in Java and C++, you can implement very sophisticated ideas, but with Ruby it becomes possible to hide the details of your implementations much more effectively. As you will see on the pages that follow, many of the design patterns that require many lines of endlessly repeated boilerplate code in traditional static languages require only one or two lines in Ruby. You can turn a class into a singleton with a simple `include Singleton` command. You can delegate as easily as you can inherit. Because Ruby enables you to say more interesting things in each line of code, you end up with less code.

This is not just a question of keyboard laziness; it is an application of the DRY (Don't Repeat Yourself) principle. I don't think anyone today would mourn the passing of my old object-oriented pattern in C. It worked for me, but it made me work for it, too. In the same way, the traditional implementations of many design patterns work, but they make you work, too. Ruby represents a real step forward in that you become able to do work only once and compress it out of the bulk of your code. In short, Ruby allows you to concentrate on the real problems that you are trying to solve instead of the plumbing. I hope that this book will help you see how.

Who Is This Book For?

Simply put, this book is intended for developers who want to know how to build significant software in Ruby. I assume that you are familiar with object-oriented programming, but you don't really need any knowledge of design patterns—you can pick that up as you go through the book.

You also don't need a lot of Ruby knowledge to read this book profitably. You will find a quick introduction to the language in Chapter 2, and I try to explain any Ruby-specific language issues as we go.

How Is This Book Organized?

This book is divided into three parts. First come a couple of introductory chapters, starting with the briefest outline of the history and background of the whole design patterns movement, and ending with a quick tour of the Ruby language at the "just enough to be dangerous" level.

Part 2, which takes up the bulk of these pages, looks at a number of the original Gang of Four patterns from a Ruby point of view. Which problem is this pattern trying to solve? What does the traditional implementation of the pattern—the implementation given by the Gang of Four—look like in Ruby? Does the traditional implementation make sense in Ruby? Does Ruby provide us with any alternatives that might make solving the problem easier?

Part 3 of this book looks at three patterns that have emerged with the introduction and expanded use of Ruby.

A Word of Warning

I cannot sign my name to a book about design patterns without repeating the mantra that I have been muttering for many years now: Design patterns are little spring-loaded solutions to common programming problems. Ideally, when the appropriate problem comes along, you should trigger the design pattern and your problem is solved. It is that first part—the bit about waiting for the appropriate problem to come along—that some engineers have trouble with. You cannot say that you are correctly applying a design pattern *unless you are confronting the problem that the pattern is supposed to solve.*

The reckless use of every design pattern on the menu to solve nonexistent problems has given design patterns a bad name in some circles. I would contend that Ruby makes it easier to write an adapter that uses a factory method to get a proxy to the builder, which then creates a command, which will coordinate the operation of adding two plus two. Ruby will make that process easier, but even in Ruby it will not make any sense.

Nor can you look at program construction as a simple process of piecing together some existing design patterns in new combinations. Any interesting program will always have unique sections, bits of code that fit that specific problem perfectly and no other. Design patterns are meant to help you recognize and solve the common problems that arise repeatedly when you are building software. The advantage of design patterns is that they let you rapidly wing your way past the problems that someone has already solved, so that you can get on to the hard stuff, the code that is unique to your situation. Design patterns are not the universal elixir, the magic potion that will fix all of your design problems. They are simply one technique—albeit a very useful technique—that you can use to build programs.

About the Code Style Used in This Book

One thing that makes programming in Ruby so pleasant is that the language tries to stay out of your way. If there are several sensible ways of saying something, Ruby will usually support them all:

```ruby
# One way to say it

if (divisor == 0)
  puts 'Division by zero'
end

# And another

puts 'Division by zero' if (divisor == 0)

# And a third

(divisor == 0) && puts 'Division by zero'
```

Ruby also tries not to insist on syntax for syntax's sake. Where possible, it will let you omit things when the meaning is clear. For example, you can usually omit the parentheses around the argument list when calling a method:

```
puts('A fine way to call puts')
puts 'Another fine way to call puts'
```

You can even forget the parentheses when you are defining the argument list of a method and around the conditional part of an `if` statement:

```
def method_with_3_args a, b, c
  puts "Method 1 called with #{a} #{b} #{c}"
  if a == 0
    puts 'a is zero'
  end
end
```

The trouble with all of these shortcuts, convenient as they are in writing real Ruby programs, is that when liberally used, they tend to confuse beginners. Most programmers who are new to Ruby are going to have an easier time with

```
if file.eof?
  puts( 'Reached end of file' )
end
```

or even

```
puts 'Reached end of file' if file.eof?
```

than with

```
file.eof? || puts('Reached end of file')
```

Because this book is more about the deep power and elegance of Ruby than it is about the details of the language syntax, I have tried to strike a balance between making my examples actually look like real Ruby code on the one hand while still being beginner friendly on the other hand. In practice, this means that while I take advantage of some obvious shortcuts, I have deliberately avoided the more radical tricks. It is not that I am unaware of, or disapprove of, the Ruby syntactical shorthand. It is just that I am more interested getting the conceptual elegance of the language across to readers who are new to Ruby. There will be plenty of time to learn the syntactical shortcuts after you have fallen hopelessly in love with the language.

Acknowledgments

I have always thought that whoever said that no man is an island got it pretty much backward. Most islands are the very tops of underwater mountains, the tiny green part that you see supported by a massive and invisible structure just below the waves. So, if the point is that no one does anything unaided, and that credit for everything we do should be spread among our friends and families and colleagues, then we are all islands, propped up by folks who help but who are not seen. Certainly this book would have never gotten started or completed without the help of a mountain of very generous people.

I would like to particularly thank my good friend Bob Kiel, who probably told me no less than 17,827 times that I should write a book. Thanks also to Xandy Johnson, for his generous support and encouragement throughout the writing of this book.

I would also like to say "thank you" to everyone who reviewed this book in its various drafts, including the aforementioned Bob and Xandy, along with Mike Abner, Geoff Adams, Peter Cooper, Tom Corbin, Bill Higgins, Jason Long, Steve Metsker, Glenn Pruitt, Rob Sanheim, Mike Stok, and Gary Winklosky. And special thanks to Andy Lynn and Arild Shirazi, who both went over early drafts of the manuscript with an invaluable, if sometimes painful, fine-toothed comb. Special thanks to Rob Cross for finding that "last" typo.

Thanks also to Heli Roosild, a very professional writer who took the time to look over some things I had written and said, "Yes, this will do."

Thanks also to Lara Wysong, Raina Chrobak, and Christopher Guzikowski, all of Addison-Wesley—especially Chris, who read a 900-word blog article and saw a 384-page book. Thanks also to Jill Hobbs, who copyedited this book with a sharp eye and an even sharper pen.

I'd also like to thank the fine folks at FGM for creating the kind of intellectual environment that makes efforts like this book possible.

Thanks, too, to Steve McMaster and his band of merry men at SamSix for their support and encouragement.

On a more personal level, I would like to thank my wife Karen for her encouragement and suggestions, and for lending me the end of the kitchen table for all those months. Thanks, too, to my son Jackson for letting me tell stories about him here and there in these pages. Many thanks to Diana Greenberg, a good friend in the best of times, and a great friend in the worst of times.

Thanks to my brother Charles for setting an example of courage and persistence that I try to live up to every day.

Finally, thanks to my sister Dolores for awakening my interest in reading. I clearly remember the day she dragged me across the library, away from the trash I had been browsing and over to a shelf of serious books. She pulled one down and said, "*This* is the kind of thing you should be reading." I can still picture the book. It was *The Rise and Fall of the Third Reich* by William L. Shirer, all 1,264 pages of it. I think I was seven at the time.

About the Author

Russ Olsen is a software engineer with more than twenty-five years of experience. Russ has built software in such diverse areas as CAD/CAM, GIS, document management, and enterprise integration. Currently, he is involved in building SOA service discovery and security solutions for large enterprises.

Russ has been involved in Ruby since 2002 and was the author of ClanRuby, an early attempt to bring multimedia capabilities to Ruby. He is currently a committer on a number of open source projects, including UDDI4R.

Russ's technical articles have been featured on Javalobby, O'Reilly's On Java, and the Java Developer's Journal Web site.

Russ holds a B.S. from Temple University and lives with his family, two turtles, and an indeterminate number of guppies outside of Washington, D.C.

You can reach Russ via e-mail at russ@russolsen.com.

PART I

Patterns and Ruby

CHAPTER 1

Building Better Programs with Patterns

It's funny, but design patterns always remind me of a certain grocery store. You see, my very first steady job was a part-time gig that I landed in high school. For a couple of hours every weekday and all day on Saturday, I would help out at the local mom-and-pop grocery store. I stocked the shelves, swept the floor, and generally did whatever unskilled labor needed doing. At first, the goings-on at that little store were a complex blur of sights (I have never liked the look of raw liver), sounds (my boss had been a Marine Corps drill instructor and knew how to express himself for effect), and smells (better left to the imagination).

But the longer I worked at Conrad Market, the more all those disconnected events began to form themselves into understandable chunks. In the morning you unlocked the front door, disarmed the alarm, and put out the "Yes! We're Open" sign. At the end of the day you reversed the process. In between there were a million jobs to be done—everything from stocking the shelves to helping customers find the ketchup. As I got to know my colleagues in other grocery stores, it turned out that those other markets were run pretty much the same way.

This is how people deal with the problems they confront, with the complexity that life forces on them. The first few times we see a problem we may improvise and invent a solution on the spot, but if that same problem keeps reappearing, we will come up with a standard operating procedure to cover it. Don't, as the old saying goes, keep reinventing the wheel.

The Gang of Four

Wheel reinvention is a constant problem for software engineers. It is not that we like doing things over and over. It is just that sometimes when you are designing systems it is hard to realize that the circular friction reduction device with a central axis that you have just built is, in fact, a wheel. Software design can be so numbingly complex that it is easy to miss the patterns of challenges and solutions that pop up repeatedly.

In 1995, Erich Gamma, Richard Helm, Ralph Johnson, and John Vlissides set out to redirect all the effort going into building redundant software wheels into something more useful. That year, building on the work of Christopher Alexander, Kent Beck, and others, they published *Design Patterns: Elements of Reusable Object-Oriented Software*. The book was an instant hit, with the authors rapidly becoming famous (at least in software engineering circles) as the Gang of Four (GoF).

The GoF did two things for us. First, they introduced most of the software engineering world to the idea of design patterns, where each pattern is a prepackaged solution to a common design problem. We should look around, they wrote, and identify common solutions to common problems. We should give each solution a name, and we should talk about what that solution is good for, when to use it, and when to reach for something else. And we should write all of this information down, so that over time our palette of design solutions will grow.

Second, the GoF identified, named, and described 23 patterns. The original 23 solutions were the recurring patterns that the GoF saw as key to building clean, well-designed object-oriented programs. In the years since *Design Patterns* was published, people have described patterns in everything from real-time micro-controllers to enterprise architectures. But the original 23 GoF patterns stuck to the middle ground of object-oriented design—bigger than a hash table, smaller than a database—and focused on some key questions: How do objects like the ones you tend to find in most systems relate to one another? How should they be coupled together? What should they know about each other? How can we swap out parts that are likely to change frequently?

Patterns for Patterns

In trying to answer these questions, the GoF opened their book with a discussion of some general principles, a set of meta-design patterns. For me, these ideas boil down to four points:

- Separate out the things that change from those that stay the same.

- Program to an interface, not an implementation.

- Prefer composition over inheritance.
- Delegate, delegate, delegate.

To these, I would like to add one idea that is not really mentioned in *Design Patterns,* but that guides much of my own approach to building programs:

- You ain't gonna need it.

In the following sections, we will look at each of these principles in turn, to see what they can tell us about building software.

Separate Out the Things That Change from Those That Stay the Same

Software engineering would be a lot easier if only things would stay the same. We could build our classes serene in the knowledge that, once finished, they would continue to do exactly what we built them to do. Of course, things never stay the same, not in the wider world and certainly not in software engineering. Changes in computing hardware, operating systems, and compilers, combined with ongoing bug fixes and ever-migrating requirements, all take their toll.

A key goal of software engineering is to build systems that allow us to contain the damage. In an ideal system, all changes are local: You should never have to comb through *all* of the code because A changed, which required you to change B, which triggered a change in C, which rippled all the way down to Z. So how do you achieve—or at least get closer to—that ideal system, the one where all changes are local?

You get there by separating the things that are likely to change from the things that are likely to stay the same. If you can identify which aspects of your system design are likely to change, you can isolate those bits from the more stable parts. When requirements change or a bug fix comes along, you will still have to modify your code, but perhaps, just perhaps, the changes can be confined to those walled-off, change-prone areas and the rest of your code can live on in stable peace.

But how do you effect this quarantine? How do you keep the changing parts from infecting the stable parts?

Program to an Interface, Not an Implementation

A good start is to write code that is less tightly coupled to itself in the first place. If our classes are to do anything significant, they need to know about each other. But *what* exactly do they need to know? The following Ruby fragment[1] creates a new instance of the `Car` class and calls the `drive` method on that instance:

```
my_car = Car.new
my_car.drive(200)
```

Clearly, this bit of code is married to the `Car` class. It will work as long as the requirement is that we need to deal with exactly one type of vehicle: a car. Of course, if the requirement changes and the code needs to deal with a second type of transport (such as an airplane), we suddenly have a problem. With only two flavors of vehicle to deal with, we might be able to get away with the following monstrosity:

```
# Deal with cars and planes

if is_car
  my_car = Car.new
  my_car.drive(200)
else
  my_plane = AirPlane.new
  my_plane.fly(200)
end
```

Not only is this code messy, but it is now also coupled to both cars and airplanes. This fix may just about hold things together . . . until a boat comes along. Or a train. Or a bike. A better solution, of course, is to return to Object-Oriented Programming 101 and apply a liberal dose of polymorphism. If cars and planes and boats all implement a common interface, we could improve things by doing something like the following:

```
my_vehicle = get_vehicle
my_vehicle.travel(200)
```

In addition to being good, straightforward object-oriented programming, this second example illustrates the principle of **programming to an interface.** The original

---

1. If you are new to Ruby, don't fret: The code in this chapter is very, very basic, and the next chapter offers a reasonably full introduction to the language. So just sit back for the next few pages and try to hum along.

code worked with exactly one type of vehicle—a car—but the new and improved version will work with any `Vehicle`.

Java and C# programmers sometimes take the advice to "program to an interface" literally, as the **interface** is an actual construct in those languages. They carefully abstract out all the important functionality into many separate interfaces, which their classes then implement. This is usually a good idea, but it is not really what the principle of programming to an interface is suggesting. The idea here is to program to the most general type you can—not to call a car a car if you can get away with calling it a vehicle, regardless of whether `Car` and `Vehicle` are real classes or abstract interfaces. And if you can get away with calling your car something more general still, such as a movable object, so much the better. As we shall see in the pages that follow, Ruby (a language that lacks interfaces in the built-in syntax sense)[2] actually encourages you to program to your interfaces in the sense of programming to the most general types.

By writing code that uses the most general type possible—for example, by treating all of our planes and trains and cars like vehicles whenever we can—we reduce the total amount of coupling in our code. Instead of having 42 classes that are all tied to cars and boats and airplanes, perhaps we end up with 40 classes that know only about vehicles. Chances are that the remaining two classes will still give us trouble if we have to add another kind of vehicle, but at least we have limited the damage. In fact, if we have to change only a couple of classes, we have succeeded in separating out the parts that need to change (the two classes) from the parts that stay the same (the other 40 classes). The cumulative effect of turning down the coupling volume is that our code tends to be less likely to shatter in a horrendous chain reaction in the face of change.

Even so, programming to an interface is not the only step that we can take to make our code more change resistant. There is also composition.

Prefer Composition over Inheritance

If your introduction to object-oriented programming was like mine, you spent 10 minutes on information hiding, 22 minutes on scope and visibility issues, and the rest of the semester talking about inheritance. Once you got past the basic ideas of objects, fields, and methods, inheritance was the interesting thing, the most object-oriented part of object-oriented programming. With inheritance you could get implementation

---

2. The Ruby language does support modules, which bear a "first cousin" relationship to Java interfaces. We will have a lot more to say about Ruby modules in Chapter 2.

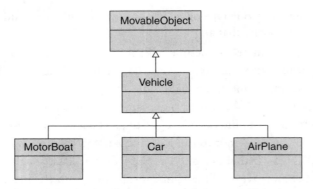

Figure 1-1   Getting the maximum mileage out of inheritance

for free: Just subclass `Widget` and you magically can take advantage of all the good stuff in the `Widget` class.

Inheritance sometimes seems like the solution to every problem. Need to model a car? Just subclass `Vehicle`, which is a kind of `MovableObject`. Similarly, as shown in Figure 1-1, an `AirPlane` might branch off to the right under `Vehicle` while `MotorBoat` might go off to the left. At each level we have succeeded in taking advantage of all the workings of the higher-level superclasses.

The trouble is that inheritance comes with some unhappy strings attached. When you create a subclass of an existing class, you are not really creating two separate entities: Instead, you are making two classes that are bound together by a common implementation core. Inheritance, by its very nature, tends to marry the subclass to the superclass. Change the behavior of the superclass, and there is an excellent chance that you have also changed the behavior of the subclass. Further, subclasses have a unique view into the guts of the superclass. Any of the interior workings of the superclass that are not carefully hidden away are clearly visible to the subclasses. If our goal is to build systems that are not tightly coupled together, to build systems where a single change does not ripple through the code like a sonic boom, breaking the glassware as it goes, then probably we should not rely on inheritance as much as we do.

If inheritance has so many problems, what is the alternative? We can assemble the behaviors we need through **composition.** Instead of creating classes that inherit most of their talents from a superclass, we can assemble functionality from the bottom up. To do so, we equip our objects with references to other objects—namely, objects that supply the functionality that we need. Because the functionality is encapsulated in these other objects, we can call on it from whichever class needs that functionality. In short, we try to avoid saying that an object *is a kind of* something and instead say that it *has* something.

Returning to our car example, assume we have a method that simulates taking a Sunday drive. A key part of taking that drive is to start and stop the engine:

```ruby
class Vehicle

  # All sorts of vehicle-related code...

  def start_engine
    # Start the engine
  end

  def stop_engine
    # Stop the engine
  end
end

class Car < Vehicle
  def sunday_drive
    start_engine
    # Cruise out into the country and return
    stop_engine
  end
end
```

The thinking behind this code goes something like this: Our car needs to start and stop its engine, but so will a lot of other vehicles, so let's abstract out the engine code and put it up in the common `Vehicle` base class (see Figure 1-2).

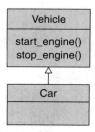

Figure 1-2   Abstracting out the engine code into the base class

That is great, but now all vehicles are required to have an engine. If we come across an engine-less vehicle (for example, a bicycle or a sailboat), we will need to perform some serious surgery on our classes. Further, unless we take extraordinary care in building the `Vehicle` class, the details of the engine are probably exposed to the `Car` class—after all, the engine is being managed by `Vehicle` and a `Car` is nothing but a flavor of a `Vehicle`. This is hardly the stuff of separating out the changeable from the static.

We can avoid all of these issues by putting the engine code into a class all of its own—a completely stand-alone class, not a superclass of `Car`:

```
class Engine

  # All sorts of engine-related code...

  def start
    # Start the engine
  end

  def stop
    # Stop the engine
  end
end
```

Now, if we give each of our `Car` objects a reference to its own `Engine`, we are ready for a drive, courtesy of composition.

```
class Car
  def initialize
    @engine = Engine.new
  end

  def sunday_drive
    @engine.start
    # Cruise out into the country and return...
    @engine.stop
  end
end
```

Assembling functionality with composition (Figure 1-3) offers a whole trunkload of advantages: The engine code is factored out into its own class, ready for reuse

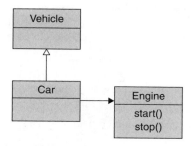

Figure 1-3 Assembling a car with composition

(via composition, of course!). As a bonus, by untangling the engine-related code from Vehicle, we have simplified the Vehicle class.

We have also increased encapsulation. Separating out the engine-related code from Vehicle ensures that a firm wall of interface exists between the car and its engine. In the original, inheritance-based version, all of the details of the engine implementation were exposed to all of the methods in Vehicle. In the new version, the only way a car can do anything to its engine is by working through the public—and presumably well-thought-out—interface of the Engine class.

We have also opened up the possibility of other kinds of engines. The Engine class itself could actually be an abstract type and we might have a variety of engines, all available for use by our car, as shown in Figure 1-4.

On top of that, our car is not stuck with one engine implementation for its whole life. We can now swap our engines at runtime:

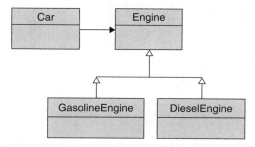

Figure 1-4 A car can now have different kinds of engines

```
class Car
  def initialize
    @engine = GasolineEngine.new
  end

  def sunday_drive
    @engine.start
    # Cruise out into the country and return...
    @engine.stop
  end

  def switch_to_diesel
    @engine = DieselEngine.new
  end
end
```

Delegate, Delegate, Delegate

There is a subtle functional difference between our current `Car` class (the one with the separate `Engine` object) and the original inheritance-based implementation. The original `Car` class exposed the `start_engine` and `stop_engine` methods to the world at large. Of course, we can do the same thing in our latest implementation of `Car` by simply foisting off the work onto the `Engine` object:

```
class Car
  def initialize
    @engine = GasolineEngine.new
  end

  def sunday_drive
    @engine.start
    # Cruise out into the country and return...
    @engine.stop
  end

  def switch_to_diesel
    @engine = DieselEngine.new
  end

  def start_engine
    @engine.start
  end
```

```
    def stop_engine
      @engine.stop
    end
  end
```

This simple "pass the buck" technique goes by the somewhat pretentious name of **delegation.** Someone calls the `start_engine` method on our `Car`. The car object says, "Not my department," and hands the whole problem off to the engine.

The combination of composition and delegation is a powerful and flexible alternative to inheritance. We get most of the benefits of inheritance, much more flexibility, and none of the unpleasant side effects. Of course, nothing comes for free. Delegation requires an extra method call, as the delegating object passes the buck along. This extra method call will have some performance cost—but in most cases, it will be very minor.

Another cost of delegation is the boilerplate code you need to write—all of those boring delegating methods such as `start_engine` and `stop_engine` that do nothing except pass the buck on to the object that really knows what to do. Fortunately, this is a book about design patterns in Ruby and, as we shall see in Chapters 10 and 11, in Ruby we don't have to write all of those dull methods.

You Ain't Gonna Need It

So much for the principles originally cited by the GoF in 1995. To this formidable set, I would like to add one more principle that I think is critical to building, and actually finishing, real systems. This design principle comes out of the Extreme Programming world and is elegantly summed up by the phrase **You Ain't Gonna Need It** (**YAGNI** for short). The YAGNI principle says simply that you should not implement features, or design in flexibility, that you don't need *right now*. Why? Because chances are, *you ain't gonna need it later,* either.

Look at it this way: A well-designed system is one that will flex gracefully in the face of bug fixes, changing requirements, the ongoing march of technology, and inevitable redesigns. The YAGNI principle says that you should focus on the things that you need right now, building in only the flexibility that you know you need. If you are not sure that you need it right now, postpone implementing the functionality until you really do need it. If you do not need it now, do not implement it now; instead, spend your time and energy implementing the things that you definitely need right now.

At the heart of the YAGNI idea is the simple realization that we tend to be wrong when we try to anticipate exactly what we will need in the future. When you put in some feature or add some new bit of flexibility to your system before you really need it, you are making a two-pronged bet.

First, you are betting that you will eventually need this new feature. If you make your persistence layer database independent today, you are betting that someday you will need to port to a new database. If you internationalize your GUI now, you are betting that someday you will have users in some foreign land. But as Yogi Berra is supposed to have said, predictions are hard, especially about the future. If it turns out that you never need to work with another database, or if your application never makes it out of its homeland, then you have done all of that up-front work and lived with all of the additional complexity for naught.

The second prong of the bet that you make when you build something before you actually need it is perhaps even more risky. When you implement some new feature or add some new flexibility before its time, you are betting that you can get it right, that you know how to correctly solve a problem that you haven't really encountered yet. You are betting that the database independence layer you so lovingly installed last year will be able to handle the database the system actually does move to: "What! Marketing wants us to support xyzDB? I've never heard of it!" You are betting that your GUI internationalization will be able to deal with the specific languages that you need to support: "Gee, I didn't realize that we would need to support a language that reads from right to left . . ."

Look at it this way: Barring a sharp blow to the head, as you stand here today you are as dumb as you ever will be. We are all learning, getting smarter every day. This is especially true in software projects: You can be sure that you will have a better grasp of the requirements, technology, and design of any software system that you work on at the end of the project than at the beginning. Whenever you put in a feature before you really need it, you are guilty of programming while stupid; if you wait until you really need the thing, you are likely to have a better understanding of what you need to do and how you should go about doing it.

Design patterns are all about making your systems more flexible, more able to roll smoothly with change. But the use of design patterns has somehow become associated with a particularly virulent strain of over-engineering, with code that tries to be infinitely flexible at the cost of being understandable, and maybe even at the cost of just plain working. The proper use of design patterns is the art of making your system just flexible enough to deal with the problems you have today, but no more. Patterns are useful techniques, rather than ends in themselves. They can help you construct a working system, but your system will not work better because you used all 23 of the GoF design patterns in every possible combination. Your code will work better only if it focuses on the job it needs to do right now.

Fourteen Out of Twenty-Three

The patterns presented in *Design Patterns* are tools for building software. Like the real-world tools that you can buy in a hardware store, they are not all equally useful in all situations. Some are like your trusty hammer, absolutely required for every job. Others are more like that laser level that I got for my last birthday—great when you need it, which is not really all that often. In this book we will look at 14 of the original 23 GoF patterns. In picking which patterns to discuss, I have tried to concentrate on the most widely used and useful. For example, I find it hard to imagine coding without iterators (Chapter 7), so that one is definitely in. I have also leaned toward the patterns that morph in the translation to Ruby. Here again, the iterator is a good example: I can't live without iterators, but iterators in Ruby are not quite the same as iterators in Java or C++.

To give you a preview of what lies in store for you, here is a quick overview of the GoF patterns covered in this book:

- Every pattern has a problem that it is trying to solve. For example, perhaps your code always wants to do exactly the same thing, except at step 44. Sometimes step 44 wants to do this, and sometimes it wants to do that. Perhaps you need a **Template Method.**

- Maybe it is not step 44 that wants to vary but the whole algorithm. You have a well-defined job, something that needs to get done, but there are a lot of ways to do it. You might need to remove the outer covering from a feline creature, and there is more than one technique you might employ. You might want to wrap those techniques—those algorithms—in a **Strategy** object.

- What if you have a class A, which needs to know what is happening over there in class B? But you don't want to couple the two classes together because you never know when class C (or even class D!) might come along. You might want to consider using the **Observer** pattern.

- Sometimes you need to treat a collection of objects just like a single object—I can delete or copy or move an individual file, but I can also delete or copy or move a whole directory of files. If you need to build a collection of objects that looks just like one of the individual objects, you probably need the **Composite** pattern.

- Now suppose you are writing some code that hides a collection of objects, but you don't want the collection hidden *too* well: You would like your client to be able to access the objects in your collection in sequence without knowing how or where you have stored those objects. You definitely need the **Iterator** pattern.

- Sometimes we need to wrap instructions in a kind of a postcard: *Dear database, when you get this, delete row number 7843.* Postcards are hard to come by in code, but the **Command** pattern is tailor made for this situation.

- What do you do when an object does what you need it to do, but its interface is wrong? Your interface mismatch might be very deep and complex, or it might be as simple as needing an object that can `write` but having an object that calls it `save`. The GoF would recommend an **Adapter** to you.

- Maybe you have the right object, but it is over there, someplace else on the network, and you don't want the client code to care about its location. Or perhaps you want to delay creating your object as long as possible, or control access to it. In this circumstance, you may need a **Proxy.**

- Sometimes you need to add responsibilities to your objects on the fly, at runtime. If you have a need for objects that implement some core capabilities but must sometimes take on additional responsibilities, perhaps you need the **Decorator** pattern.

- Perhaps you have an instance of a class, and it needs to be the only instance of that class—that is, the single instance that everybody uses. Sounds like you have a **Singleton.**

- Now suppose you are writing a base class, one that is meant to be extended. As you are happily coding away at your base class, you realize that it needs to produce a new object and only the subclass will know exactly which kind of object to produce. You may need a **Factory Method** here.

- How do you create families of compatible objects? Suppose you have a system that models various types of cars, but not all engines are compatible with all fuel or cooling systems. How do you ensure that you don't end up with the automotive equivalent of Frankenstein's monster? You might build a class devoted to creating all of those objects and call it an **Abstract Factory.**

- Perhaps you are building an object so complex that its construction requires a significant bit of code. Even worse, the process of construction needs to vary according to the circumstances. Perhaps you need the **Builder** pattern?

- Ever have the feeling that you are using the wrong programming language to solve your problem? As crazy as it sounds, perhaps you should stop trying to solve your problem directly and build an **Interpreter** for a language that solves your problem more easily.

Patterns in Ruby?

So much for the theory of patterns.[3] But why Ruby? Isn't Ruby just some scripting language, only suitable for system administration tasks and building Web GUIs?

In a word, no.

Ruby is an elegant, general-purpose, object-oriented programming language. It is not suited for every situation—for example, if you need very high performance, perhaps you should look elsewhere (at least for the moment). But for many programming jobs Ruby is more than suitable. Ruby code is terse but expressive. Ruby brings with it a rich and sophisticated model of programming.

As we shall see in the coming chapters, Ruby has its own way of doing things, a way that changes how we approach many programming problems, including the problems addressed by the classic GoF design patterns. Given that, it would be surprising if the combination of Ruby and the classic design patterns did not lead to something a little bit different, a new twist on the traditional. Sometimes Ruby is different enough that its use permits completely new solutions to programming problems. In fact, three new patterns have come into focus with the recent popularity of Ruby. So, the catalog of patterns in this book will close out with the following:

- The **Internal Domain-Specific Language (DSL),** a very dynamic twist on building specialized little languages

- **Meta-programming,** a technique for creating just the classes and objects that you need, dynamically at runtime

- **Convention Not Configuration,** a cure for the (mostly XML) configuration blues

Let's get started . . .

---

3. Of course, I have just barely made the faintest of scratches on the surface of this huge and interesting topic. Take a look at Appendix B, Digging Deeper, to learn more.

CHAPTER 2

Getting Started with Ruby

I first found Ruby because of my eight-year-old son and his love of a certain electrically charged, but very sweet yellow mouse. Back in 2002, my son was spending his free time playing a certain computer game that involved finding and taming various magical creatures, including the energetic rodent.[1] In my mind's eye, I see the glowing light bulb suddenly appear over his head. "My dad," I imagine him thinking, "is a programmer. This thing that I'm playing, this thing with the magical islands and wonderful creatures, is a program. My dad makes programs. My dad can teach me to make a game!"

Well, maybe. After a blast of begging and pleading that only the parents of young children can truly comprehend, I set out to teach my son to program. The first thing I needed, I thought, was a simple, clear, and easy-to-understand programming language. So I went looking—and I found Ruby. My son, as kids do, rapidly moved on to other things. But in Ruby I had found a keeper. Yes, it was clean and clear and simple—a good language for learning. But the professional software engineer in me, the guy who has built systems in everything from assembly language to Java, saw something else: Ruby is concise, sophisticated, and wickedly powerful.

But Ruby is also solidly mainstream. The basic moving parts of the language are the old gears and pulleys familiar to all programmers. Ruby has all of the data types with which you are familiar: strings, integers, and floating-point numbers, along with arrays and our old friends, `true` and `false`. The basics of Ruby are familiar and commonplace. It is the way they are assembled and the higher-level stuff that makes the language such an unexpected joy.

---

1. Thankfully, the Pokemon craze has abated a bit since then.

If you already know the basics of Ruby, if you know how to pull the third character out of a string and how to raise 2 to the 437th power, and if you have written a class or two, then you can probably dive right into Chapter 3. This chapter will still be here if you get stuck.

If you are very new to Ruby, then this chapter is for you. In this chapter I will take you through the basics of the language as quickly as possible. After all, Alan Turing was right: Past a certain level of complexity, all programming languages are equivalent. If you already know another mainstream language, then the basics of Ruby will present no problem to you; you will just be relearning all of the things that you already know. My hope is that by the end of this chapter you will know just enough of the language to be dangerous.

Interactive Ruby

The easiest way to run Ruby[2] is to use the interactive Ruby shell, irb. Once you start up irb, you can type in Ruby code interactively and see the results immediately. To run irb, you simply enter irb at the command prompt. The following example starts up irb and then uses Ruby to add 2 plus 2:

```
$ irb
irb(main):001:0> 2 + 2
=> 4
irb(main):002:0>
```

The interactive Ruby shell is great for trying out things on a small scale. There is nothing like immediate feedback for exploring a new programming language.

Saying Hello World

Now that you have Ruby safely up and running, the next step is obvious: You need to write the familiar hello world program. Here it is in Ruby:

```
#
# The traditional first program in any language
#
puts('hello world')
```

---

2. See Appendix A if you need guidance in installing Ruby on your system.

You could simply start up irb and type in this code interactively. Alternatively, you could use a text editor and type the hello world program into a text file with a name such as hello.rb. You can then use the Ruby interpreter, appropriately called ruby, to run your program:

```
$ ruby hello.rb
```

Either way, the result is the same:

```
hello world
```

You can learn an awful lot about a programming language from the hello world program. For example, it looks like the `puts` method prints things out, and so it does. You can also see that Ruby comments start with the # character and continue until the end of the line. Comments may fill the entire line, as in the earlier example, or you can tack on a comment after some code:

```
puts('hello world')     # Say hello
```

Another thing to notice about our Ruby hello world program is the absence of semicolons to end the statements. In Ruby, a program statement generally ends with the end of a line. Ruby programmers tend to use semicolons only to separate multiple statements on the same line on those rare occasions when they decide to jam more than one statement on a line:

```
#
# A legal, but very atypical Ruby use of the semicolon
#
puts('hello world');
#
# A little more de rigueur, but still rare use of semicolons
#
puts('hello '); puts('world')
```

The Ruby parser is actually quite smart and will look at the next line if your statement is obviously unfinished. For example, the following code works just fine because the Ruby parser deduces from the dangling plus sign that the calculation continues on the second line:

```
x = 10 +
    20 + 30
```

You can also explicitly extend a statement onto the next line with a backslash:

```
x = 10 \
    + 10
```

There is a theme here: The Ruby design philosophy is to have the language help you whenever possible but to otherwise stay out of the way. In keeping with this philosophy, Ruby lets you omit the parentheses around argument lists when the meaning is clear without them:

```
puts 'hello world'
```

For clarity, most of the examples in this book include the parentheses when calling a method, unless there are no arguments, in which case the empty parentheses are omitted.

While our hello world program wrapped its string with single quotes, you can also use double quotes:

```
puts("hello world")
```

Single or double quotes will result in exactly the same kind of string object, albeit with a twist. Single-quoted strings are pretty much a case of "what you see is what you get": Ruby does very little interpretation on single-quoted strings. Not so with double-quoted strings. These strings are preprocessed in some familiar ways: \n becomes a single linefeed (also known as a newline) character, while \t becomes a tab. So while the string 'abc\n' is five characters long (the last two characters being a backslash and the letter "n"), the string "abc\n" is only four characters long (the last character being a linefeed character).

Finally, you may have noticed that no \n appeared at the end of the 'hello world' string that we fed to puts. Nevertheless, puts printed our message with a newline. It turns out that puts is actually fairly clever and will stick a newline character on the end of any output that lacks one. This behavior is not necessarily desirable for precision formatting, but is wonderful for the kind of examples you will find throughout this book.

Variables

Ordinary Ruby variable names—we will meet several extraordinary variables in a bit—start with a lowercase letter or an underscore.[3] This first character can be followed by uppercase or lowercase letters, more underscores, and numbers. Variable names are case sensitive, and other than your patience there is no limit on the length of a Ruby variable name. All of the following are valid Ruby variable names:

- `max_length`

- `maxLength`

- `numberPages`

- `numberpages`

- `a_very_long_variable_name`

- `_flag`

- `column77Row88`

- `___`

The first two variable names in this list, `max_length` and `maxLength`, bring up an important point: While camelCase variable names are perfectly legal in Ruby, Ruby programmers tend not to use them. Instead, the well-bred Ruby programmer uses words_separated_by_underscores. Also, because variable names are case sensitive, `numberPages` and `numberpages` are different variables. Finally, the last variable name listed above consists of three underscores, which is legal in the way that many very bad ideas are legal.[4]

Okay, let's put our strings and variables together:

```
first_name = 'russ'
last_name = 'olsen'
full_name = first_name + ' ' + last_name
```

---

3. In fact, for most parsing purposes in Ruby, an underscore actually counts as a lowercase letter. This, of course, raises the question of what an uppercase underscore would look like, and whether it would be called an overscore.

4. Another good reason to avoid using all-underscore variable names is that irb has already beat you to the punch. irb sets the variable _ (that is, one underscore) to the last expression it evaluated.

What we have here are three basic assignments: The variable `first_name` is assigned the string `'russ'`, `last_name` is assigned a value of `'olsen'`, and `full_name` gets the concatenation of my first and last names separated by a space.

You may have noticed that none of the variables were declared in the previous example. There is nothing declaring that the variable `first_name` is, and always will be, a string. Ruby is a dynamically typed language, which means that variables have no fixed type. In Ruby, you simply pull a variable name out of thin air and assign a value to it. The variable will take on the type of the value it happens to hold. Not only that, but at different times in the same program a variable might hold radically different types. Early in a program, the value of `pi` might be the number 3.14159; later in the same program, the value might be a reference to a complex mathematical algorithm; still later, it might be the string `"apple"`. We will revisit dynamic typing a number of times in this book (starting with the very next chapter, if you can't wait), but for now just remember that variables take on the types of their values.

Aside from the garden-variety variables that we have examined so far, Ruby supports constants. A constant is similar to a variable, except that its name starts with an uppercase letter:

```
POUNDS_PER_KILOGRAM = 2.2
StopToken = 'end'
FACTS = 'Death and taxes'
```

The idea of a constant is, of course, that the value should not change. Ruby is not overly zealous about enforcing this behavior, however. You *can* change the value of a constant, but you will get a warning for your trouble:

```
StopToken = 'finish'
(irb):2: warning: already initialized constant StopToken
```

For the sake of sanity, you should probably avoid changing the values of constants.

Fixnums and Bignums

To no one's great surprise, Ruby supports arithmetic. You can add, subtract, multiply, and divide in Ruby with the usual results:

```
x = 3
y = 4
sum = x+y
product = x*y
```

Ruby enforces some standard rules about numbers. There are two basic flavors, integers and floating-point numbers. Integers, of course, lack a fractional part: 1, 3, 6, 23, –77, and 42 are all integers, whereas 7.5, 3.14159, and –60000.0 are all floating-point numbers.

Integer division in Ruby comes as no surprise: Divide two integers and your answer will be another integer, with any decimal part of the quotient silently truncated (not rounded!):

```
6/3           # Is 2
7/3           # Is still 2
8/3           # 2 again
9/3           # Is 3 finally!
```

Reasonably sized integers—anything you can store in 31 bits—are of type `Fixnum`, while larger integers are of type `Bignum`; a `Bignum` can hold an arbitrarily gigantic number. Given that the two types convert back and forth more or less seamlessly, however, you can usually forget that there is any distinction between them:

```
2                       # A Fixnum
437                     # A Fixnum
2**437                  # Very definitely a big Bignum
1234567890              # Another Bignum
1234567890/1234567890   # Divide 2 Bignums, and get 1, a Fixnum
```

Ruby also supports the familiar assignment shortcuts, which enable you to shorten expressions such as a = a+1 to a += 1:

```
a = 4
a += 1        # a is now 5
a -= 2        # a is now 3
a *= 4        # a is now 12
a /= 2        # a is now 6
```

Sadly, there are no increment (++) and decrement (--) operators in Ruby.

Floats

If only the world were as exact as the integers. To deal with messy reality, Ruby also supports floating-point numbers or, in Ruby terminology, floats. A float is easy to spot—it is a number with a decimal point:

```
3.14159
-2.5
6.0
0.0000000111
```

You can add, subtract, and multiply floats with the results you would expect. Floats even obey the more familiar rules of grammar-school division:

```
2.5+3.5          # Is 6.0
0.5*10           # Is 5.0
8.0/3.0          # Is 2.66666666
```

There Are No Primitives Here

You do not have to take my word about the types of these different flavors of numbers. You can simply ask Ruby by using the `class` method:

```
7.class                  # Gives you the class Fixnum
888888888888.class       # Gives you the class Bignum
3.14159.class            # Gives you the class Float
```

The slightly strange-looking syntax in this code is actually a tip-off to something deep and important: In Ruby, everything—and I mean *everything*—is an object. When we say `7.class`, we are actually using the familiar object-oriented syntax to call the `class` method on an object, in this case the object representing the number seven. In fact, Ruby numbers actually have quite a wide selection of methods available:

```
3.7.round          # Gives us 4.0
3.7.truncate       # Gives us 3
-123.abs           # Absolute value, 123
1.succ             # Successor, or next number, 2
```

Unlike Java, C#, and many other widely used languages, Ruby does not have any primitive data types. It is objects all the way down. The fact that everything is an object in Ruby drives much of the elegance of the language. For example, the universal object orientation of Ruby is the secret that explains how `Fixnums` and `Bignums` can be so effortlessly converted back and forth.

If you follow the class inheritance hierarchy of any Ruby object upward, from its class up through the parent class or superclass, and on to its super-duper-class, eventually you will reach the `Object` class. Because every Ruby object can trace its class ancestry back to `Object`, all Ruby objects inherit a minimum set of methods, a sort of object-oriented survival kit. That was the source of the `class` method that we encountered earlier. We can also find out whether an object is an instance of a given class:

```
'hello'.instance_of?(String)   # true
```

We can also see if it is `nil`:

```
'hello'.nil?                  # false
```

Perhaps the `Object` method that gets the most use is `to_s`, which returns a string representation of the object—a suitably brief name for the Ruby equivalent of the Java `toString` method:

```
44.to_s          # Returns a two-character string '44'
'hello'.to_s     # A fairly boring conversion, returns 'hello'
```

The total object orientation of Ruby also has some implications for variables. Because everything in Ruby is an object, it is not really correct to say that the expression x = 44 assigns the value 44 to the variable x. Instead, what is really happening is that x receives a reference to an object that happens to represent the number after 43.

But Sometimes There Is No Object

If everything is an object, what happens when you do not really have an object? For exactly those occasions, Ruby supplies us with a special object that represents the idea of not having an object, of being utterly object-less, sans object. This special value is `nil`.

In the last section, we said that everything in Ruby is an object, and so it is: `nil` is every bit as much a Ruby object as `"hello world"` or 43. For example, you can get the class of `nil`:

```
puts(nil.class)
```

That turns out to be something very predictable:

```
NilClass
```

Sadly, `nil` is destined to live out its life alone: There is only one instance of `NilClass` (called `nil`) and you cannot make any new instances of `NilClass`.

Truth, Lies, and nil

Ruby supports the usual set of Boolean operators. For example, we can find out if two expressions are equal, if one expression is less than the other, or if one expression is greater than the other.

```
1 == 1                    # true
1 == 2                    # false
'russ' == 'smart'         # sadly, false
(1 < 2)                   # true
(4 > 6)                   # nope

a = 1
b = 10000
(a > b)                   # no way
```

We also have less than or equal and its cousin, greater than or equal:

```
(4 >= 4)                  # yes!
(1 <= 2)                  # also true
```

All of these comparison operators evaluate to one of two objects—`true` or `false`. Like `nil`, the `true` and `false` objects are the only instances of their respective classes: `true` is the only instance of `TrueClass` and `false` is the sole instance of (you guessed it)

`FalseClass`. Oddly, both `TrueClass` and `FalseClass` are direct subclasses of `Object`. I keep expecting a `BooleanClass` to slip in somewhere, but alas, no.

Ruby also has an `and` operator—in fact, several of them. For example, you might say

```
(1 == 1) and (2 == 2)     # true
(1 == 1) and (2 == 3)     # false
```

You might also say

```
(1 == 1) && (2 == 2)     # true
(1 == 1) && (2 == 3)     # false
```

Both amount to the same thing. Essentially, `and` and `&&` are synonyms.[5] Matched up with `and` and `&&` is `or` and `||`, which do about what you would expect:[6]

```
(1 == 1) or (2 == 2)      # yup
(2 == 1) || (7 > 10)      # nope
(1 == 1) or (3 == 2)      # yup
(2 == 1) || (3 == 2)      # nope
```

Finally, Ruby has the usual `not` operator and its twin `!`:

```
not (1 == 2)   # true
! (1 == 1)     # false
not false      # true
```

One thing to keep in mind is that Ruby can come up with a Boolean value for any expression. We can, therefore, mix strings, integers, and even dates into Boolean

---

5. Okay, not quite. The `&&` operator has a higher precedence—it is stickier in expressions—than `and`. The same is true of the `||` and `or` operators.
6. Ruby also has `&` and `|` operators—note that they are single characters. These guys are bitwise logical operators, useful in their own right but probably not what you would want to use in your average `if` statement.

expressions. The evaluation rule is very simple: `false` and `nil` evaluate to false; every-thing else evaluates to true. So the following are perfectly legal expressions:

```
true and 'fred'   # true, because 'fred' is neither nil nor false
'fred' && 44      # true, because both 'fred' and 44 are true
nil || false      # false, because both nil and false are false
```

If you come from the world of C or C++, you will be shocked to learn that in Ruby, zero, being neither `false` nor `nil`, evaluates to `true` in a Boolean expression. Surprisingly, this expression

```
if 0
  puts('Zero is true!')
end
```

will print out

```
Zero is true!
```

Decisions, Decisions

That last example was a sneak preview of the `if` statement, which has the usual optional `else`:

```
age = 19

if (age >= 18)
  puts('You can vote!')
else
  puts('You are too young to vote.')
end
```

As you can see from the example, each `if` statement always has its own terminating `end`. If you have more than one condition, you can use an `elsif`:

```
if(weight < 1)
  puts('very light')
elsif(weight < 10)
  puts('a bit of a load')
elsif(weight < 100)
  puts('heavy')
else
  puts('way too heavy')
end
```

Note that the keyword is `elsif`—five letters, one word. It is not `else if`, `elseif`, and certainly not `elif`.

As usual, Ruby tries its best to make the code as concise as possible. Because the parentheses after the `if` and `elsif` really do not add much to the meaning, they are optional:

```
if weight < 1
  puts('very light')
elsif weight < 10
  puts('a bit of a load')
elsif weight < 100
  puts('heavy')
else
  puts('way too heavy')
end
```

There is also an idiom for those times when you need to decide whether you want to execute a single statement. Essentially, you can hang the `if` on the end of a statement:

```
puts('way too heavy') if weight >= 100
```

There is also an `unless` statement, which reverses the sense of an `if` statement: The body of the statement executes only if the condition is false. As with the `if` statement, you can have a long form of `unless`:

```
unless weight < 100
  puts('way too heavy')
end
```

A short form is also available:

```
puts('way too heavy') unless weight < 100
```

Loops

Ruby has two flavors of loops. First, we have the classic `while` loop, which, like the `if` statement, is always terminated with an `end`. Thus this loop

```
i = 0
while i < 4
  puts("i = #{i}")
  i = i + 1
end
```

will print out this:

```
i = 0
i = 1
i = 2
i = 3
```

The evil twin of the `while` loop is the `until` loop, which is more or less identical to the `while` loop except that it keeps looping until the condition becomes true. Thus we might have written the preceding example as follows:

```
i = 0
until i >= 4
  puts("i = #{i}")
  i = i + 1
end
```

Ruby also has a `for` loop, which you can use, among other things, to sequence through arrays:

```
array = ['first', 'second', 'third']
array.each do |x|
  puts(x)
end
```

Surprisingly, `for` loops are rare in real Ruby programs. A Ruby programmer is much more likely to write this equivalent code instead:

```ruby
array.each do |x|
  puts(x)
end
```

We will have much more to say about this odd-looking loop thing in Chapter 7. For now, just think of the `each` syntax as another way to write a `for` loop.

If you need to break out of a loop early, you can use a `break` statement:

```ruby
names = ['george', 'mike', 'gary', 'diana']

names.each do |name|
  if name == 'gary'
    puts('Break!')
    break
  end
  puts(name)
end
```

Run this code and it will never print out `gary`:

```
george
mike
Break!
```

Finally, you can skip to the next iteration of a loop with the `next` statement:

```ruby
names.each do |name|
  if name == 'gary'
    puts('Next!')
    next
  end
  puts(name)
end
```

This code will skip right over `gary` but keep going:

```
george
mike
Next!
diana
```

More about Strings

Since we are already using Ruby strings, let's get to know them a little better. As we have seen, we can build string literals with both single and double quotes:

```
first = 'Mary had'
second = " a little lamb"
```

We have also seen that the plus sign is the concatenation operator, so that

```
poem = first + second
```

will give us this:

```
Mary had a little lamb
```

Strings have a whole range of methods associated with them. You can, for example, get the length of a string:

```
puts(first.length)      # Prints 8
```

You can also get an all-uppercase or all-lowercase version of a string:

```
puts(poem.upcase)
puts(poem.downcase)
```

This code will print out

```
MARY HAD A LITTLE LAMB
mary had a little lamb
```

In many ways, Ruby strings act like arrays: You can set individual characters in a string by indexing the string in a very array-like fashion. Thus, if you execute

```
poem[0] = 'G'
puts(poem)
```

you will get a very different sort of poem:

```
Gary had a little lamb
```

You can also get at individual characters in a string in the same way, albeit with a slightly annoying twist: Because Ruby lacks a special character type, when you pull an individual character out of a Ruby string you get a number—namely, the integer character code. Consider this example:

```
second_char = poem[1]    # second_char is now 97, the code for 'a'
```

Fortunately, you can also put individual characters back via the code, so perhaps there is not much harm done:

```
poem[0] = 67             # 67 is the code for 'C'
```

Now Cary is the former owner of a young sheep.

Double-quoted strings in Ruby have another feature, one that you are going to run into frequently in the examples in this book. While it is turning the familiar \n's into newlines and \t's into tabs, if the Ruby interpreter sees #{expression} inside a double-quoted string, it will substitute the value of the expression into the string. For example, if we set the variable n

```
n = 42
```

we can smoothly insert it into a string

```
puts("The value of n is #{n}.")
```

to get

```
The value of n is 42.
```

This feature (called string interpolation) is not just limited to one expression per string, nor is the expression limited to a simple variable name. For example, we can say

```
city = 'Washington'
temp_f = 84
puts("The city is #{city} and the temp is #{5.0/9.0 * (temp_f-32)} C")
```

which will print

```
The city is Washington and the temp is 28.8888888888889 C
```

While traditional quotes are great for relatively short, single-line strings, they tend to be awkward for expressing longer, multiple-line strings. To ease this pain, Ruby has another way of expressing string literals:

```
a_multiline_string = %Q{
The city is #{city}.
The temp is #{5.0/9.0 * (temp_f-32)} C
}
```

In this example, everything between the `%Q{` and the final `}` is a string literal. If you start your string literal with a `%Q{` as we did above, Ruby will treat your string as double quoted and do all of the usual double-quoted interpretation on it. If you use `%q{` (note the lowercase "q"), your text will receive the same minimal processing as a single-quoted string.[7]

Finally, if you are coming from the Java or C# world, there is a serious conceptual landmine waiting for you in Ruby. In C# and Java, strings are **immutable:** Once you create a string in either of these languages, that string can never be changed. Not so in Ruby. In Ruby, any string is liable to change just about any time. To illustrate, let us create two references to the same string:

```
name = 'russ'
first_name = name
```

---

7. Actually, you have a lot more options. You can, for example, use matched pairs of parentheses "()" or angle brackets "<>" instead of the braces that I show here to delimit your string. Thus `%q<a string>` is a fine string. Alternatively, you can use any other special character to start and end your string— for example, `%Q-a string-`.

If this were Java or C# code, I could use `first_name` essentially forever, serene in the knowledge that its value could never change out from under me. By contrast, if I change the contents of `name`:

```
name[0] = 'R'
```

I also change `first_name`, which is just a reference to the same string object. If we print out either variable

```
puts(name)
puts(first_name)
```

we will get the same, changed value:

```
Russ
Russ
```

Symbols

The merits of making strings immutable have been the subject of long debate. Strings were mutable in C and C++, were immutable in Java and C#, and went back to mutable in Ruby. Certainly there are advantages to mutable strings, but making strings mutable does leave an obvious gap: What do we do when we need to represent something that is less about data and more like an internal identifier in our program?

Ruby has a special class of object just for this situation—namely, the symbol. A Ruby symbol is essentially an immutable identifier type thing. Symbols always start with a colon:

- `:a_symbol`

- `:an_other_symbol`

- `:first_name`

If you are not used to them, symbols may seem a bit strange at first. Just remember that symbols are more or less immutable strings and that Ruby programmers use them as identifiers.

Arrays

Creating arrays in Ruby is as easy as typing a pair of square braces or `Array.new`:

```
x = []                          # An empty array
y = Array.new                   # Another one
a = [ 'neo',  'trinity',  'tank']   # A three-element array
```

Ruby arrays are indexed from zero:

```
a[0]                            # neo
a[2]                            # tank
```

You can get the number of elements in an array with the `length` or `size` method. Both do the same thing:

```
puts(a.length)                  # Is 3
puts(a.size)                    # Is also 3
```

Keep in mind that Ruby arrays do not have a fixed number of elements. You can extend arrays on the fly by simply assigning a new element beyond the end of the array:

```
a[3] = 'morpheus'
```

Our array now contains four elements.

If you add an element to an array far beyond the end, then Ruby will automatically add the intervening elements and initialize them to `nil`. Thus, if we execute the code

```
a[6] = 'keymaker'
puts(a[4])
puts(a[5])
puts(a[6])
```

we will get

```
nil
nil
keymaker
```

A convenient way to append a new element to the end of an array is with the <<
operator:

```
a << 'mouse'
```

Ruby also sticks to the spirit of dynamic typing with arrays. In Ruby, arrays are
not limited to a single type of element. Instead, you can mix and match any kind of
object in a single array:

```
mixed = ['alice', 44, 62.1234, nil, true, false]
```

Finally, because arrays are just regular objects,[8] they have a rich and varied set of
methods. You can, for example, sort your array:

```
a = [ 77, 10, 120, 3]
a.sort              # Returns [3, 10, 77, 120]
```

You can also reverse the elements in an array:

```
a = [1, 2, 3]
a.reverse           # Returns [ 3, 2, 1]
```

Keep in mind that the sort and reverse methods leave the original array
untouched: They actually return a *new* array that is sorted or reversed. If you want to
sort or reverse the original array, you can use sort! and reverse!:

```
a = [ 77, 10, 120, 3]
a.sort!             # a is now [3, 10, 77, 120]
a.reverse!          # a is now [120, 77, 10, 3]
```

---

8. We know arrays are just objects in Ruby because (all together now!) *everything* in Ruby is an object.

This convention of `method` leaving the original object untouched while `method!` modifies the original object is not limited to arrays. It is applied frequently (but sadly not quite universally) throughout Ruby.

Hashes

A Ruby hash is a close cousin to the array—you can look at a hash as an array that will take anything for an index. Oh yes, and unlike arrays, hashes are unordered. You can create a hash with a pair of braces:

```
h = {}
h['first_name'] = 'Albert'
h['last_name'] = 'Einstein'

h['first_name']      # Is 'Albert'
h['last_name']       # Is Einstein
```

Hashes also come complete with a shortcut initialization syntax. We could define the same hash with

```
h = {'first_name' => 'Albert', 'last_name' => 'Einstein'}
```

Symbols make good hash keys, so our example might be improved with

```
h = {:first_name => 'Albert', :last_name => 'Einstein'}
```

Regular Expressions

The final built-in Ruby type that we will examine is the regular expression. A regular expression in Ruby sits between a pair of forward slashes:

```
/old/
/Russ|Russell/
/.*/
```

While you can do incredibly complex things with regular expressions, the basic ideas underlying them are really very simple and a little knowledge will take you a long way.[9] Briefly, a regular expression is a pattern that either does or does not match any given string. For example, the first of the three regular expressions above will match only the string `'old'`, while the second will match two variations of my first name. The third expression will match anything.

In Ruby, you can use the `=~` operator to test whether a given regular expression matches a particular string. The `=~` operator will return either `nil` (if the expression does not match the string) or the index of the first matching character (if the pattern does match):

```
/old/ =~ 'this old house'  # 5 - the index of 'old'
/Russ|Russell/ =~ 'Fred'   # nil - Fred is not Russ nor Russell
/.*/ =~ 'any old string'    # 0 - the RE will match anything
```

There is also a `!~` operator for testing whether a regular expression does *not* match a given string.

A Class of Your Own

Ruby would not be much of an object-oriented language if you could not create classes of your own:

```
class BankAccount
  def initialize( account_owner )
    @owner = account_owner
    @balance = 0
  end

  def deposit( amount )
    @balance = @balance + amount
  end

  def withdraw( amount )
    @balance = @balance - amount
  end
end
```

---

9. If you are one of those people who have avoided learning regular expressions, let me recommend that you take some time to explore this wonderfully useful tool. You could start with some of the books listed in Appendix B, Digging Deeper.

Clearly, the Ruby class definition syntax has the same unadorned brevity as the rest of the language. We start a class definition with the keyword class followed by the name of the class:

```
class BankAccount
```

Recall that in Ruby all constants start with an uppercase letter. In Ruby's worldview, a class name is a constant. This makes sense because the name of a class always refers to the same thing—the class. Thus, in Ruby, all class names need to start with an uppercase letter, which is why our class is BankAccount with a capital "B". Also note that while the only hard requirement is that the name of a class begin with an uppercase letter, Ruby programmers typically use camel case for class names.

The first method of our BankAccount class is the initialize method:

```
def initialize( account_owner )
  @owner = account_owner
  @balance = 0
end
```

The initialize method is both special and ordinary. It is ordinary in the way it is built—the line introducing the method consists of the keyword def followed by the name of the method, followed by the argument list, if there is one. Our initialize method does have a single argument, account_owner.

Next, we have the body of the method—in this case, a couple of assignment statements. The first thing our initialize method does is to grab the value passed in through account_owner and assign it to the very strange-looking variable, @owner:

```
@owner = account_owner
```

Names that start with an @ denote **instance variables**—each instance of the BankAccount class will carry around its own copy of @owner. Likewise, each instance of BankAccount will carry around its copy of @balance, which we initialize to zero. As usual, there is no up-front declaration of @owner or @balance; we simply make up the names on the spot.

Although initialize is defined in the same, ordinary way as all other methods, it is special because of its name. Ruby uses the initialize method to set up new objects. When Ruby creates a new instance of a class, it calls the initialize method to set up the new object for use. If you do not define an initialize method on your class, Ruby will do the typical object-oriented thing: It will look upward through the class hierarchy until either it finds an `initialize` method or it reaches `Object`. Given that the `Object` class defines an `initialize` method (which does nothing), the search is guaranteed to quietly end there. Essentially, `initialize` is the Ruby version of a constructor.

To actually construct a new instance of our class, we call the `new` method on the class. The `new` method takes the same parameters as the `initialize` method:

```
my_account = BankAccount.new('Russ')
```

This statement will allocate a new `BankAccount` object, call its `initialize` method with the arguments passed into `new`, and assign the newly initialized `BankAccount` instance to `my_account`.

Our `BankAccount` class has two other methods, `deposit` and `withdraw`, which grow and shrink the size of our account, respectively. But how do we get at our account balance?

Getting at the Instance Variables

While our `BankAccount` class seems like it is almost ready for use, there is one problem: In Ruby, an object's instance variables cannot be accessed from outside the object. If we made a new `BankAccount` object and tried to get at `@balance`, we are in for an unpleasant shock. Running this code

```
my_account = BankAccount.new('russ')
puts(my_account.balance)
```

produces the following error:

```
account.rb:8: undefined method 'balance' ... (NoMethodError)
```

Nor does `my_account.@balance`, with the at sign, work. No, the instance variables on a Ruby object are just not visible outside the object. What is a coder to do? We might simply define an accessor method:

```
def balance
  @balance
end
```

One thing to note about the `balance` method is that it lacks a `return` statement. In the absence of an explicit `return` statement, a method will return the value of the last expression computed, which in this case is simply `@balance`.

We can now get at our balance:

```
puts(my_account.balance)
```

The fact that Ruby allows us to omit the parentheses for an empty argument list gives us the satisfying feeling that we are accessing a value instead of calling a method.

We might also like to be able to set the account balance directly. The obvious thing to do is to add a setter method to `BankAccount`:

```
def set_balance(new_balance)
  @balance = new_balance
end
```

Code with a reference to a `BankAccount` instance could then set the account balance:

```
my_account.set_balance(100)
```

One problem with the `set_balance` method is that it is fairly ugly. It would be much clearer if you could just write

```
my_account.balance = 100
```

Fortunately, you can. When Ruby sees an assignment statement like this one, it will translate it into a plain old method call. The method name will be variable name, followed by an equals sign. The method will have one parameter, the value of the right-hand side of the assignment statement. Thus the assignment above is translated into the following method call:

```
my_account.balance=(100)
```

Take a close look at the name of that method. No, that is not some special syntax; the method name really does end in an equals sign. To make this all work for our `BankAccount` object, we simply rename our setter method:

```
def balance=(new_balance)
  @balance = new_balance
end
```

We now have a class that looks good to the outside world: Code that uses `BankAccount` can set and get the balance with abandon, without caring that it is really calling the `balance` and `balance=` methods. Sadly, our class is a bit verbose on the inside: We seem doomed to have all of these boring `name` and `name=` methods littered throughout our class definition. Unsurprisingly, Ruby comes to our rescue yet again.

It turns out that getter and setter methods are so common that Ruby supplies us with a great shortcut to create them. Instead of going through all of the `def name...` motions, we can simply add the following line to our class:

```
attr_accessor :balance
```

This statement will create a method called `balance` whose body does nothing more than return the value of `@balance`. It will also create the `balance=(new_value)` setter method. We can even create multiple accessor methods in a single statement:

```
attr_accessor  :balance, :grace, :agility
```

The preceding code adds no less than six new methods for the enclosing class: getter and setter methods for each of the three named instance variables.[10] Instant accessors, no waiting.

You also have help if you want the outside world to be able to read your instance variables but not write them. Just use `attr_reader` instead of `attr_accessor`:

```
attr_reader :name
```

Now your class has a getter method for `name`, but no setter method. Similarly, `attr_writer` will create only the setter method, `name=(new_value)`.

---

10. There is a subtle twist of terminology going on here: The things with the at signs on the inside of the class are instance variables. When you create the getter and setter methods and expose them to the outside world, they become **attributes** of the object—hence `attr_reader` and `attr_writer`. In practice, the finer points of the terminology seem to be honored more in the breach than the observance and no one is confused.

An Object Asks: Who Am I?

Sometimes a method needs a reference to the current object, the instance to which the method is attached. For that purpose we can use self, which is always a reference to the current object:

```
class SelfCentered
  def talk_about_me
    puts("Hello I am #{self}")
  end
end


conceited = SelfCentered.new
conceited.talk_about_me
```

If you run this code, you will get something like this:

```
Hello I am #<SelfCentered:0x40228348>
```

Of course, your instance of SelfCentered is unlikely to reside at the same hex address as mine, so your output may look a little different.

Inheritance, Subclasses, and Superclasses

Ruby supports single inheritance—all the classes that you create have exactly one parent or superclass. If you do not specify a superclass, your class automatically becomes a subclass of Object. If you want your superclass to be something other than Object, you can specify the superclass right after the class name:

```
class InterestBearingAccount < BankAccount
  def initialize(owner, rate)
    @owner = owner
    @balance = 0
    @rate = rate
  end

  def deposit_interest
    @balance += @rate * @balance
  end
end
```

Take a good look at the `InterestBearingAccount initialize` method. Like the `initialize` method of `BankAccount`, the `InterestBearingAccount initialize` method sets `@owner` and `@balance` along with the new `@rate` instance variable. The key point is that the `@owner` and `@balance` instance variables in `InterestBearingAccount` are the same as the ones in the `BankAccount` class. In Ruby, an object instance has only one set of instance variables, and those variables are visible all the way up and down the inheritance tree. If we went `BankAccount` mad and built a subclass of `BankAccount` and a sub-subclass of that, and so on for 40 classes and 40 subclasses, there would still be only one `@owner` instance variable per instance.

One unfortunate aspect of our `InterestBearingAccount` class is that the `InterestBearingAccount initialize` method sets the `@owner` and `@balance` fields, essentially duplicating the contents of the `initialize` method in `BankAccount`. We can avoid this messy code duplication by calling the `Account initialize` method from the `InterestBearingAccount initialize` method:

```
def initialize(owner, rate)
  super(owner)
  @rate = rate
end
```

Our new `initialize` method replaces the duplicate code with a call to `super`. When a method calls `super`, it is saying, "Find the method with the same name as me in my superclass, and call that." Thus the effect of the call to `super` in the `initialize` method is to call the `initialize` method in the `BankAccount` class. If there is no method of the same name in the superclass, Ruby will continue looking upward through the inheritance tree until it finds a method or runs out of classes, in which case you will get an error.

Unlike many object-oriented languages, Ruby does not automatically ensure that `initialize` is called for all your superclasses. In this sense, Ruby treats `initialize` like an ordinary method. If the `InterestBearingAccount initialize` method did not make the call to super, the `BankAccount` rendition of `initialize` would never be called on `InterestBearingAccounts`.

Argument Options

So far, the methods with which we have adorned our classes have sported pretty boring lists of arguments. It turns out that Ruby actually gives us a fair number of options when it comes to method arguments. We can, for example, specify default values for our arguments:

```
def create_car( model, convertible=false)
  # ...
end
```

You can call `create_car` with one argument—in which case `convertible` defaults to `false`—or two arguments. Thus all of the following are valid calls to `create_car`:

```
create_car('sedan')
create_car('sports car', true)
create_car('minivan', false)
```

If you do write a method with default values, all of the arguments with default values must come at the end of the argument list.

While default values give you a lot of method-defining flexibility, sometimes even more freedom is handy. For those occasions you can create methods with an arbitrary number of arguments:

```
def add_students(*names)
  for student in names
    puts("adding student #{student}")
  end
end

add_students( "Fred Smith", "Bob Tanner" )
```

Run the code above and you will see

```
adding student Fred Smith
adding student Bob Tanner
```

The `add_students` method works because all of the arguments are rolled up in the `names` array—that's what the asterisk indicates. You can even mix and match regular arguments with the variable arguments array, as long as the array appears at the end of the argument list:

```
def describe_hero(name, *super_powers)
  puts("Name: #{name}")
  for power in super_powers
    puts("Super power: #{power}")
  end
end
```

The preceding method requires at least one argument but will take as many additional arguments as you care to give it. Thus all of the following are valid calls to `describe_hero`:

```
describe_hero("Batman")
describe_hero("Flash", "speed")
describe_hero("Superman", "can fly", "x-ray vision", "invulnerable")
```

Modules

Along with classes, Ruby features a second code-encapsulating entity called a module. Like a class, a module is a package of methods and constants. Unlike a class, however, you can never create an instance of a module. Instead, you include a module in a class, which will pull in all of the module's methods and constants and make them available to instances of the class. If you are a Java programmer, you might think of modules as being a bit like interfaces that carry a chunk of implementation code.

A module definition bears an uncanny resemblance to a class definition, as we can see from this simple, one-method module:

```
module HelloModule
  def say_hello
    puts('Hello out there.')
  end
end
```

Once we have defined our little module, we can pull it into any of our classes with the `include` statement:[11]

---

11. There is another way to use modules, which we will see in Chapter 12: You can just call methods directly out of the module without including the module in any class.

```
class TryIt
  include HelloModule
end
```

The effect of the `include` statement is to make all of the methods in the module available to instances of the class:

```
tryit = TryIt.new
tryit.say_hello
```

The accessibility also works in the other direction: Once a module is included in a class, the module methods have access to all of the methods and instance variables of the class. For example, the following module contains a method that prints various bits of information about the object in which it finds itself—values that it gets by calling the `name`, `title`, and `department` methods supplied by its host class:

```
module Chatty
  def say_hi
    puts("Hello, my name is #{name}")
    puts("My job title is #{title}")
    puts("I work in the #{department} department")
  end
end

class Employee
  include Chatty

  def name
    'Fred'
  end

  def title
    'Janitor'
  end

  def department
    'Maintenance'
  end
end
```

Running this code produces

```
Hello, my name is Fred
My job title is Janitor
I work in the Maintenance department
```

When you include a module in your class, the module becomes a sort of special, secret superclass of your class (see Figure 2-1). But while a class can have only one superclass, it can include as many modules as it likes.

When someone calls a method on an instance of your class, Ruby will first determine whether that method is defined directly in your class. If it is, then that method will be called. For example, if you call the `name` method on an `Employee` instance, Ruby will look first in the `Employee` class, see that a `name` method is available right there, and call it. If there is no such method defined directly by the class, Ruby will next look through all the modules included by the class. For example, if you call the `say_hi` methods, Ruby—after failing to find it in the `Employee` class itself—will look in the modules included by `Employee`. If the class includes more than one module, Ruby will search the modules from the last one included back to the first. But our `Employee` class includes only one module; right there in the `Chatty` module Ruby will find and call the `say_hi` method. If Ruby had not found the method in the `Employee` class or in any of its modules, it would have continued the search on to `Employee` superclass—and its modules.

Modules, when used in the way described here, are known as mixins—because they live to be *mixed in* (that is, to add their methods) to classes. Conceptually, mixin

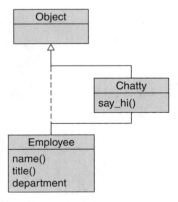

Figure 2-1 A module mixed into a class

modules resemble Java and C# interfaces. Like an interface, a module allows classes that resemble each other in some way to share a common set of methods. The difference is that while an interface is completely abstract—no implementation included— a module comes complete with an implementation.

Exceptions

Most languages these days have a facility for dealing with the computing misfortunes that sometimes befall even respectable code. Ruby is no exception. When something bad happens to a good program, the Ruby interpreter will stop processing and raise an exception. The exception will bubble up the call stack until Ruby comes across code that will handle the exception or runs off the top of the call stack. In the later case Ruby will terminate your program. You can catch exceptions with a `begin/rescue` statement:

```
begin
  quotient = 1 / 0    # Boom!
rescue
  puts('Something bad happened')
end
```

Ruby will catch any exception that might arise between the `begin` and `rescue` statements and will immediately transfer control to the code after the `rescue` statement if an exception is thrown. You can specify the errors that you will catch in greater detail by supplying a list of exception classes in the `rescue` statement:

```
begin
  quotient = 1 / 0    # Boom!
rescue ZeroDivisionError
  puts('You tried to divide by zero')
end
```

If you happen to find yourself in the role of trouble source instead of trouble sink, you can raise your own exception with `raise`:

```
if denominator == 0
  raise ZeroDivisionError
end
return numerator / denominator
```

Ruby provides a number of nice shortcuts for raising exceptions. If your `raise` statement calls out an exception class—as we did in the preceding example—Ruby will conveniently create a new instance of that class and use the instance as the exception. Conversely, if you supply `raise` with a string, Ruby will instantiate a `RuntimeException` and use the string as the message embedded in that exception:

```
irb(main):001:0> raise 'You did it wrong'
RuntimeError: You did it wrong
```

Threads

Like many recent languages, Ruby has its own built-in threading facility. Threads allow your program to do several things at once.[12] Creating new threads in Ruby is quite easy: The `Thread` constructor takes a block, which becomes the body of the thread. The thread starts executing the second you create it and continues executing until the block finishes. Here, for example, are a couple of threads that compute the sum and products of the first ten integers:

```
thread1 = Thread.new do
  sum=0
  1.upto(10) {|x| sum = sum + x}
  puts("The sum of the first 10 integers is #{sum}")
end

thread2 = Thread.new do
  product=1
  1.upto(10) {|x| product = product * x}
  puts("The product of the first 10 integers is #{product}")
end

thread1.join
thread2.join
```

---

12. Well, if you are running on a single-processor system, threads only make it seem like your program is doing several things at once. In fact, the system makes a little progress on each thing before switching to the next task. But everything happens so quickly that most of the time you can't tell the difference.

You can wait for your thread to finish by using the `join` method:

```
thread1.join
thread2.join
```

While there is great power in multithreaded code, there is also a lot of danger. A great way to introduce hard-to-find bugs into your programs is to allow two or more threads to modify the same data structure at the same time. A good way to avoid this and other **race conditions** and make your code thread safe is to use the `Monitor` class:

```
@monitor = Monitor.new

@monitor.synchronize do
  # Only one thread at a time here...
end
```

Managing Separate Source Files

One nice thing about dealing with programming examples is that they tend to be short—short enough that they can easily be stuffed into a single source file. Sadly, at some point most real applications outgrow that first file. The logical response is to break up your system into multiple files, each containing a manageable chuck of code. Of course, once you have broken your code up into those manageable chunks, you need to deal with the issue of loading all of those files. Different languages deal with this issue differently. Java, for example, has an elaborate system for loading classes automatically as a program needs them.

Ruby approaches this problem a bit differently. Ruby programs must explicitly load the classes on which they depend. For example, if your `BankAccount` class lives in a file called `account.rb` and you want to use it in your `Portfolio` class, which resides in `portfolio.rb`, you somehow need to ensure that `BankAccount` is actually loaded before `Portfolio` starts to use it. You can accomplish this with the `require` statement:

```
require 'account.rb'

class Portfolio
  # Uses BankAccount
end
```

The `require` statement will load the contents of the file into the Ruby interpreter. The `require` statement is fairly smart: It will automatically add the .rb suffix. Thus, for the code above, most Ruby programmers would simply say

```
require 'account'
```

The `require` statement also remembers whether a file has already been loaded and will not load the same file twice, so you do not have to worry about requiring the same file multiple times. Because `require` is so smart about what it has already loaded, programmers commonly `require` in everything they need at the top of each Ruby file—no need to fret about which classes have already been loaded by some other file.

All of this applies not just to the files that you produce, but also to the files included with the Ruby standard library. For example, if you need to parse some URLs, you can simply `require` in the URI class that comes with Ruby:

```
require 'uri'
yahoo = URI.parse('http://www.yahoo.com')
```

A final twist on the whole `require` saga relates to **RubyGems.** RubyGems is a software packaging system that lets coders release Ruby libraries and applications in convenient, easy-to-install bundles. If you want to use a library from a gem—perhaps from a gem called runt[13]—you need to `require` in the RubyGems support first:

```
require 'rubygems'
require 'runt'
```

Wrapping Up

From `hello_world` to modules and `require`, this chapter has been a whirlwind tour of Ruby. Fortunately, many of the Ruby basics—for example, the numbers, strings, and variables—are fairly commonplace. The quirks of the language, such as the

---

13. We will have more to say about runt, which is a library for dealing with times and schedules, in Chapter 15.

not-quite-constant constants and the fact that zero is true, are not terribly over-whelming. Even so, we can begin to see, peeking out from the subbasement foundation of the language, some of the things that make Ruby such a joy. The syntax is terse but not cryptic. Everything that lives inside a program—everything from the string 'abc' to the number 42 to arrays—is an object.

As we go through the design patterns in the chapters that follow, we shall see how Ruby enables us to say some really powerful things, clearly and concisely.

PART II

Patterns in Ruby

## CHAPTER 3

Varying the Algorithm
with the Template Method

Imagine that you have a complex bit of code—maybe an involved algorithm or just some hairy system code or perhaps something just hard enough that you want to code it once, write some unit tests, and leave it alone. The trouble is that somewhere right in the middle of your complex code is a bit that needs to vary. Sometimes this bit of code wants to do this and sometimes it wants to do that. Even worse, you are pretty sure that in the future the silly thing will need to something else. You are up against the old "defend against change" problem discussed in Chapter 1. What do you do?

To make this scenario more concrete, imagine that your first real Ruby project is to write a report generator—that is, a program that will spew out monthly status reports. Your reports need to be formatted in reasonably attractive HTML, so you come up with something like this:

```ruby
class Report
  def initialize
    @title = 'Monthly Report'
    @text = [ 'Things are going', 'really, really well.' ]
  end

  def output_report
    puts('<html>')
    puts('  <head>')
    puts("    <title>#{@title}</title>")
```

```
      puts('  </head>')
      puts('  <body>')
      @text.each do |line|
        puts("    <p>#{line}</p>" )
      end
      puts('  </body>')
      puts('</html>')
    end
end
```

Clearly, we are taking some liberties with this code in the interest of keeping this example simple. In real life, our report would not just be hard-coded into the class, and we certainly would not just include arbitrary text into an HTML file without checking for the odd "<" or ">". That said, the preceding code has some good things going for it. It is simple, it is easy to use, and it does produce HTML:

```
report = Report.new
report.output_report
```

If all you want to do is generate some basic HTML, this code or something like it is all you really need.

Keeping Up with What Life Throws at You

Unfortunately, even when life starts out simple, it rarely stays that way. Just months after you finished the preceding programming masterpiece, you get a new requirement: Your formatting object needs to produce plain text reports along with the current HTML. Oh, and we will probably need PostScript and maybe RTF output before the year is out.

Sometimes the simplest solutions are the best, so you just code your way around the problem in the dumbest possible way:

```
class Report
  def initialize
    @title = 'Monthly Report'
    @text = ['Things are going', 'really, really well.']
  end
```

```
    def output_report(format)
      if format == :plain
        puts("*** #{@title} ***")
      elsif format == :html
        puts('<html>')
        puts('  <head>')
        puts("    <title>#{@title}</title>")
        puts('  </head>')
        puts('  <body>')
      else
        raise "Unknown format: #{format}"
      end

      @text.each do |line|
        if format == :plain
          puts(line)
        else
          puts("    <p>#{line}</p>" )
        end
      end

      if format == :html
        puts('  </body>')
        puts('</html>')
      end
    end
  end
end
```

Yuk. This second version may work, but it is a mess. The code to handle the plain text formatting is tangled up with the HTML code. Worse, as you add more formats (remember that looming requirement for PostScript!), you will have to go back and rework the `Report` class to accommodate each new format. The way the code stands right now, each time you add a new format you risk breaking the code for the other formats. In short, our first attempt to add a new output format violates one of the guiding principles for design patterns: It mixes up code that is changing with code that is not changing.

Separate the Things That Stay the Same

The way out of this quandary is to refactor this mess into a design that separates the code for the various formats. The key in doing so is to realize that no matter which format is involved—whether plain text or HTML or the future PostScript—the basic flow of `Report` remains the same:

1. Output any header information required by the specific format.

2. Output the title.

3. Output each line of the actual report.

4. Output any trailing stuff required by the format.

With this sequence in mind, we can reach back to the lessons we learned in Object-Oriented Programming 101: Define an abstract base class with a master method that performs the basic steps listed above, but that leaves the details of each step to a subclass. With this approach, we have one subclass for each output format. Here is our new, abstract `Report` class:

```ruby
class Report
  def initialize
    @title = 'Monthly Report'
    @text =  ['Things are going', 'really, really well.']
  end

  def output_report
    output_start
    output_head
    output_body_start
    output_body
    output_body_end
    output_end
  end

  def output_body
    @text.each do |line|
      output_line(line)
    end
  end

  def output_start
    raise 'Called abstract method: output_start'
  end

  def output_head
    raise 'Called abstract method: output_head'
  end
```

```
    def output_body_start
      raise 'Called abstract method: output_body_start'
    end

    def output_line(line)
      raise 'Called abstract method: output_line'
    end

    def output_body_end
      raise 'Called abstract method: output_body_end'
    end

    def output_end
      raise 'Called abstract method: output_end'
    end
  end
```

Of course, this new `Report` class is not really an abstract class. While we might talk in theory about abstract methods and classes, the fact is that Ruby supports neither. The ideas of abstract methods and classes do not really fit with Ruby's easygoing, dynamic view of life. The closest we can come is to raise exceptions should anyone try to call one of our "abstract" methods.

With our new `Report` implementation in hand, we can now define a `Report` subclass for each of our two formats. Here is the HTML class:

```
class HTMLReport < Report
  def output_start
    puts('<html>')
  end

  def output_head
    puts('  <head>')
    puts("    <title>#{@title}</title>")
    puts('  </head>')
  end

  def output_body_start
    puts('<body>')
  end

  def output_line(line)
    puts("  <p>#{line}</p>")
  end
```

```ruby
  def output_body_end
    puts('</body>')
  end

  def output_end
    puts('</html>')
  end
end
```

Here is the plain text version:

```ruby
class PlainTextReport < Report
  def output_start
  end

  def output_head
    puts("**** #{@title} ****")
    puts
  end

  def output_body_start
  end

  def output_line(line)
    puts(line)
  end

  def output_body_end
  end

  def output_end
  end
end
```

Using our new report classes is straightforward:

```ruby
report = HTMLReport.new
report.output_report

report = PlainTextReport.new
report.output_report
```

Picking a format is now as easy as selecting the right formatting class.

Discovering the Template Method Pattern

Congratulations! You have just rediscovered what is probably the simplest of the original GoF patterns, the Template Method pattern.

As shown in Figure 3-1, the general idea of the Template Method pattern is to build an abstract base class with a skeletal method. This skeletal method (also called a **template method**) drives the bit of the processing that needs to vary, but it does so by making calls to abstract methods, which are then supplied by the concrete subclasses. We pick the variation that we want by selecting one of those concrete subclasses.

In our example, the basic outline is all the things you need to do to generate a report: output any header information, the report title, and then each line of the report. In this case, the detail-supplying methods of the subclasses deal with writing out the report in the correct format, either plain text or HTML. If we engineer all of these tasks correctly, we will end up separating the stuff that stays the same (the basic algorithm expressed in the template method) from the stuff that changes (the details supplied by the subclasses).

One characteristic that the HTMLReport and PlainTextReport classes share with all properly written Template Method pattern concrete subclasses is that they look fragmentary. Like the good concrete subclasses that they are, both HTMLReport and PlainTextReport override output_line and the other abstract methods. The subclasses get their fragmentary appearance from the fact that they do *not* override the key template method, output_report. In the Template Method pattern, the abstract base class controls the higher-level processing through the template method; the subclasses simply fill in the details.

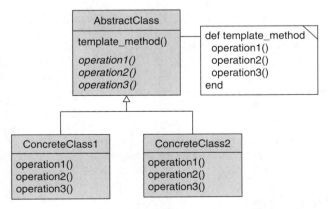

Figure 3-1   Class Diagram for the Template Method pattern

Hook Methods

If you go back and look at `PlainTextReport`, you will see that while it does override
the `output_start` and `output_end` methods as well as the start and end methods for the
body, there is no actual code in any of the `PlainTextReport` versions of these methods.
This is reasonable enough: Unlike an HTML document, a plain text document does not
need any leading or trailing formatting. But there really is no reason to force a class such
as `PlainTextReport`, which has no use for all of these start and stop methods, to define
them anyway. It makes more sense for the base `Report` class to simply supply a default
implementation of these methods for the convenience of its subclasses:

```ruby
class Report
  def initialize
    @title = 'Monthly Report'
    @text =  ['Things are going', 'really, really well.']
  end

  def output_report
    output_start
    output_head
    @text.each do |line|
      output_line(line)
    end
    output_end
  end

  def output_start
  end

  def output_head
    raise 'Called abstract method: output_head'
  end

  def output_body_start
  end

  def output_line(line)
    raise 'Called abstract method: output_line'
  end

  def output_body_end
  end
```

```
  def output_end
  end
end
```

Non-abstract methods that can be overridden in the concrete classes of the Template Method pattern are called **hook methods.** Hook methods permit the concrete classes to choose (1) to override the base implementation and do something different or (2) to simply accept the default implementation. Frequently, the base class will define hook methods solely to let the concrete subclass know what is going on. When the `Report` class calls `output_start`, for example, it is telling its subclasses, "We are ready to start outputting the report, so if you need to do something, do it now." The default implementations of these informative hook methods are frequently empty. They exist merely to let the subclasses know what is happening but do not require the subclasses to override methods that do not interest them.

Sometimes, however, the default implementation of a hook method may actually contain some code. In our `Report` example, we might default to treating the title like just another line of text:

```
class Report
  def initialize
    @title = 'Monthly Report'
    @text =  ['Things are going', 'really, really well.']
  end

  def output_report
    output_start
    output_head
    @text.each do |line|
      output_line(line)
    end
    output_end
  end

  def output_start
  end

  def output_head
    output_line(@title)
  end

  def output_body_start
  end
```

```
    def output_line(line)
      raise 'Called abstract method: output_line'
    end

    def output_body_end
    end

    def output_end
    end
  end
```

But Where Are All the Declarations?

Given that this chapter describes our first Ruby pattern, it is worth taking a moment to consider the issues of types and type safety in Ruby. If you are recently arrived from the world of statically typed languages, you may be wondering how our `Report` class and its subclasses can get away with the almost total lack of declarations. Nowhere in the `Report` class, you may have noticed, do we declare that `@title` is a string or that `@text` is an array of strings. In the same vein, when our client code creates a new `HTMLReport`, we never actually say that the variable `formatter` holds a reference to an instance of `HTMLReport` or `Report`—it just does:

```
    report = HTMLReport.new
```

Ruby is dynamically typed, which means that the language does no checking to ensure that the objects being passed around have any particular class ancestry. The only thing that matters is that an object actually implements the methods that its clients want to call. In the preceding example, the `Report` class simply expects the `@text` object to behave like an array of strings. If `@text` looks like an array of strings—that is, if you can get the third string out of it with `@text[2]`—then whatever its actual class, it is the correct type.

This "I am what I am" approach to typing has been called **duck typing.** The name comes from the old bit of wisdom that goes, "If it looks like a duck and quacks like a duck, then it is a duck." Another way to look at this issue is to think of static typing as working like an aristocracy: Statically typed languages are constantly asking about your parent or grandparent, or perhaps, in the case of Java-style interfaces, your aunts and uncles. In a statically typed language, an object's family tree matters deeply. Dynamically typed languages, by contrast, are meritocracies:

They are concerned with which methods you have, rather than where those methods came from. Dynamically typed languages rarely ask about an object's ancestry; instead, they simply say, "I don't care who you are related to, Mac. All I want to know is what you can do."[1]

Types, Safety, and Flexibility

People who are used to programming in statically typed languages often wonder how all of this could possibly work. You might think that all of this free and easy duck typing stuff will certainly lead to disaster, with programs constantly crashing as they try to format some HTML with a database connection or attempt to tell the number 42 to generate a monthly report. Surprisingly, it turns out that these kinds of outrageous typing problems rarely occur.

You can find evidence of this robustness in the world of Java programs, of all places. Almost all Java programs written before the advent of Java 1.5—and that covers the bulk of existing Java programs—use the containers from the java.util package, things like `HashMap` and `ArrayList`. The pre-1.5 versions of these containers provided no type safety at all, and even post-1.5 Java continues to provide non-type-safe versions of these containers for backward compatibility. Despite this cavalier attitude toward type safety, most Java programs do not mix up their socket objects with their `Employee` objects and crash while trying to give a network connection a pay raise.

Statically typed languages are so pervasive these days that a key question is rarely asked: What is the cost of static typing? My answer is that static typing costs a lot. In fact, in the currency of programming effort and code clutter, static typing costs a fortune. Look at a Java or C# program and count the number of tokens devoted to parameter and variable declarations. Add in most of the interfaces. Don't forget those pesky class casts, where you convince the typing system that, yes, that really is a String over there. Add a bonus for each complex generic declaration. All of this code clutter is not free.[2]

---

1. And, in my mind at least, they say it with the accent of a New York cab driver.
2. In fairness, I must point out that static typing is very expensive in terms of code clutter as it is implemented in the languages in wide use today. There are, however, a number of much less widely used languages, such as OCaml and Scala, that manage to handle static typing with much less noise.

And it is not just programming effort. There is a very real, albeit hidden cost to static typing: It tends to couple your system together much more tightly than necessary. Consider the following Java isEmpty() method:

```java
public boolean isEmpty(String s)
{
   return s.length() == 0;
}
```

Now look at its Ruby twin:

```ruby
def empty?(s)
  s.length == 0
end
```

On the surface, the two methods seem pretty much the same. Now consider that the Java version works only on arguments of type java.lang.String. The Ruby version will work on strings, to be sure—but it will also work with arrays, queues, sets, and hashes. In fact, the Ruby empty? method will work with any argument that has a length method. It doesn't care what the exact type of the argument is, and perhaps it should not.

The arguments for dynamic typing might sound counterintuitive to the statically typed ear. If you are used to static typing, in which you declare everything all the time, it might seem unrealistic to suppose that you can build large, reliable systems without strong type checking. But it is possible—and there are two very obvious examples that demonstrate just how possible it is.

Ruby on Rails is by far the most prominent evidence that you can write reliable code in a dynamically typed language. Rails consists of tens of thousands of lines of dynamically typed Ruby code, and Rails is rock stable. If Rails does not persuade you, think about that other large lump of Ruby code in constant use everyday: the standard library that comes with Ruby. The Ruby standard library consists of more than 100,000 lines of Ruby. It is nearly impossible to write a Ruby program that does not use the Ruby standard library—and it works.

Ruby on Rails and the Ruby standard library are the existence proof: You can write large bodies of reliable code in a dynamically typed language. The fear that dynamic typing will produce code chaos is mostly unfounded. Yes, type problems do occasionally cause Ruby programs to crash. But Ruby programs do not crash with anything like the frequency that you might expect given the lengths that statically typed languages go to in to avoid even the remote possibility of type errors.

Does this mean that dynamically typed languages are just better, and that we should give up on statically typed languages completely? The jury is still out on this question. As with most software engineering questions, the answer involves seeing the two options as a balance. Static typing is probably worth the price on large, complex systems built by huge teams. But dynamic typing has some significant advantages: Programs written in Ruby are generally a fraction of the size of their statically typed equivalents. And, as we saw with the `empty?` example and shall see in the chapters to come, dynamic typing offers a huge flexibility bonus.

If all of this seems crazy to you, stick with me through the rest of this book, and give all of this dynamically typed insanity a chance. You may be pleasantly surprised.

Unit Tests Are Not Optional

One way that you can increase the chances that the surprise will be a pleasant one is to write unit tests. No matter whether you are writing in Java, C#, or Ruby, you should be writing unit tests: The second oldest[3] joke in programming is "It compiles, so it must work."

While tests are important no matter which language you are using, they are critical when you are working in a dynamic language such as Ruby. There is no compiler in Ruby to make that first sanity check—and perhaps give you a false sense of security. Instead, the only way to know that the program is working is to run some tests. The good news is that the same unit tests that you need to show that your code works will also tend to ferret out the vast bulk of those pesky type-related problems.

The even better news is that if you know how to use JUnit, NUnit, or any of the other familiar XUnit-style libraries, then you already know how to write unit tests in Ruby. For example, the following class tests our Ruby `empty?` method:

```
require 'test/unit'
require 'empty'

class EmptyTest < Test::Unit::TestCase
  def setup
    @empty_string = ''
    @one_char_string = 'X'
    @long_string = 'The rain in Spain'
```

---

3. The oldest is that dead moth taped in the log book.

```
  @empty_array = []
  @one_element_array = [1]
  @long_array = [1, 2, 3, 4, 5, 6]
end

def test_empty_on_strings
  assert empty?(@empty_string)
  assert ! empty?(@one_char_string)
  assert ! empty?(@long_string)
end

def test_empty_on_arrays
  assert empty?(@empty_array)
  assert ! empty?(@one_element_array)
  assert ! empty?(@long_array)
end
end
```

True to its XUnit roots, Test::Unit runs each of the methods whose name starts with test as a test. If your test class has a setup method (as the preceding class does), it is run before *each* test method. If your class has a teardown method (and the preceding class does not), it is run after *each* test method.

Test::Unit comes equipped with a whole menagerie of assert methods. You can assert that something is true, or you can assert_equal that two objects are equal. If you want to be sure that you have something and not nothing, you can assert_not_nil.

Running the unit tests could not be easier. If the test case above is found in a file called string_test.rb, then you can run the tests by simply executing the file as a Ruby program:

```
$ ruby empty_test.rb
Loaded suite empty_test
Started
..
Finished in 0.000708 seconds.

2 tests, 6 assertions, 0 failures, 0 errors
```

Nothing like the feeling of a test that completes without complaint.

Using and Abusing the Template Method Pattern

Given that it is possible to write a reliable implementation of the Template Method pattern in Ruby, how do you actually go about doing so? The best approach is an evolutionary one: Start with one variation and simply code as though it was the only problem that you need to solve. In our report example, you might have started with HTML:

```ruby
class Report
  def initialize
    @title = 'MonthlyReport'
    @text = ['Things are going', 'really, really well.']
  end

  def output_report
    puts('<html>')
    puts('  <head>')
    puts('    <title>#{@title}</title>')
    # output the rest of the report ...
  end
end
```

Next, you could refactor the method that will become the template method so that it calls other methods for the variable parts of the algorithm, but still just focus on the one case:

```ruby
class Report
  # ...

  def output_report
    output_start
    output_title(@title)
    output_body_start
    for line in @text
      output_line(line)
    end
    output_body_end
    output_end
  end

  def output_start
    puts('<html>')
  end
```

```
def output_title(title)
  puts('  <head>')
  puts("    <title>#{title}</title>")
  puts('  </head>')
end

# ...
```

end

Finally, you could create a subclass for your first case and move your specific implementation into that subclass. At this point, you are ready to start coding the rest of the variations.

As mentioned in Chapter 1, the worst mistake you can make is to overdo things in an effort to cover every conceivable possibility. The Template Method pattern is at its best when it is at its leanest—that is, when every abstract method and hook is there for a reason. Try to avoid creating a template class that requires each subclass to override a huge number of obscure methods just to cover every conceivable possibility. You also do not want to create a template class that is encrusted with a multitude of hook methods that no one will ever override.

Templates in the Wild

You can find a classic example of the Template Method pattern in WEBrick, the lightweight, all-Ruby library for building TCP/IP servers. A key part of WEBrick is the `GenericServer` class, which implements all of the details of being a network server. Of course, `GenericServer` has no idea what you want to actually accomplish in your server. Thus, to use `GenericServer`, you simply extend it and override the `run` method:

```
require 'webrick'

class HelloServer < WEBrick::GenericServer
  def run(socket)
    socket.print('Hello TCP/IP world')
  end
end
```

The template method buried inside `GenericServer` contains all the code for listening on a TCP/IP port, accepting new connections, and cleaning up when a connection is broken. And right in the middle of all that code, right when it has its hands on a new connection, it calls your `run` method.[4]

There is another very common example of the Template Method pattern that is perhaps so pervasive that it is hard to see. Think about the `initialize` method that we use to set up our objects. All we know about `initialize` is that it is called sometime toward the end of the process of creating a new object instance and that it is a method that we can override in our class to do any specific initialization. Sounds like a hook method to me.

Wrapping Up

In this chapter we looked in detail at our first pattern, the Template Method pattern. The Template Method pattern is simply a fancy way of saying that if you want to vary an algorithm, one way to do so is to code the invariant part in a base class and to encapsulate the variable parts in methods that are defined by a number of subclasses. The base class can simply leave the methods completely undefined—in that case, the subclasses *must* supply the methods. Alternatively, the base class can provide a default implementation for the methods that the subclasses *can* override if they want.

Given that this was our first pattern, we also took a bit of a detour in which we explored one of the most important aspects of programming in Ruby: duck typing. Duck typing is a trade-off: You give up the compile-time safety of static typing, and in return you get back a lot of code clarity and programming flexibility.

Looking ahead, we will soon see that the Template Method pattern is such a basic object-oriented technique that it pops up in other patterns. In Chapter 13, for example, we will learn that the Factory Method pattern is simply the Template Method pattern applied to creating new objects. The problem that the Template Method pattern attacks is also reasonably pervasive. In fact, in the next chapter we will look at the Strategy pattern, which offers a different solution to the same problem—a solution that does not rely on inheritance in the same way that the Template Method pattern does.

---

4. I know this because I have looked. One of the advantages of dealing with an interpreted language is that all of the Ruby standard library source code is sitting somewhere on your system, just waiting to teach you all sorts of things. I can't imagine a better way to learn a new programming language than to look at actual, working code.

CHAPTER 4

Replacing the Algorithm with the Strategy

We kicked off the last chapter by posing the following question: How do you vary part of an algorithm? How can you get step 3 of a five-step process to sometimes do one thing and sometimes do another thing? The answer that we came up with in Chapter 3 is to use the Template Method pattern, to create a base class with a template method that controls the overall processing and then to use subclasses to fill in the details. If we want to sometimes do this and other times to do that, we create two subclasses, one for this and another for that.

Unfortunately, the Template Method pattern has some drawbacks, most of which stem from the fact that this pattern is built around inheritance. As we saw in Chapter 1, basing your design on inheritance has some significant disadvantages. No matter how carefully you design your code, your subclasses are tangled up with their superclass: It is in the nature of the relationship. On top of this, inheritance-based techniques such as the Template Method pattern limit our runtime flexibility. Once we have selected a particular variation of the algorithm—in our example, once we have created an instance of `HTMLReport`—changing our mind is hard. With the Template Method pattern, if we change our mind about the format of the report, we need to create a whole new report object—perhaps a `PlainTextReport`—just to switch to a different output format. But what is the alternative?

Delegate, Delegate, and Delegate Again

The alternative is to follow that bit of GoF advice mentioned in Chapter 1: Prefer delegation. What if, instead of creating a subclass for each variation, we tear out the whole annoyingly varying chunk of code and isolate it in its own class? Then we could create a whole family of classes, one for each variation. Here for example, is our HTML formatting code from the report example, surgically transplanted into its own class:

```
class Formatter
  def output_report( title, text )
    raise 'Abstract method called'
  end
end

class HTMLFormatter < Formatter
  def output_report( title, text )
    puts('<html>')
    puts('  <head>')
    puts("    <title>#{title}</title>")
    puts('  </head>')
    puts('  <body>')
    text.each do |line|
      puts("    <p>#{line}</p>" )
    end
    puts('  </body>')
    puts('</html>')
  end
end
```

Here's the formatter for plain text:

```
class PlainTextFormatter < Formatter
  def output_report(title, text)
    puts("***** #{title} *****")
    text.each do |line|
      puts(line)
    end
  end
end
```

Now that we have completely removed the details of formatting the output from our `Report` class, that class becomes much simpler:

```ruby
class Report
  attr_reader :title, :text
  attr_accessor :formatter

  def initialize(formatter)
    @title = 'Monthly Report'
    @text =  [ 'Things are going', 'really, really well.' ]
    @formatter = formatter
  end

  def output_report
    @formatter.output_report( @title, @text )
  end
end
```

Using the new `Report` class is only slightly more complicated. We now need to supply `Report` with the correct formatting object:

```ruby
report = Report.new(HTMLFormatter.new)
report.output_report
```

The GoF call this "pull the algorithm out into a separate object" technique the Strategy pattern (Figure 4-1). The key idea underlying the Strategy pattern is to define a family of objects, the **strategies,** which all do the same thing—in our example, format the report. Not only does each strategy object perform the same job, but all of the objects support exactly the same interface. In our example, both of the strategy objects

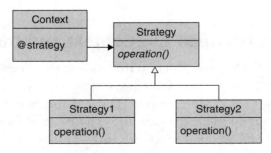

Figure 4-1   The Strategy pattern

support the `output_report` method. Given that all of the strategy objects look alike from the outside, the user of the strategy—called the **context** class by the GoF—can treat the strategies like interchangeable parts. Thus, it does not matter which strategy you use, because they all look alike and they all perform the same function.

But it does matter which strategy you pick, because each one does its thing a little differently. In the example, one of our formatting strategies produces HTML while the other produces plain text. If we were doing tax calculations, we might have use the Strategy pattern for state income tax calculations: one strategy to compute taxes for residents of Virginia, and another to do the calculations according to the California tax code.

The Strategy pattern has some real advantages. As we saw in the report example, we can achieve better separation of concerns by pulling out a set of strategies from a class. By using the Strategy pattern, we relieve the `Report` class of any responsibility for or knowledge of the report file format.

In addition, because the Strategy pattern is based on composition and delegation, rather than on inheritance, it is easy to switch strategies at runtime. We simply swap out the strategy object:

```
report = Report.new(HTMLFormatter.new)
report.output_report

report.formatter = PlainTextFormatter.new
report.output_report
```

The Strategy pattern does have one thing in common with the Template Method pattern: Both patterns allow us to concentrate the decision about which variation we are using in one or a few places. With the Template Method pattern, we make our decision when we pick our concrete subclass. In the Strategy pattern, we make our decision by selecting a strategy class at runtime.

Sharing Data between the Context and the Strategy

A real advantage of the Strategy pattern is that because the context and the strategy code are in different classes, a nice wall of data separation divides the two. The bad news is that we now need to figure a way to get the information that the context has but the strategy needs up and over that wall. We have essentially two choices here.

First, we can continue with the approach that we have used so far—that is, pass in everything that the strategy needs as arguments when the context calls the methods on the strategy object. Recall that in our `Report` example, the report object passed in everything that the formatter needed to know in the arguments to `output_report`. Passing in all of the data has the advantage of keeping the context and the strategy objects crisply separated. The strategies have their interface; the context simply uses that interface. The downside of doing things this way is that if there is a lot of complex data to pass between the context and the strategy, then, well, you are going to be passing a lot of complex data around without any guarantee that it will get used.

Second, we can get the data from the context to the strategy by having the context object pass a reference to itself to the strategy object. The strategy object can then call methods on the context to get at the data it needs. Returning to our reporting example, we might do something like this:

```ruby
class Report
  attr_reader :title, :text

  attr_accessor :formatter

  def initialize(formatter)
    @title = 'Monthly Report'
    @text = ['Things are going', 'really, really well.']
    @formatter = formatter
  end

  def output_report
    @formatter.output_report(self)
  end
end
```

Here `Report` passes a reference to itself to the formatting strategy, and the formatter class calls the new `title` and `text` methods to get the data it needs. Here is a refactored `HTMLFormatter` to go with this self-passing `Report` class:

```ruby
class Formatter
  def output_report(context)
    raise 'Abstract method called'
  end
end
```

```ruby
class HTMLFormatter < Formatter
  def output_report(context)
    puts('<html>')
    puts('  <head>')
    puts("    <title>#{context.title}</title>")
    puts('  </head>')
    puts('  <body>')
    context.text.each do |line|
      puts("    <p>#{line}</p>")
    end
    puts('  </body>')
    puts('</html>')
  end
end
```

Although this technique of passing the context to the strategy does simplify the flow of data, it also increases the coupling between the context and the strategy. This magnifies the danger that the context class and the strategy classes will get tangled up with each other.

Duck Typing Yet Again

The formatting example that we have built so far mirrors the GoF approach to the Strategy pattern. Our family of formatting strategies consists of the "abstract" `Formatter` base class with two subclasses, `HTMLFormatter` and `PlainTextFormatter`. This is, however, a very un-Ruby implementation, because the `Formatter` class does not actually do anything: It simply exists to define the common interface for all the formatter subclasses. There is certainly nothing wrong with this approach in the sense of it working or not working—it does work. Nevertheless, this kind of code runs counter to Ruby's duck typing philosophy. The ducks would argue (quack?) that `HtmlFormatter` and `PlainTextFormatter` already share a common interface because both implement the `output_report` method. Thus there is no need to artificially grind in the point by creating what is essentially a do-nothing superclass.

We can eliminate the `Formatter` base class with a few swipes of the delete key. We end up with the following code:

```
class Report
  attr_reader :title, :text
  attr_accessor :formatter

  def initialize(formatter)
    @title = 'Monthly Report'
    @text = ['Things are going', 'really, really well.']
    @formatter = formatter
  end

  def output_report()
    @formatter.output_report(self)
  end
end

class HTMLFormatter
  def output_report(context)
    puts('<html>')
    puts('  <head>')
    # Output The rest of the report ...

    puts("    <title>#{context.title}</title>")
    puts('  </head>')
    puts('  <body>')
    context.text.each do |line|
      puts("    <p>#{line}</p>")
    end
    puts('  </body>')

    puts('</html>')
  end
end

class PlainTextFormatter
  def output_report(context)
    puts("***** #{context.title} *****")
    context.text.each do |line|
      puts(line)
    end
  end
end
```

If you compare this code with the previous version, you will see that we eliminated the base Formatter class but not much else has changed. Thanks to dynamic typing, we still get the same reports proclaiming that all is well. Although both versions do work, the Ruby world would firmly vote for skipping the `Formatter` base class.

Procs and Blocks

It turns out that ripping out the base class is not the only way we can recast the Strategy pattern to give it a more Ruby-colored tint. But before we can take the next step, we need to explore one of the most interesting aspects of Ruby, code blocks and the `Proc` object.

As users of object-oriented programming languages, we spend a lot of our time thinking about objects and how they go together. But there is an asymmetry regarding how we tend to think about our objects. We have no problem separating out data from an object—we can pull out the `@text` from a report and pass it around independently of the rest of the report. Yet we tend to think of our code as tightly bound, inseparable from the object to which it is attached. Of course, it doesn't have to be this way. What if we could pull out chunks of code from our objects and pass those chunks around just like objects? It turns out that Ruby allows us to do exactly that.

In Ruby, a `Proc` is an object that holds a chunk of code. The most common way to make a `Proc` is with the `lambda` method:

```
hello = lambda do
  puts('Hello')
  puts('I am inside a proc')
end
```

Ruby calls the chunk of code between the `do` and the `end` a **code block.**[1] The `lambda` method returns a new `Proc` object, a container for all of the code between the `do` and the `end`. Our `hello` variable points at the `Proc` object. We can run the code buried inside the `Proc` by calling the (what else?) `call` method. In our example, if we call the `call` method on the `Proc` object

```
hello.call
```

we will get

```
Hello
I am inside a proc
```

---

1. Other terms for the same concept are **closure** and **lambda,** which explains the name of our `Proc`-producing method.

An extremely useful aspect of the `Proc` object is that it picks up the surrounding environment when it is created. Thus any variables that are visible when a `Proc` is created remain visible inside the `Proc` when it is run. For example, there is only one variable `name` in the following code fragment:

```
name = 'John'
proc = Proc.new do
  name = 'Mary'
end

proc.call
puts(name)
```

When we run this code, `name` will be set to "John" in the first statement, then reset to "Mary" when the `Proc` is called. Ultimately, Ruby will print "Mary".

If `do` and `end` seem like too much typing for you, Ruby provides a slightly more concise syntax using curly braces. Here is a quicker way to create our hello `Proc`:

```
hello = lambda {
  puts('Hello, I am inside a proc')
}
```

Ruby programmers have adopted the convention of using `do`/`end` for multiple-line code blocks and braces for one liners.[2] A more socially acceptable version of our example, then, is this:

```
hello = lambda {puts('Hello, I am inside a proc')}
```

`Proc` objects have a lot in common with methods. For example, not only are `Proc` objects and methods bundles of code, but both can also return a value. A `Proc` always returns the last value computed in the code block; thus, to return a value from

---

2. Actually, there is one real difference between `do`/`end` and the braces. In Ruby expressions, the braces have a higher precedence than the `do`/`end` pair. Essentially, the braces are stickier in an expression. This difference usually rears its head only when you start dropping all of those optional parentheses.

a `Proc`, you just make sure that the value you want returned is computed by the last expression in the `Proc` object. Whatever value is returned by the `Proc` is passed back through by `call`. Thus the code

```
return_24 = lambda {24}
puts(return_24.call)
```

will print

```
24
```

You can also define parameters for your `Proc` object, although the syntax is a little strange. Instead of wrapping your parameter list with the usual round parentheses "()", you open and close the list with a vertical bar character "|":

```
multiply = lambda {|x, y| x * y}
```

This code defines a `Proc` object that takes two parameters, multiplies them together, and returns the result. To call a `Proc` with parameters, we simply add the parameters to the `call` method:

```
n = multiply.call(20, 3)
puts(n)
n = multiply.call(10, 50)
puts(n)
```

Running this code will produce the following printout:

```
60
500
```

The ability to pass around blocks of code is so useful that Ruby has defined a special shorthand syntax for it. If we want to pass a block of code into a method, we simply append the block to the end of the method call. The method can then execute the code block by using the `yield` keyword. For example, here is a method that prints a message, executes its code block, and prints a second message:

```
def run_it
  puts("Before the yield")
  yield
  puts("After the yield")
end
```

And here is the call to run_it. Notice that we just append the code block to the end of the method call:

```
run_it do
  puts('Hello')
  puts('Coming to you from inside the block')
end
```

When we slap a code block on the end of a method call as we did above, the block (actually the Proc object) is passed along as a sort of invisible parameter to the method. The yield keyword will then execute that parameter. For instance, running the code above will produce the following output:

```
Before the yield
Hello
Coming to you from inside the block
After the yield
```

If the block that is passed into your method takes parameters, you supply the parameters to the yield. For instance, the code

```
def run_it_with_parameter
  puts('Before the yield')
  yield(24)
  puts('After the yield')
end

run_it_with_parameter do |x|
  puts('Hello from inside the proc')
  puts("The value of x is #{x}")
end
```

will print

```
Before the yield
Hello from inside the proc
The value of x is 24
After the yield
```

Sometimes we want to make the code block parameter explicit—that is, we want to capture the block passed into our method as a `Proc` object in an actual parameter. We can do so by adding a special parameter to the end of our parameter list. This special parameter, which is preceded by an ampersand, is assigned the `Proc` object created from the code block that came after the method call. Thus an equivalent rendition of the `run_it_with_parameters` method is

```
def run_it_with_parameter(&block)
  puts('Before the call')
  block.call(24)
  puts('After the call')
end
```

The ampersand works in the other direction, too. If we have a `Proc` object in a variable and we want to pass it to a method that is looking for a code block, we can convert the `Proc` object back into a code block by sticking an ampersand in front of it:

```
my_proc = lambda {|x| puts("The value of x is #{x}")}
run_it_with_parameter(&my_proc)
```

Quick-and-Dirty Strategies

What does all of this code block and `Proc` stuff have to do with the Strategy pattern? Simply put, you can look at a strategy as a lump of executable code that knows how to do something—format text, for example—and is wrapped up in an object. This should sound familiar because it is also a good description of a `Proc`—a chunk of code wrapped in an object.

Recasting our report formatting example to use a `Proc` strategy is trivial. The only changes we need to make to the `Report` class are to add an ampersand to pick up any code block that is passed in the `initialize` method and to rename the method that we call from `output_report` to `call`:

```
class Report
  attr_reader :title, :text
  attr_accessor :formatter

  def initialize(&formatter)
    @title = 'Monthly Report'
    @text = [ 'Things are going', 'really, really well.' ]
    @formatter = formatter
  end

  def output_report
    @formatter.call( self )
  end
end
```

Building the formatters is a little different, however. We now need to create `Proc` objects instead of instances of our special formatter classes:

```
HTML_FORMATTER = lambda do |context|
  puts('<html>')
  puts('  <head>')
  puts("    <title>#{context.title}</title>")
  puts('  </head>')
  puts('  <body>')
  context.text.each do |line|
    puts("    <p>#{line}</p>" )
  end
  puts('  </body>')
  puts
```

With our new `Proc`-based formatters in hand, we are ready to create some reports. Given that we have a `Proc` object and the `Report` constructor expects a code block, we need to stick an ampersand in front of our `Proc` object when we create a new `Report` instance:

```
report = Report.new &HTML_FORMATTER
report.output_report
```

Why bother with a `Proc`-based strategy at all? For one thing, we do not have to define special classes for our strategy—we just wrap the code in a `Proc`. More importantly, we can now create a strategy out of thin air by passing a code block right into the method. As an example, here is our plain text formatter, recast as an on-the-fly code block:

```
report = Report.new do |context|
  puts("***** #{context.title} *****")
  context.text.each do |line|
    puts(line)
  end
end
```

If you are not used to them, code blocks can seem a little bizarre. But consider that with code blocks, we have simplified the Strategy pattern from a context, a base strategy class, some number of concrete strategies, and associated instances here and there, to a context class and some code blocks.

Does all of this mean we should just forget about the class-based strategies? Not really. Code block-based strategies work only when the strategy interface is a simple, one-method affair. After all, the only method that we can call on a `Proc` object is `call`. If you need more than that for your strategy, by all means build some classes. But if your requirement calls for a simple strategy, the code block may just be the way to go.

Using and Abusing the Strategy Pattern

The easiest way to go wrong with the Strategy pattern is to get the interface between the context and the strategy object wrong. Bear in mind that you are trying to tease an entire, consistent, and more or less self-contained job out of the context object and delegate it to the strategy. You need to pay particular attention to the details of the interface between the context and the strategy as well as to the coupling between them. Remember, the Strategy pattern will do you little good if you couple the context and your first strategy so tightly together that you cannot wedge a second or a third strategy into the design.

The Strategy Pattern in the Wild

The rdoc utility, which came packaged with your Ruby distribution, contains a couple of instances of the classic GoF class-based Strategy pattern. The purpose of `rdoc` is to extract documentation from programs. Besides Ruby, rdoc can distill documentation from C and (goodness help us!) FORTRAN programs. The rdoc utility uses the

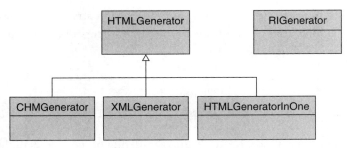

Figure 4-2   The generator classes of rdoc

Strategy pattern to handle each of the different programming languages—there is a C parser, a Ruby parser, and a FORTRAN parser, each of which is a strategy for handling its respective input.

The rdoc utility also gives you a choice of output formats—you can choose to output your documentation in several flavors of HTML, or in XML, or in the format used by the Ruby-supplied `ri` command. As you have probably guessed, each of these output formats is also handled by its own strategy. The relationship between the various rdoc strategy classes is a good illustration of the typical Ruby attitude toward inheritance. The class relationship between the various strategies is depicted in Figure 4-2.

As you can see from Figure 4-2, there are four related output strategies (or generators, as rdoc calls them) and one stand-alone strategy. The four related strategies all generate similar output—that familiar `<stuff>` wrapped in angle brackets `</stuff>`.[3] The final strategy generates output for the Ruby `ri` command, which does not resemble either XML or HTML. As you can see from the UML diagram in Figure 4-2, the class relationships are purely a reflection of implementation issues: The classes that generate HTML, CHM, and XML will naturally share a lot of common code and, therefore, have an inheritance relationship. The `RIGenerator` produces very different output and is completely unrelated to the XML/HTML family. The rdoc code gives no thought to making all of the generators share a common superclass simply because they need to implement the same interface. Each generator implements the right methods, and that is the end of it.

---

3. CHM is an HTML flavor used to generate Microsoft help files. And please remember it is the rdoc code—and not me—that suggests XML is a kind of HTML.

A good example of the `Proc` object as a lightweight strategy object is as close at hand as the familiar array. If you want to sort the contents of a Ruby array, you can simply call the `sort` method:

```
a = ['russell', 'mike', 'john', 'dan', 'rob']
a.sort
```

By default, `sort` will sort by the "natural" ordering of the objects in the array. But what if we want to use some other ordering? For example, what if we want to sort by the length of the strings? We simply pass in a comparison strategy—as a code block:

```
a.sort { |a,b| a.length <=> b.length }
```

The `sort` method will call your code block each time it needs to compare two elements in the array. Your block should return 1 if the first element is larger, 0 if they are equal, and -1 if the second element is larger. Not so coincidentally, this is exactly what the `<=>` operator does.

Wrapping Up

The Strategy pattern is a delegation-based approach to solving the same problem as the Template Method pattern. Instead of teasing out the variable parts of your algorithm and pushing them down into subclasses, you simply implement each version of your algorithm as a separate object. You can then vary the algorithm by supplying different strategy objects to the context—one strategy for producing HTML and a different one for outputting PDF files, for example, or perhaps one strategy for calculating Virginia taxes and a different one for computing Pennsylvania taxes.

We have a couple of choices regarding how we get the appropriate data from the context object over to the strategy object. We can pass all of the data as parameters as we call methods on the strategy object, or we can simply pass a reference to the whole context object to the strategy.

Ruby code blocks, which are essentially code wrapped up in an instant object (the `Proc` object), are wonderfully useful for creating quick, albeit simple, strategy objects.

As we shall see in coming chapters, the Strategy pattern resembles, at least superficially, several other patterns. For example, in the Strategy pattern we have an object—the context—that is trying to get something done. But to get that thing done, we need to supply the context with a second object—the strategy object—that helps get the thing done. Superficially, the Observer pattern works in much the same way: An object does something, but along the way it makes calls to a second object, which we need to supply.

The difference between these two patterns relates to their intent. The motive behind the Strategy pattern is to supply the context with an object that knows how to perform some variation on an algorithm. The intent of the Observer pattern is very different—the intent of the Observer pattern is . . . Well, perhaps we should leave that distinction to another chapter (the next one, in fact).

CHAPTER 5

Keeping Up with the Times with the Observer

One of the knottiest design challenges is the problem of building a system that is highly integrated—that is, a system where every part is aware of the state of the whole. Think about a spreadsheet, where editing the contents of one cell not only changes the number in the grid but also changes the column totals, alters the height of one of the bars in a bar chart, and enables the Save button. Even more simply, how about a personnel system that needs to let the payroll department know when someone's salary changes?

Building this kind of system is hard enough, but throw in the requirement that the system be maintainable and now you are talking truly difficult. How can you tie the disparate parts of a large software system together without increasing the coupling between classes to the point where the whole thing becomes a tangled mess? How do you construct a spreadsheet that properly displays changes in the data without hard-coding a link between the spreadsheet editing code and the bar chart renderer? How can you make the `Employee` object spread the news about salary changes without tangling it up with the payroll system?

Staying Informed

One way to solve this problem is to focus on the fact that the spreadsheet cell and the `Employee` object are both acting as a source of news. Fred gets a raise and his `Employee` record shouts out to the world (or at least to anyone who seems interested), "Hello! I've got something going on here!" Any object that is interested in the state of

Fred's finances need simply register with his `Employee` object ahead of time. Once registered, that object would receive timely updates about the ups and downs of Fred's paycheck.

How would all of this work in code? Here is a basic version of an `Employee` object with no code to tell anyone anything—it just goes about its business of keeping track of an employee:

```ruby
class Employee
  attr_reader :name
  attr_accessor  :title, :salary

  def initialize( name, title, salary )
    @name = name
    @title = title
    @salary = salary
  end
end
```

Because we have made the salary field accessible with `attr_accessor`, our employees can get raises:[1]

```ruby
fred = Employee.new("Fred Flintstone", "Crane Operator", 30000.0)

# Give Fred a raise

fred.salary=35000.0
```

Let's now add some fairly naive code to keep the payroll department informed of pay changes:

```ruby
class Payroll
  def update( changed_employee )
    puts("Cut a new check for #{changed_employee.name}!")
    puts("His salary is now #{changed_employee.salary}!")
  end
end
```

---

1. Of course, the employees can also suffer pay cuts, but we will silently pass over such unpleasant matters.

```
class Employee
  attr_reader :name, :title
  attr_reader :salary

  def initialize( name, title, salary, payroll)
   @name = name
   @title = title
   @salary = salary
   @payroll = payroll
  end

  def salary=(new_salary)
    @salary = new_salary
   @payroll.update(self)
  end
end
```

We can now change Fred's wages:

```
payroll = Payroll.new
fred = Employee.new('Fred', 'Crane Operator', 30000, payroll)
fred.salary = 35000
```

And the payroll department will know all about it:

```
Cut a new check for Fred!
His salary is now 35000!
```

Note that since we need to inform the payroll department about changes in salary, we cannot use `attr_accessor` for the salary field. Instead, we need to write the `salary=` method out by hand.

A Better Way to Stay Informed

The trouble with this code is that it is hard-wired to inform the payroll department about salary changes. What do we do if we need to keep other objects—perhaps some accounting-related classes—informed about Fred's financial state? As the code stands right now, we must go back in and modify the Employee class. Needing to change the Employee class in this situation is very unfortunate because nothing in the Employee

class is really changing. It is the other classes—the payroll and accounting classes—
that are actually driving the changes to Employee. Our Employee class seems to be
showing very little change resistance here.

Perhaps we should step back and try to solve this notification problem in a more
general way. How can we separate out the thing that is changing—who gets the news
about salary changes—from the real guts of the Employee object? What we seem to
need is a list of objects that are interested in hearing about the latest news from the
Employee object. We can set up an array for just that purpose in the initialize
method:

```ruby
def initialize( name, title, salary )
  @name = name
  @title = title
  @salary = salary
  @observers = []
end
```

We also need some code to inform all of the observers that something has
changed:

```ruby
def salary=(new_salary)
  @salary = new_salary
  notify_observers
end

def notify_observers
  @observers.each do |observer|
    observer.update(self)
  end
end
```

The key moving part of notify_observers is observer.update(self). This
bit of code calls the update method on each observer,[2] telling it that something—in
this case, the salary—has changed on the Employee object.

---

2. Recall that array.each is Ruby terminology for a loop that runs through all of the elements in an
array. We will have more to say about this array.each in Chapter 7.

The only job left is to write the methods that add and delete observers from the `Employee` object:

```ruby
def add_observer(observer)
  @observers << observer
end

def delete_observer(observer)
  @observers.delete(observer)
end
```

Now any object that is interested in hearing about changes in Fred's salary can simply register as an observer on Fred's `Employee` object:

```ruby
fred = Employee.new('Fred', 'Crane Operator', 30000.0)

payroll = Payroll.new
fred.add_observer( payroll )

fred.salary=35000.0
```

By building this general mechanism, we have removed the implicit coupling between the `Employee` class and the `Payroll` object. `Employee` no longer cares which or how many other objects are interested in knowing about salary changes; it just forwards the news to any object that said that it was interested. In addition, instances of the `Employee` class will be happy with no observers, one, or several:

```ruby
class TaxMan
  def update( changed_employee )
    puts("Send #{changed_employee.name} a new tax bill!")
  end
end

tax_man = TaxMan.new
fred.add_observer(tax_man)
```

Suppose we change Fred's salary again:

```ruby
fred.salary=90000.0
```

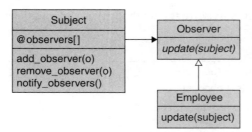

Figure 5-1   The Observer pattern

Now both the payroll department and the tax man will hear about it:

```
Cut a new check for Fred!
His salary is now 80000.0!
Send Fred a new tax bill!
```

The GoF called this idea of building a clean interface between the source of the news that some object has changed and the consumers of that news the Observer pattern (Figure 5-1). The GoF called the class with the news the **subject** class. In our example, the subject is the `Employee` class. The **observers** are the objects that are interested in getting the news. In our employee example, we have two observers: `Payroll` and `TaxMan`. When an object is interested in being informed of the state of the subject, it registers as an observer on that subject.

It has always seemed to me that the Observer pattern is somewhat misnamed. While the observer object gets top billing—in fact, the only billing—it is actually the subject that does most of the work. It is the subject that is responsible for keeping track of the observers. It is also the subject that needs to inform the observers that a change has come down the pike. Put another way, it is much harder to publish and distribute a newspaper than to read one.

Factoring Out the Observable Support

Implementing the Observer pattern in Ruby is usually no more complex than our `Employee` example suggested: just an array to hold the observers and a couple of methods to manage the array, plus a method to notify everyone when something changes. But surely we can do better than to repeat this code every time we need to make an object observable. We could use inheritance. By factoring out the code that manages the observers, we end up with a functional little base class:

```ruby
class Subject
  def initialize
    @observers=[]
  end

  def add_observer(observer)
    @observers << observer
  end

  def delete_observer(observer)
    @observers.delete(observer)
  end

  def notify_observers
    @observers.each do |observer|
      observer.update(self)
    end
  end
end
```

Now we can make `Employee` a subclass of `Subject`:

```ruby
class Employee < Subject
  attr_reader :name, :address
  attr_reader :salary

  def initialize( name, title, salary)
    super()
    @name = name
    @title = title
    @salary = salary
  end

  def salary=(new_salary)
    @salary = new_salary
    notify_observers
  end
end
```

This is not a completely unreasonable solution; in fact, Java has gone exactly this route with its `java.util.Observable` class. But, as we saw in Chapter 1, using inheritance can cause grief. The problem with using `Subject` as a base class is that it shuts out the possibility of having anything else as a base class. Ruby allows each class to have exactly one superclass: Use up your single superclass of `Employee` on `Subject` and you are done. If our domain model demands that we make `Employee` a subclass of `OrganizationalUnit` or `DatabaseObject`, we are out of luck; we cannot also make it a subclass of `Subject`.

The problem is that sometimes we want to share code between otherwise unrelated classes. Our `Employee` class wants to be a `Subject`, but perhaps so does that spreadsheet cell. So how can we share the `Subject` implementation without using up our one allotted superclass?

The solution to this dilemma is to use a module. Recall that a module is a package of methods and constants that we can share among classes, but that does not soak up the single allotted superclass. If we recast our `Subject` class as a module, it does not really look all that different:

```ruby
module Subject
  def initialize
    @observers=[]
  end

  def add_observer(observer)
    @observers << observer
  end

  def delete_observer(observer)
    @observers.delete(observer)
  end

  def notify_observers
    @observers.each do |observer|
      observer.update(self)
    end
  end
end
```

Using the new `Subject` module is simplicity itself. We include the module and call `notify_observers` when something changes:

```ruby
class Employee
  include Subject

  attr_reader :name, :address
  attr_reader :salary
```

```
    def initialize( name, title, salary)
     super()
     @name = name
     @title = title
     @salary = salary
    end

    def salary=(new_salary)
      @salary = new_salary
      notify_observers
    end
  end
end
```

By including the Subject module, our new Employee class gains all of the Subject methods: It is now fully equipped to play the subject in the Observer pattern. Note that we needed to call super() in the initialize method of Employee, which has the effect of calling initialize in the Subject module.[3]

Building our own Subject module was great fun and a good exercise in creating a mixin module. But would you really want to use the Subject that we just cooked up? Probably not. The Ruby standard library comes with a fine, prebuilt Observable module that provides all of the support you need to make your object, well, observable. Using it is not all that different from using the Subject module that we built:

```
require 'observer'

class Employee
  include Observable

  attr_reader :name, :address
  attr_reader :salary

  def initialize( name, title, salary)
   @name = name
   @title = title
   @salary = salary
  end
```

---

3. Calling super() is one of the few places in Ruby where you need to supply the parentheses for an empty argument list. Calling super the way we do here, with the parentheses, calls the method in the superclass with no arguments. If you omit the parentheses, you will be calling super with the original set of arguments to the current method—in this case, name, title, salary, and payroll_manager.

```
def salary=(new_salary)
  @salary = new_salary
  changed
  notify_observers(self)
end
end
```

The standard `Observable` module does feature one twist that we omitted from our hand-built version. To cut down on redundant notifications to the observers, the standard `Observable` module requires that you call the `changed` method before you call `notify_observers`. The `changed` method sets a Boolean flag that says the object really has changed; the `notify_observers` method will not actually make any notifications if the changed flag is not set to `true`. Each call to `notify_observers` sets the changed flag back to `false`.

Code Blocks as Observers

A common Ruby variation on the Observer pattern is our old friend the code block. The code becomes a lot simpler if we can just pass in a code block as our listener. Because the Ruby library `Observable` does not support code blocks, perhaps we can find a use for a slightly modified version of our `Subject` module after all:

```
module Subject
  def initialize
    @observers=[]
  end

  def add_observer(&observer)
    @observers << observer
  end

  def delete_observer(observer)
    @observers.delete(observer)
  end

  def notify_observers
    @observers.each do |observer|
      observer.call(self)
    end
  end
end
```

```ruby
class Employee
  include Subject

  attr_accessor :name, :title, :salary

  def initialize( name, title, salary )
    super()
    @name = name
    @title = title
    @salary = salary
  end

  def salary=(new_salary)
    @salary = new_salary
    notify_observers
  end
end
```

The advantage of using code blocks as observers is that they simplify the code; we no longer need a separate class for the observers. To add an observer, we just call add_observer and pass in a code block:

```ruby
fred = Employee.new('Fred', 'Crane Operator', 30000)

fred.add_observer do |changed_employee|
    puts("Cut a new check for #{changed_employee.name}!")
    puts("His salary is now #{changed_employee.salary}!")
end
```

This example passes a two-line code block as an observer into Employee object. By the time those two lines reach the Employee object, they are all wrapped up in a convenient Proc object and are set to act as a ready-made observer. When Fred's salary changes, the Employee object calls the call method on the Proc, and the two puts get fired.

Variations on the Observer Pattern

The key decisions that you need to make when implementing the Observer pattern all center on the interface between the subject and the observer. At the simple end of the spectrum, you might do what we did in the example above: Just have a single method in the observer whose only argument is the subject. The GoF term for this strategy is the *pull* method, because the observers have to pull whatever details about the change that they need out of the subject. The other possibility—logically enough termed the *push* method—has the subject send the observers a lot of details about the change:

```
observer.update(self, :salary_changed, old_salary, new_salary)
```

We can even define different update methods for different events. For example, we could have one method for a salary update

```
observer.update_salary(self, old_salary, new_salary)
```

and a different method for title changes

```
observer.update_title(self, old_title, new_title)
```

The advantage in providing more details is that the observers do not have to work quite as hard to keep track of what is going on. The disadvantage of the push model is that if all of the observers are not interested in all of the details, then the work of passing the data around goes for naught.

Using and Abusing the Observer Pattern

Most of the problems that come up in using the Observer pattern revolve around the frequency and timing of the updates. Sometimes the sheer volume of updates can be a problem. For example, an observer might register with a subject, unaware that the subject is going to spew out thousands of updates each second. The subject class can help with all of this by avoiding broadcasting redundant updates. Just because someone updates an object, it does not mean that anything really changed. Remember the salary= method on the Employee object? We probably should not notify the observers if nothing has actually changed:

```
def salary=(new_salary)
  old_salary = @salary
  @salary = new_salary
  if old_salary != new_salary
    changed
    notify_observers(self)
  end
end
```

Another potential problem lies in the consistency of the subject as it informs its observers of changes. Imagine we enhance our employee example a bit so that it informs its observers of changes in an employee's title as well as his or her salary:

```
def title=(new_title)
  old_title = @title
  @title = new_title
  if old_title != new_title
    changed = true
    notify_observers(self)
  end
end
```

Now imagine that Fred gets a big promotion and a big raise to go along with it. We might code that as follows:

```
fred = Employee.new("Fred", "Crane Operator", 30000)

fred.salary = 1000000
# Warning! Inconsistent state here!
fred.title = 'Vice President of Sales'
```

The trouble with this approach is that because he receives his raise before his new title takes effect, Fred will briefly be the highest-paid crane operator in the world. This would not matter, except that all of our observers are listening and experiencing that inconsistent state. You can deal with this problem by not informing the observers until a consistent set of changes is complete:

```
# Don't inform the observers just yet

fred.salary = 1000000
fred.title = 'Vice President of Sales'

# Now inform the observers!

fred.changes_complete
```

One final thing to look out for is badly behaved observers. Although we have used the analogy of the subject delivering news to its observer, we are really talking about one object calling a method on another object. What happens if you update an observer with the news that Fred has gotten a raise, and that observer responds by raising an exception? Do you simply log the exception and soldier on, or do you do something more drastic? There is no standard answer: It really depends on your specific application and the amount of confidence you have in your observers.

Observers in the Wild

The Observer pattern is not hard to find in the Ruby code base. It is, for example, used by `ActiveRecord`. `ActiveRecord` clients that want to stay informed of the goings on as database records are created, read, written, and deleted can define observers that look like this:[4]

```ruby
class EmployeeObserver < ActiveRecord::Observer
  def after_create(employee)
    # New employee record created
  end

  def after_update(employee)
    # Employee record updated
  end

  def after_destroy(employee)
    # Employee record deleted
  end
end
```

In a nice example of the Convention Over Configuration pattern (see Chapter 18), `ActiveRecord` does not require you to register your observer: It just figures out that `EmployeeObserver` is there to observe `Employees`, based on the class name.

You can find an example of the code block-based observer in REXML, the XML parsing package that ships as part of the standard Ruby library. The REXML SAX2Parser class is a streaming XML parser: It will read an XML file and you are welcome to add observers that will be informed when specific XML constructs get read.

---

4. If the `ActiveRecord::Observer` syntax looks a little odd to you, it is because we haven't talked about it. This syntax exists because the `Observer` class is defined inside of a module and you need the `::` to dig inside the module to get to the class.

While SAX2Parser supports the more formal, separate object observer style, you can also pass in code blocks that act as your observer:

```ruby
require 'rexml/parsers/sax2parser'
require 'rexml/sax2listener'

#
# Create an XML parser for our data
#
xml = File.read('data.xml')
parser = REXML::Parsers::SAX2Parser.new( xml )

#
# Add some observers to listen for start and end elements...
#
parser.listen( :start_element ) do |uri, local, qname, attrs|
  puts("start element: #{local}")
end

parser.listen( :end_element ) do |uri, local, qname|
  puts("end element #{local}")
end

#
# Parse the XML
#
parser.parse
```

Feed the code above an XML file, and you can sit back and observe as the elements go flying by.

Wrapping Up

The Observer pattern allows you to build components that know about the activities of other components without having to tightly couple everything together in an unmanageable mess of code-flavored spaghetti. By creating a clean interface between the source of the news (the observable object) and the consumer of that news (the observers), the Observer pattern moves the news without tangling things up.

Most of the work in implementing the Observer pattern occurs in the subject or observable class. In Ruby, we can factor that mechanism out into either a superclass or (more likely) a module. The interface between observer and observable can be a complex as you like, but if you are building a simple observer, code blocks work well.

As pointed out in Chapter 4, the Observer pattern and the Strategy pattern look a bit alike: Both feature an object (called the observable in the Observer pattern and the context in the Strategy pattern) that makes calls out to some other object (either the observer or the strategy). The difference is mostly one of intent. In the case of the observer, we are informing the other object of the events occurring back at the observable. In the case of the strategy, we are getting the strategy object to do some computing.

The Observer pattern also serves more or less the same function as hook methods in the Template Method pattern; both are there to keep some object informed of current events. The difference is, of course, that the Template Method pattern will only talk to its relatives: If you are not a subclass, you will not get any news from a Template Method pattern hook.

CHAPTER 6

Assembling the Whole from the Parts with the Composite

When I was about 11 or 12 years old, I developed a theory of the universe. You see, I had just learned about the solar system and about atoms, and the similarities between the two seemed to be more than a coincidence. While our solar system has planets whirling around the sun, the atom (at least when you learn about it in elementary school) has electrons spinning around its nucleus. I remember wondering whether our whole world wasn't just an electron in some larger universe. And maybe there was some fantastically tiny adolescent living out his whole life in a world that was part of the last atom at the tip of my pencil.

Although my theory almost certainly involved faulty physics, the idea of things being built of similar sub-things is actually a powerful one that you can apply to writing programs. In this chapter, we will look at the Composite pattern—a pattern that suggests that we build up bigger objects from small sub-objects, which might themselves be made up of still smaller sub-sub-objects. We will see how we can use the Composite pattern to model situations as diverse as organizational structures and the layout of graphical user interfaces. And who knows, in the unlikely event that my old theory of the universe proves correct, we might just be able to use the Composite pattern as a Model of Everything.

The Whole and the Parts

Building object-oriented software is the process of taking relatively simple objects, such as integers and strings, and combining them into slightly more complex objects, such as personnel records and song lists. We can then use the resulting objects to build even more interesting objects. What usually emerges at the end of this process are a few very sophisticated objects that look nothing like the component bits and pieces that we used to assemble them.

But not always. Sometimes we want a complex object to look and act exactly like the components we use to build it. Imagine you are working for TasteeBite Ltd., a gourmet bakery. You have been asked to build a system that keeps track of the manufacturing of the new ChocOBite chocolate cake. A key requirement is that your system must be able to keep track of the time it takes to manufacture a cake. Of course, making a cake is a fairly complicated process. First you have to make the cake batter, put the batter in a pan, and put the pan in the oven. Once the cake is baked, you need to frost it and package it for sale. Making the batter is also a reasonably complicated process in itself, involving a fairly long sequence of steps such as measuring out the flour, cracking the eggs, and licking the spoon.

As you can see from Figure 6-1, you can think of the cake-baking process as a tree, where the master task of making a cake is built up from subtasks such as baking the cake and packaging it, which are themselves made up of even simpler tasks.

Naturally, you do not want to subdivide the cake manufacturing process infinitely ("Now move the 1,463,474th speck of flour to the bowl . . ."). Instead, you need to identify the lowest-level, most-fundamental tasks of cake making and stop there. It is probably reasonable to stop at the "add dry ingredients" and "put cake in oven" level

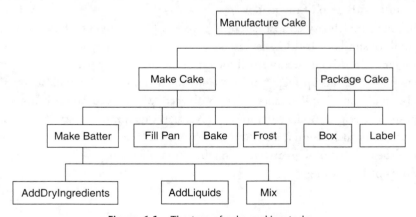

Figure 6-1   The tree of cake-making tasks

and model each of these steps as a separate class. Clearly, all of classes will need to share a common interface—an interface that will let them report back how much time they take. In your TasteeBite project, you decide to use a common base class, called `Task`, and you start by creating a bunch of subclasses, one for the each basic job: `AddDryIngredientsTask`, `AddLiquidsTask`, and `MixTask`.

So much for the simple tasks. But what about the more complex tasks, such as "make batter" or even "manufacture cake," which are built up of smaller subtasks? On the one hand, these are perfectly respectable tasks. In exactly the same way that we might want to know how long it takes to do something basic such as add the dry ingredients, we might want to know how long it takes to make the batter, package the cake, or even make the whole cake. But, these higher-level tasks are not quite the same as the simple ones: They are built up from other tasks.

Obviously, you will need some kind of container object to deal with these complex (or shall we say, *composite*) tasks. But there is one other point to keep in mind about these higher-level tasks: While they are built up internally of any number of subtasks, from the outside they look just like any other `Task`.

This approach works on two levels. First, any code that uses the `MakeBatterTask` object does not have to worry about the fact that making batter is more complex than, say, measuring flour. Simple or complex, everything is just a `Task`. The same is true for the `MakeBatter` class itself: `MakeBatter` does not have to concern itself with the details of its subtasks; simple or complex, they are just `Tasks` to `MakeBatter`. That brings us to the second elegant aspect of this technique: Because `MakeBatter` simply manages a list of `Tasks`, any of those subtasks could themselves be made up of sub-subtasks. We can, in short, make the tree of tasks and subtasks go as deep as we like.

It turns out that this situation, in which you group together a number of components to create a new super-component, actually occurs fairly frequently. Think about how large companies are organized. Any company is fundamentally made up of people—the executives and the accountants and the factory workers. But we rarely think of a big company as simply a collection of individuals. Instead, we might look at a big company and see a conglomeration of divisions, which are made of departments, which are assembled from teams, which are staffed by people.

Departments and divisions have a lot in common with individual workers. For instance, all of them cost the company money in salaries: Fred in shipping might be grossly underpaid, for example, but so is the whole public relations department. Both workers and departments report to someone: Sally is Fred's boss, while Lori is the vice president of the entire public relations department. Finally, both workers and whole departments can leave the company: Fred might find a better-paying job, while the public relations department could be sold off to a different firm. In terms of modeling, the people in a big company are analogous to the simple steps in cake baking, while the departments and divisions are higher-level elements akin to the more complex tasks involved in making a cake.

Creating Composites

The GoF called the design pattern for our "the sum acts like one of the parts" situation the Composite pattern. You will know that you need to use the Composite pattern when you are trying to build a hierarchy or tree of objects, and you do not want the code that uses the tree to constantly have to worry about whether it is dealing with a single object or a whole bushy branch of the tree.

To build the Composite pattern (Figure 6-2), you need three moving parts. First, you need a common interface or base class for all of your objects. The GoF call this base class or interface the **component.** Ask yourself, "What will my basic and higher-level objects all have in common?" In baking cakes, both the simple task of measuring flour and the much more complex task of making the batter take a certain amount of time.

Second, you need one or more **leaf** classes—that is, the simple, indivisible building blocks of the process. In our cake example, the leaf tasks were the simple jobs, such as measuring flour or adding eggs. In our organization example, the individual workers were the leaves. The leaf classes should, of course, implement the `Component` interface.

Third, we need at least one higher-level class, which the GoF call the **composite** class. The composite is a component, but it is also a higher-level object that is built from subcomponents. In the baking example, the composites are the complex tasks such as making the batter or manufacturing the whole cake—that is, the tasks that are

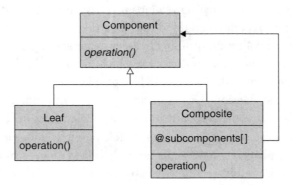

Figure 6-2   The Composite pattern

made up of subtasks. For organizations, the composite objects are the departments and divisions.

To make this discussion a little more concrete, let's look at the process of making a cake in terms of some code. We'll start with the component base class:

```ruby
class Task
  attr_reader :name

  def initialize(name)
    @name = name
  end

  def get_time_required
    0.0
  end
end
```

`Task` is an abstract base class in the sense that it is not really complete: It just keeps track of the name of the task and has a do-nothing `get_time_required` method.

Now let's build two leaf classes:

```ruby
class AddDryIngredientsTask < Task

  def initialize
    super('Add dry ingredients')
  end

  def get_time_required
    1.0                    # 1 minute to add flour and sugar
  end
end

class MixTask < Task

  def initialize
    super('Mix that batter up!')
  end

  def get_time_required
    3.0                    # Mix for 3 minutes
  end
end
```

The `AddDryIngredientsTask` and `MixTask` classes are very simple subclasses of `Task`; they simply supply a real `get_time_required` method. Obviously, we could go on and on defining all of the basic cake-baking tasks, but let's just use our imagination and skip ahead to the punch line—a composite task:

```ruby
class MakeBatterTask < Task
  def initialize
    super('Make batter')
    @sub_tasks = []
    add_sub_task( AddDryIngredientsTask.new )
    add_sub_task( AddLiquidsTask.new )
    add_sub_task( MixTask.new )
  end

  def add_sub_task(task)
    @sub_tasks << task
  end

  def remove_sub_task(task)
    @sub_tasks.delete(task)
  end

  def get_time_required
    time=0.0
    @sub_tasks.each {|task| time += task.get_time_required}
    time
  end
end
```

While the `MakeBatterTask` class looks to the outside world like any other simple task—it implements the key `get_time_required` method—it is actually built up from three subtasks: `AddDryIngredientsTask` and `MixTask`, which we saw earlier, plus `AddLiquidsTask`, a task whose implementation I will leave to your imagination. A key part of `MakeBatterTask` is the way it handles the `get_time_required` method. Specifically, `MakeBatterTask` totals up all of the times required by its child tasks.

Because we will have a number of composite tasks in our baking example (packaging the cake as well as the master task of manufacturing the cake), it makes sense to factor out the details of managing the child tasks into another base class:

```
class CompositeTask < Task
  def initialize(name)
    super(name)
    @sub_tasks = []
  end

  def add_sub_task(task)
    @sub_tasks << task
  end

  def remove_sub_task(task)
    @sub_tasks.delete(task)
  end

  def get_time_required
    time=0.0
    @sub_tasks.each {|task| time += task.get_time_required}
    time
  end
end
```

Our `MakeBatterTask` then reduces to the following code:

```
class MakeBatterTask < CompositeTask
  def initialize
    super('Make batter')
    add_sub_task( AddDryIngredientsTask.new )
    add_sub_task( AddLiquidsTask.new )
    add_sub_task( MixTask.new )
  end
end
```

The key point to keep in mind about composite objects is that the tree may be arbitrarily deep. While `MakeBatterTask` goes down only one level, that will not be true in general. For example, when we really finish out our bakery project, we will need a `MakeCake` class:

```
class MakeCakeTask < CompositeTask
  def initialize
    super('Make cake')
    add_sub_task( MakeBatterTask.new )
    add_sub_task( FillPanTask.new )
```

```
    add_sub_task( BakeTask.new )
    add_sub_task( FrostTask.new )
    add_sub_task( LickSpoonTask.new )
  end
end
```

Any one of the subtasks of `MakeCakeTask` might be a composite. In fact, we have already seen that `MakeBatterTask` actually is a composite.

Sprucing Up the Composite with Operators

We can make our composite code even more readable if we realize that composite objects fulfill a dual role. On the one hand, the composite object is a component; on the other hand, it is a collection of components. As we have written it, our `CompositeTask` does not look much like any of the standard Ruby collections, such as `Array` or `Hash`. It would be nice, for example, to be able to add tasks to a `CompositeTask` with the `<<` operator, just as we could in an array:

```
composite = CompositeTask.new('example')
composite << MixTask.new
```

It turns out that we can get this done by simply renaming the `add_sub_task` method:

```
  def <<(task)
    @sub_tasks << task
  end
```

We might also want to get at our subtasks by the familiar array indexing syntax, something like this:

```
puts(composite[0].get_time_required)
composite[1] = AddDryIngredientsTask.new
```

This is once again a simple matter of picking the right name for our method. Ruby will translate `object[i]` into a call to a method with the odd name of `[]`, which takes one parameter, the index. To add support for this operation to our `CompositeTask` class, we simply add a method:

```ruby
def [](index)
  @sub_tasks[index]
end
```

In the same way, `object[i] = value` is translated into a call to the method with the even stranger name of `[]=`, which takes two parameters, the index and the new value:

```ruby
def []=(index, new_value)
  @sub_tasks[index] = new_value
end
```

An Array as a Composite?

We could also get the same container operator effect with our `CompositeTask` by simply making it a subclass of `Array` instead of `Task`:

```ruby
class CompositeTask < Array
  attr_reader :name

  def initialize(name)
    @name = name
  end

  def get_time_required
    time=0.0
    each {|task| time += task.get_time_required}
    time
  end
end
```

Given the dynamic typing rules of Ruby, this approach will work. By making `CompositeTask` a subclass of `Array`, we get a container and its associated `[]`, `[]=`, and `<<` operators for free via inheritance. But is this a good approach?

I vote no. A `CompositeTask` is not some specialized kind of array; it is a specialized kind of `Task`. If `CompositeTask` is going to be related to any class, it should be related to `Task`, not `Array`.

An Inconvenient Difference

Any implementation of the Composite pattern needs to deal with one other sticky issue. We began by saying that the goal of the Composite pattern is to make the leaf objects more or less indistinguishable from the composite objects. I say "more or less" here because there is one unavoidable difference between a composite and a leaf: The composite has to manage its children, which probably means that it needs to have a method to get at the children and possibly methods to add and remove child objects. The leaf classes, of course, really do not have any children to manage; that is the nature of leafyness.

How we handle this inconvenient fact is mostly a matter of taste. On the one hand, we can make the composite and leaf objects different. For example, we can supply the composite object with `add_child` and `remove_child` methods (or the equivalent array-like operators) and simply omit these methods from the leaf class. This approach has certain logic behind it: After all, leaf objects are childless, so they do not need the child management plumbing.

On the other hand, our main goal with the Composite pattern is to make the leaf and composite objects indistinguishable. If the code that uses your composite has to know that only some of the components—the composite ones—have `get_child` and `add_child` methods while other components—the leaves—do not, then the leaf and composite objects are not the same. But if you do include the child-handling methods in the leaf object, what happens if someone actually calls them on a leaf object? Responding to `remove_child` is not so bad—leaf objects do not have children so there is never anything to remove. But what if someone calls `add_child` on a leaf object? Do you ignore the call? Throw an exception? Neither response is very palatable.

As I say, how you handle this decision is mostly a matter of taste: Make the leaf and composite classes different, or burden the leaf classes with embarrassing methods that they do not know how to handle. My own instinct is to leave the methods off of the leaf classes. Leaf objects cannot handle child objects, and we may as well admit it.

Pointers This Way and That

So far, we have looked at the Composite pattern as a strictly top-down affair. Because each composite object holds references to its subcomponents but the child components do not know a thing about their parents, it is easy to traverse the tree from the root to the leaves but hard to go the other way.

It is easy to add a parent reference to each participant in the composite so that we can climb back up to the top of the tree. The best place to put the parent-reference handling code is in the component class. You can centralize the code to handle the parent there:

```ruby
class Task
  attr_accessor :name, :parent

  def initialize(name)
    @name = name
    @parent = nil
  end

  def get_time_required
    0.0
  end
end
```

Given that the composite class is the place where the parent–child relationships are managed, it is also the logical place to set the parent attribute:

```ruby
class CompositeTask < Task
  def initialize(name)
    super(name)
    @sub_tasks = []
  end

  def add_sub_task(task)
    @sub_tasks << task
    task.parent = self
  end

  def remove_sub_task(task)
    @sub_tasks.delete(task)
    task.parent = nil
  end

  def get_time_required
    time=0.0
    @sub_tasks.each {|task| time += task.get_time_required}
    time
  end
end
```

With the parent references in place, we can now trace any composite component up to its ultimate parent:

```
while task
  puts("task: #{task}")
  task = task.parent
end
```

Using and Abusing the Composite Pattern

The good news about the Composite pattern is that there is only one really common mistake people make when they implement it; the bad news is that they make this mistake a lot. The error that crops up so frequently with the Composite pattern is assuming that the tree is only one level deep—that is, assuming that all of the child components of a composite object are, in fact, leaf objects and not other composites. To illustrate this misstep, imagine we needed to know how many leaf steps are involved in our cake-baking process. We could simply add the following code to the `CompositeTask` class:

```
#
# Wrong way of doing it
#
class CompositeTask < Task

  # Lots of code omitted...

  def total_number_basic_tasks
    @sub_tasks.length
  end

end
```

We could do that, but it would be wrong. This implementation ignores the fact that any one of those subtasks could itself be a huge composite with many of its own sub-subtasks. The right way to handle this situation is to define the `total_num_of_tasks` method in the component class:

```
class Task
  # Lots of code omitted...

  def total_number_basic_tasks
    1
  end

end
```

Next we override this method in the composite class to run recursively down the tree:

```
class CompositeTask < Task

  # Lots of code omitted...

  def total_number_basic_tasks
    total = 0
    @sub_tasks.each {|task| total += task.total_number_basic_tasks}
    total
  end

end
```

Remember, the power of the Composite pattern is that it allows us to build arbitrarily deep trees. Do not go to all this trouble and then throw the advantage away by writing a few sloppy lines of code.

Composites in the Wild

If you look around for real examples of the Composite pattern in the Ruby code base, the graphical user interface (GUI) libraries jump out. All modern GUIs support a pallet of basic components, things like labels and text fields and menus. These basic GUI components have a lot in common with each other: No matter whether they are buttons or labels or menu items, all of them have a font, and a background and foreground color, and all of them take up a certain amount of screen real estate. Of course, any real, modern GUI is not just a simple collection of the basic GUI components. No, a real GUI is built as a hierarchy: Start with a label and a field, position them just so, and then join them together into a single visual thing that prompts the user for his or her first name. Combine this first-name prompter with a similar last-name prompter and a prompter that asks for a Social Security number. Combine those elements into a still larger and more complex GUI component. If you have read this chapter carefully, this process should sound very familiar: We have just built a GUI composite.

A good example of the use of composites in a GUI toolkit can be found in FXRuby. FXRuby is a Ruby extension that brings FOX—an open-source cross-platform GUI toolkit—to the Ruby world. FXRuby supplies you with a wide variety of user interface widgets, ranging from the mundane FXButton and FXLabel to the very elaborate FXColorSelector and FXTable. You can also build your own, arbitrarily complex widgets with FXHorizontalFrame and its cousin FXVerticalFrame. The two frame classes act as containers, allowing you to add sub-widgets to create a single unified GUI element. The difference between these two frame classes is the way they display their sub-widgets visually: One lines up the sub-widgets in a horizontal line, while the other stacks them vertically. Horizontal or vertical, both FOX frame widgets are subclasses of FXWindow, as are all of the basic widgets.

By way of example, here is an application that uses FXRuby to build a tiny, mock text editor:

```ruby
require 'rubygems'
require 'fox16'

include Fox

application = FXApp.new("CompositeGUI", "CompositeGUI")
main_window = FXMainWindow.new(application, "Composite",
                              nil, nil, DECOR_ALL)
main_window.width = 400
main_window.height = 200

super_frame = FXVerticalFrame.new(main_window,
                                LAYOUT_FILL_X|LAYOUT_FILL_Y)
FXLabel.new(super_frame, "Text Editor Application")

text_editor = FXHorizontalFrame.new(super_frame,
                                LAYOUT_FILL_X|LAYOUT_FILL_Y)

text = FXText.new(text_editor, nil, 0,
       TEXT_READONLY|TEXT_WORDWRAP|LAYOUT_FILL_X|LAYOUT_FILL_Y)
```

```
    text.text = "This is some text."

    # Button bar along the bottom

    button_frame = FXVerticalFrame.new(text_editor,
                                LAYOUT_SIDE_RIGHT|LAYOUT_FILL_Y)

    FXButton.new(button_frame,  "Cut")
    FXButton.new(button_frame, "Copy")
    FXButton.new(button_frame, "Paste")

    application.create
    main_window.show(PLACEMENT_SCREEN)
    application.run
```

The entire GUI is built as a series of nested composites. At the top of the tree is FXMainWindow, which has exactly one child element, a vertical frame. The frame has a horizontal frame for a child element, which has . . . Well, you get the picture—and if you don't, have a look at Figure 6-3. It shows a neat Composite pattern that you can see on your screen.

Wrapping Up

Once you grasp its recursive nature, the Composite pattern is really quite simple. Sometimes we need to model objects that naturally group themselves into larger components. These more complex objects fit into the Composite pattern if they share some characteristics with the individual components: The whole looks a lot like one of the parts. The Composite pattern lets us build arbitrarily deep trees of objects

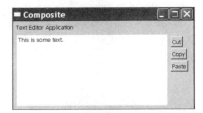

Figure 6-3   A mock text editor, built with FXRuby

in which we can treat any of the interior nodes—the composites—just like any of the leaf nodes.

The Composite pattern is so fundamental that it is not surprising that it reappears, sometimes in disguise, in other patterns. As we will see in Chapter 15, the Interpreter pattern is nothing more than a specialization of the Composite pattern.

Finally, it is difficult to imagine the Composite pattern without the Iterator pattern. The reasons behind this hand-in-glove relationship are about to be revealed, because the Iterator pattern is the topic of the very next chapter.

CHAPTER 7

Reaching into a Collection with the Iterator

In Chapter 6, we looked at composites—objects that appear to be simple components but are actually made up of a collection of subcomponents. Of course, an object does not have to be a composite to know about collections of other objects. An `Employee` object might know about several dependents, or phone numbers, or, in the case of a well-paid executive, the addresses of many palatial estates. In this kind of situation, it would be helpful if we could sequence through all of the sub-objects without needing to know any of the details of how the aggregate object is storing them.

In this chapter, we will explore the Iterator pattern, a technique that allows an aggregate object to provide the outside world with a way to access its collection of sub-objects. We will see how iterators come in two basic flavors and learn how the Iterator pattern explains those funny-looking `each` loops that we encounter in Ruby.

External Iterators

The GoF tell us that the Iterator pattern will do the following:

> Provide a way to access the elements of an aggregate object sequentially without exposing its underlying representation

In other words, an Iterator provides the outside world with a sort of movable pointer into the objects stored inside an otherwise opaque aggregate object.

If you are a Java programmer, iterators will be most familiar to you in the guise of the `java.util.Iterator` interface and its older brother, `java.util.Enumeration`. A typical use of the Java iterator is shown here:

```java
ArrayList list = new ArrayList();
list.add("red");
list.add("green");
list.add("blue");

for( Iterator i = list.iterator(); i.hasNext();) {
        System.out.println( "item: " + i.next());
}
```

Iterators also show up in slightly more unexpected places. For example, you can look at `java.util.StringTokenizer` as an iterator that allows you to run through all of the tokens in a string. Similarly, JDBC includes `ResultSet`, which allows us to iterate over each row in a SQL query result.

This style of iterator is sometimes referred to as an **external iterator**—"external" because the iterator is a separate object from the aggregate. We will see in a minute that this is not the only iterator on the menu, but first let's see what an external iterator might look like in Ruby.

It is actually quite easy to construct Java-like external iterators in Ruby. A simple, if somewhat less than vitally needed, implementation of an iterator for Ruby arrays might look something like this:

```ruby
class ArrayIterator
  def initialize(array)
    @array = array
    @index = 0
  end

  def has_next?
    @index < @array.length
  end

  def item
    @array[@index]
  end
```

```
      def next_item
        value = @array[@index]
        @index += 1
        value
      end
    end
```

ArrayIterator is a straightforward translation of a Java-style iterator into Ruby, albeit with the addition of item, a method that retrieves the current item (something that is oddly missing from the Java rendition). Here's how we might use this new iterator:

```
    array = ['red', 'green', 'blue']

    i = ArrayIterator.new(array)
    while i.has_next?
      puts("item: #{i.next_item}")
    end
```

Running this code will give us the output we expect:

```
    item: red
    item: green
    item: blue
```

With just a few lines of code, our ArrayIterator gives us just about everything we need to iterate over any Ruby array. As a free bonus, Ruby's flexible dynamic typing allows ArrayIterator to work on any aggregate class that has a length method and can be indexed by an integer. String is just such a class, and our ArrayIterator will work fine with strings:

```
    i = ArrayIterator.new('abc')

    while i.has_next?
      puts("item: #{i.next_item.chr}")
    end
```

Run the code above and you will see this output:

```
item: a
item: b
item: c
```

The only wrinkle in using `ArrayIterator` on strings is that `string[n]` returns the nth character in the string as a number, the character code. Hence we need the `chr` method in the example above.

Given how easy it was to build `ArrayIterator`, it is surprising that external iterators are so rare in Ruby. It turns out that Ruby has something better—and that this something better is based on our old friends the code block and the `Proc` object.

Internal Iterators

If you think about it, the purpose of an iterator is to introduce your code to each sub-object of an aggregate object. Traditional external iterators do so by providing a long grappling hook, the iterator object, that you can use to pull the sub-objects out of the aggregate without getting messily involved in the aggregate details. But by using a code block, you can pass your logic down into the aggregate. The aggregate can then call your code block for each of its sub-objects. Because all of the iterating action occurs inside the aggregate object, the code block-based iterators are called **internal iterators.**

Building an internal iterator for arrays is very easy—we just define a method that calls (via `yield`) the passed-in code block for each element:[1]

```
def for_each_element(array)
  i = 0
  while i < array.length
    yield(array[i])
    i += 1
  end
end
```

---

1. Actually, a real Ruby program would likely add the `for_each_element` method to the `String` class—something that you can do easily in Ruby. For much more on this topic, see Chapter 9.

To use our internal iterator, we hang a code block on the end of the method call:

```
a = [10, 20, 30]
for_each_element(a) {|element| puts("The element is #{element}")}
```

It turns out that we don't really need `for_each_element`—the `Array` class sports a fine iterator method call called `each`. Just like our `for_each_element` method, `each` takes a one-parameter code block and calls that code block for each element in the array:

```
a.each {|element| puts("The element is #{element}")}
```

Run either version of the preceding code and you will get this output:

```
The element is 10
The element is 20
The element is 30
```

The `each` method is the explanation for all of those funny-looking `each` loops that you have been seeing in this book. Those loops are not, in fact, actual "built-into-the-language" loops, but rather applications of internal iterators.

Internal Iterators versus External Iterators

While either an internal iterator or an external iterator will do the basic job of stepping through an aggregate, there are some practical differences to consider. External iterators certainly have some advantages. For example, when you use an external iterator, the client drives the iteration. With an external iterator, you won't call `next` until you are good and ready for the next element. With an internal iterator, by contrast, the aggregate relentlessly pushes the code block to accept item after item.

Most of the time, this difference does not matter. But what if you are trying to merge the contents of two sorted arrays into a single array that was itself sorted? This kind of merge is actually fairly easy with an external iterator like `ArrayInterator`: We simply create an iterator for the two input arrays and then merge the arrays by repeatedly pushing the smallest value from either of the iterators onto the output array.

```ruby
def merge(array1, array2)
  merged = []

  iterator1 = ArrayIterator.new(array1)
  iterator2 = ArrayIterator.new(array2)

  while( iterator1.has_next? and iterator2.has_next? )
    if iterator1.item < iterator2.item
      merged << iterator1.next_item
    else
      merged << iterator2.next_item
    end
  end

  # Pick up the leftovers from array1

  while( iterator1.has_next?)
    merged << iterator1.next_item
  end

  # Pick up the leftovers from array2

  while( iterator2.has_next?)
    merged << iterator2.next_item
  end

  merged
end
```

I am not sure how you would implement a merge like this using internal iterators. A second advantage of external iterators is that, because they are external, you can share them—you can pass them around to other methods and objects. Of course, this is a bit of a double-edged sword: You get the flexibility but you also have to know what you are doing. In particular, beware of multiple threads getting hold of a non-thread-safe external iterator.

The main thing that internal iterators have going for them is simplicity and code clarity. External iterators have that extra moving part, the iterator object. In our array example, we not only have the array and the client code, but also the separate `ArrayInterator` object. With internal iterators, there is no separate iterator object to manage ("Did I call `next` yet?"), just a stretch of more or less in-line code.

The Inimitable Enumerable

If you do find yourself creating an aggregate class and equipping it with an internal iterator, you should probably consider including the `Enumerable` mixin module in your class. `Enumerable` is like one of those late-night gadget commercials: To mix in `Enumerable`, you need only make sure that your internal iterator method is named `each` and that the individual elements that you are going to iterate over have a reasonable implementation of the `<=>` comparison operator. For this one low, low price, `Enumerable` will add to your class a whole range of useful methods. Among the handy things you get from `Enumerable` are `include?(obj)`, which returns `true` if the object supplied as a parameter is part of your aggregate object, plus `min` and `max`, which return exactly what you would expect.

The `Enumerable` mixin also includes more exotic methods such as `all?`, which takes a block and returns `true` if the block returns `true` for *all* of the elements. The `Array` class includes `Enumerable`, so we can write one line of code to return `true` if all the strings in an array are less than four characters long:

```
a = [ 'joe', 'sam', 'george' ]
a.all? {|element| element.length < 4}
```

The string `'george'` is longer than four characters, so the call to `all?` in this example will evaluate to `false`. Along the same lines of `all?` we have `any?`, which will return `true` if the block returns `true` for *any* of the iterator elements. Since `'joe'` and `'sam'` are both less than four characters long, the following will return `true`:

```
a.any? {|element| element.length < 4}
```

Finally, `Enumerable` supplies your class with a `sort` method, which returns all of the subitems in an array, sorted.

To see just how easy it is to include all of this functionality in one of your own classes, imagine that you have two classes: one that models a single financial account and one that manages a portfolio of accounts.

```
class Account
  attr_accessor :name, :balance

  def initialize(name, balance)
    @name = name
    @balance = balance
  end

  def <=>(other)
    balance <=> other.balance
  end
end

class Portfolio
  include Enumerable

  def initialize
    @accounts = []
  end

  def each(&block)
    @accounts.each(&block)
  end

  def add_account(account)
    @accounts << account
  end
end
```

By simply mixing the `Enumerable` module into `Portfolio` and defining an each method, we have equipped `Portfolio` with all kinds of `Enumerable` goodness. For example, we can now find out whether any of the accounts in our portfolio has a balance of at least $2,000:

```
my_portfolio.any? {|account| account.balance > 2000}
```

We can also find out whether all of our accounts contain at least $10:

```
my_portfolio.all? {|account| account.balance > = 10}
```

Using and Abusing the Iterator Pattern

While Iterator is one of the most commonly used and useful patterns, it does have some pointy bits sticking out waiting to snag the unwary. The main danger is this: What happens if the aggregate object changes while you are iterating through it?

Suppose you are sequencing through a list and just before you get to the third element, someone deletes that element from the list. What happens? Does the iterator show you the now-defunct third element anyway? Does the iterator quietly go on to the fourth element as though nothing has happened? Does it throw an exception?

Unfortunately, none of the iterators that we have built in this chapter so far react particularly well to change. Recall that our external `ArrayIterator` worked by holding on to the index of the current item. Deleting elements from the array that we have not seen yet is not a problem, but making modifications to the beginning of the array will wreak havoc with the indexing.

We can make our `ArrayIterator` resistant to changes to the underlying array by simply making a copy of the array in the iterator constructor:

```ruby
class ChangeResistantArrayIterator
  def initialize(array)
    @array = Array.new(array)
    @index = 0
  end
  ...
```

This new iterator makes a shallow copy of the array—the copy points to the original contents, which are not themselves copied—and sequences through the new array. Thanks to this new iterator, we have a change-resistant snapshot of the array and can iterate through that.

Internal iterators have exactly the same concurrent modification problems as external iterators. For example, it is probably a very bad idea to do the following:

```ruby
array=['red', 'green', 'blue', 'purple']

array.each do | color |
  puts(color)
  if color == 'green'
    array.delete(color)
  end
end
```

This code will print

```
red
green
purple
```

By deleting the 'green' entry, we managed to mess up the indexing of the iterator just enough to cause it to miss 'blue'.

Internal iterators can also defend against the crime of modifying while iterating by working on a separate copy of the aggregate, just as we did in our ChangeResistantArrayIterator class. This might look something like the following code:

```
def change_resistant_for_each_element(array)
  copy = Array.new(array)
  i = 0
  while i < copy.length
    yield(copy[i])
    i += 1
  end
end
```

Finally, a multithreaded program is a particularly dangerous home for iterators. You need to take all of the usual care to ensure that one thread does not rip the aggregate rug out from under your iterator.

Iterators in the Wild

Iterators—mostly internal but occasionally external—are so common in Ruby that it is hard to know where to start. Ruby arrays actually have two other internal iterators beside each: reverse_each cycles through the array elements from the end of the array to the beginning, while each_index calls the block passed in with each index in the array instead of each element.

The String class has an each method that cycles through each line (yes, each *line,* not each character) in the string as well as each_byte. Strings also have a wonderful scan method, which takes a regular expression and iterates over each match that is found in the string. For example, we might search for all words that begin with the letter 'p' in a well-known tongue twister:

```
s = 'Peter Piper picked a peck of pickled peppers'
s.scan(/[Pp]\w*/) {|word| puts("The word is #{word}")}
```

If you run this code, you will get lots of 'p' words:

```
The word is Peter
The word is Piper
The word is picked
The word is peck
The word is pickled
The word is peppers
```

Unsurprisingly, the Hash class supports a rich assortment of iterators. We have each_key, which calls the code block for each key in the hash:

```
h = {'name'=>'russ', 'eyes'=>'blue', 'sex'=>'male'}
h.each_key {|key| puts(key)}
```

This code produces the following output:

```
name
sex
eyes
```

The Hash class also has an each_value method:

```
h.each_value {|value| puts(value)}
```

This code produces the following output:

```
russ
male
blue
```

Finally, a vanilla each method is also available:

```
h.each {|key, value| puts("#{key} #{value}")}
```

The `each` method iterates over every key/value pair in the hash, so this code will output

```
name russ
sex male
eyes blue
```

External iterators are harder to find in Ruby, but the `IO` object presents an interesting example. The `IO` class is the base class for input and output streams. The neat thing about the `IO` object is that it is amphibious—it does both internal and external iterators. You can open a file and read each line in a very traditional style by using the open file handle as an external iterator:

```
f = File.open('names.txt')
while not f.eof?
  puts(f.readline)
end
f.close
```

The `IO` object also has an `each` method (also known as `each_line`) that implements an internal iterator over the lines in the file:

```
f = File.open('names.txt')
f.each {|line| puts(line)}
f.close
```

For the non-line-oriented files, `IO` supplies an `each_byte` iterator method:

```
f.each_byte {|byte| puts(byte)}
```

If your programs do a lot of IO, you will probably want to know about the `Pathname` class. `Pathname` tries to offer one-stop shopping for all your directory and path manipulation needs. You create a `Pathname` by supplying the constructor with a path:

```
pn = Pathname.new('/usr/local/lib/ruby/1.8')
```

Along with a raft of useful methods that have nothing to do with iterators, `Pathname` supplies the `each_filename` iterator, which cycles through the components of the path that you supplied. So if you run

```
pn.each_filename {|file| puts("File: #{file}")}
```

you will get something like this:

```
File: usr
File: local
File: lib
File: ruby
File: 1.8
```

But you can also go in the other dimension—the `each_entry` method will iterate over the contents of the directory pointed at by the `Pathname`. So if you run

```
pn.each_entry {|entry| puts("Entry: #{entry}")}
```

you will see the contents of `/usr/local/lib/ruby/1.8`:[2]

```
Entry: .
Entry: ..
Entry: i686-linux
Entry: shellwords.rb
Entry: mailread.rb
...
```

Finally, my very favorite internal iterator in Ruby is one supplied by the `ObjectSpace` module. `ObjectSpace` provides a window into the complete universe of objects that exist within your Ruby interpreter. The fundamental iterator supplied by `ObjectSpace` is the `each_object` method. It iterates across all of the Ruby objects—everything that is loaded into your Ruby interpreter:

```
ObjectSpace.each_object {|object| puts("Object: #{object}")}
```

---

2. Well, you will see this if you happen to be using a UNIX-style operating system and Ruby is installed in `/usr/local/lib`.

The `each_object` method takes an optional argument that can be either a class or a module. If you supply the argument, `each_object` will iterate over only the instances of that class or module. And yes, subclasses count. So if I wanted to print out all of the numbers known to my Ruby interpreter, I might do this:

```
ObjectSpace.each_object(Numeric) {|n| puts("The number is #{n}")}
```

This level of introspection is reasonably breathtaking. You can, for example, use `ObjectSpace` to implement your own memory profiling system: Simply start a thread that looks for the objects of interest and prints a report about them. A class might use `ObjectSpace` to hunt down all instances of itself, for example. Rails uses `ObjectSpace` to build a method that finds all of the subclasses of a given class:

```
def subclasses_of(superclass)
  subclasses = []
  ObjectSpace.each_object(Class) do |k|
    next if !k.ancestors.include?(superclass) || superclass == k ||
            k.to_s.include?('::') || subclasses.include?(k.to_s)
    subclasses << k.to_s
  end
  subclasses
end
```

If we call

```
subclasses_of(Numeric)
```

we will get back an array containing `Bignum'`, `'Float'`, `'Fixnum'`, and `'Integer'`. As I say, reasonably breathtaking.

Wrapping Up

In this chapter, we explored the two basic forms of iterators. The first, and probably more familiar, version is the external iterator, where an object points down at a member of some collection. With an internal iterator, instead of passing some sort of pointer up, we pass the code that needs to deal with the sub-objects down.

We also met the `Enumerable` module, which can enhance the iterator experience for just about any collection. In addition, we peeked into the dark side of iterators, the shady part of town where your collection can change under your feet as you are iterating through it. Finally, we became iterator tourists, taking in the sights provided by ObjectSpace, which can reach into the Ruby interpreter and show you things you never thought you would see.

Iterators in Ruby are a great example of what is right with the language. Instead of providing special-purpose external iterator objects for each aggregate class, Ruby relies on the very flexible idea of Proc objects and code blocks to build internal iterators. Because internal iterators are very easy to write—you build only one new method instead of a whole new class—Ruby encourages programmers to build whatever iterators make sense. We can see the power of this approach in the wide array of iterators available in the standard Ruby library, where we can get at everything from each_byte in a single string to each_object in the whole Ruby interpreter.

CHAPTER 8

Getting Things Done with Commands

I mentioned in Chapter 1 that I spent a lot of my high school and early college waking hours working in a grocery store. My tiny store was struggling to compete with the big supermarkets, so we tried to offer services that you wouldn't find at the local MegaMart. In particular, you could call us and dictate your shopping list over the phone, and we would be more than happy to gather up your beans, butter, and baloney and deliver it right to your door for free. Some of our customers even had standing orders. They would call us up and ask that we deliver their regular shipment—and there I would be, list in hand, pulling together yet another delivery order.

The grocery lists of my youth are a lot like the commands that give the Command pattern its name. Like a grocery list, a Command pattern command is an instruction to do something, something specific. Like a grocery list, a Command pattern command can be filled—or executed—right now, or later, or when something specific happens.

Because the Command pattern is one of the more versatile patterns covered in this book, our discussion here will necessarily be something of a survey. We will start with the very common use of the Command pattern in GUIs and then move on to their use in recording what we need to do or what we have already done. Finally, we will see how we can use the Command pattern to undo things that we have done and, occasionally, to redo thing things that we have undone.

An Explosion of Subclasses

Imagine that you are building SlickUI, a new GUI framework. You are busily creating beautiful buttons, delightful dialogs, and eye-popping icons. But once you are finished making your user interface framework attractive, you face a critical problem: How do you get that interface to do something useful?

Imagine that you have built your button class so that the on_button_push method is called whenever the user clicks the button on the screen:

```
class SlickButton
  #
  # Lots of button drawing and management
  # code omitted...
  #

  def on_button_push
    #
    # Do something when the button is pushed
    #
  end
end
```

But what should you do inside the on_button_push method? You are hoping that SlickUI will be massively popular, used by thousands of programmers the world over, who will create millions of instances of SlickButton. Perhaps one team of programmers will be building a word processor and will need buttons to create new documents and save the current document. Another team might be working on a network utility; they might need a button to initialize a network connection. The trouble is that while you are constructing the SlickButton class, you have no idea what any of those buttons are supposed to do.

One solution to this problem is to pull out our nearly universal, but now somewhat tarnished silver hammer—inheritance. You could ask your users to create a new subclass for each different type of button:

```
class SaveButton < SlickButton
  def on_button_push
    #
    # Save the current document...
    #
  end
end
```

```
class NewDocumentButton < SlickButton
  def on_button_push
    #
    # Create a new document...
    #
  end
end
```

Unfortunately, a complex GUI application will have tens or even hundreds of buttons, and so tens or hundreds of SlickButton subclasses. And then there are the other GUI elements: things like menu items and radio buttons. On top of that, inheritance is so permanent—what if you want your button to do one thing before the user has actually opened the spreadsheet and something else after the spreadsheet is open? If you subclass Button, either you need two separate Button subclasses or you need to code the "Is the file open?" logic into a single Button subclass. Either approach is messy. Is there an easier way?

An Easier Way

The way to deal with this problem is to package up the idea of what to do when the button is pushed or the menu item is selected. That is, we want to bundle up the code to handle the button push or menu selection in its own object—an object that does nothing but wait to be executed and, when executed, goes out and performs an application-specific task. These little packages of action are the **commands** of the Command pattern.

To apply the Command pattern to our button example, we simply store a command object with each button:

```
class SlickButton
  attr_accessor :command

  def initialize(command)
    @command = command
  end

  #
  # Lots of button drawing and management
  # code omitted...
  #

  def on_button_push
    @command.execute if @command
  end
end
```

We can then define different commands for all of the things that our buttons might do:

```
class SaveCommand
  def execute
    #
    # Save the current document...
    #
  end
end
```

We supply the actual commands when we create the button:

```
save_button = SlickButton.new( SaveCommand.new )
```

The idea of factoring out the action code into its own object is the essence of the Command pattern. This pattern separates out something that changes—the thing that we want to happen when the button is pushed—from something that does not change—the generic button class supplied with the GUI framework. Because the connection between the button and the command is a runtime thing—the button simply has a reference to the command that it should fire when pushed—it is easy to change commands on the fly, thereby changing the behavior of the button at runtime.

As you can see from the UML diagram in Figure 8-1, the Command pattern is structurally very simple. It consists of a number of classes that all share a common interface.

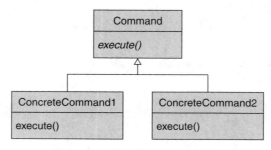

Figure 8-1   The Command pattern

Code Blocks as Commands

We have seen that a command is simply a wrapper around some code that knows how to do one specific thing, whose only reason for existence is to run some code at the right time. This should sound familiar: It is a fairly accurate description of a Ruby code block object or a `Proc`. Recall that a `Proc` object encapsulates a chunk of code, just sitting there, ready to be run.

The Command pattern translates very smoothly into code blocks. Here is our `SlickButton` class reworked to use code blocks:

```ruby
class SlickButton
  attr_accessor :command

  def initialize(&block)
    @command = block
  end

  #
  # Lots of button drawing and management
  # code omitted...
  #

  def on_button_push
    @command.call if @command
  end
end
```

To create our new, code block-based `SlickButton`, we simply pass in a code block when we create the button:

```ruby
new_button = SlickButton.new do
  #
  # Create a new document...
  #
end
```

In the world of Ruby code blocks and `Proc` objects, are hand-coded command classes like our `SaveCommand` class passé? Not really—it all depends on the complexity of the job at hand. If you simply want a command that executes some straightforward actions when it is run, by all means use a `Proc` object. But if you are doing something fairly complex, if you need to create a command that will carry around a lot of state information or that naturally decomposes into several methods, by all means create a command class.

Commands That Record

While buttons and the commands that go with them are a good example of the Command pattern, commands are by no means limited to GUIs. For example, the Command pattern can be useful in keeping track of what you have already done. Imagine that you are building an installation program, a utility that will set up software on the user's system. Installation programs typically need to create, copy, move, and sometimes delete files. The user might want to know exactly what the installer is going to do before it actually does it. The user might also want to know what the installer did, after the fact. Keeping track of this information is easy if you organize each change as a command.

Because these installation commands will be carrying a bit of state information around, we will make them separate classes in the classic Command pattern style. Let's start by defining a few file manipulation commands, all of which will implement a describe method along with execute.

First we have the base command class:

```ruby
class Command
  attr_reader :description

  def initialize(description)
    @description = description
  end

  def execute
  end
end
```

Next we have a command to create a file and write the contents of a string out to the new file:

```ruby
class CreateFile < Command
  def initialize(path, contents)
    super("Create file: #{path}")
    @path = path
    @contents = contents
  end
```

```
  def execute
    f = File.open(@path, "w")
    f.write(@contents)
    f.close
  end
end
```

We might also need a command to delete a file:

```
class DeleteFile < Command
  def initialize(path)
    super("Delete file: #{path}")
    @path = path
  end

  def execute
    File.delete(@path)
  end
end
```

And perhaps a command to copy one file to another:

```
class CopyFile < Command
  def initialize(source, target)
    super("Copy file: #{source} to #{target}")
    @source = source
    @target = target
  end

  def execute
    FileUtils.copy(@source, @target)
  end
end
```

Clearly, we could go on, building even more classes to move or rename files, to change file permissions, or to create directories, but let's stop here. Because we are trying to keep track of what we are about to do—or have done—we will need a class to collect all of our commands. Hmm, a class that acts like a command, but really is just a front for a number of subcommands. Sounds like a composite:

```ruby
class CompositeCommand < Command
  def initialize
    @commands = []
  end

  def add_command(cmd)
    @commands << cmd
  end

  def execute
    @commands.each {|cmd| cmd.execute}
  end

  def description
    description = ''
    @commands.each {|cmd| description += cmd.description + "\n"}
    description
  end
end
```

Other than being a nice use of another pattern, `CompositeCommand` allows us to tell the user exactly what we are doing to his or her system. We could, for example, create a new file, copy it to a second file, and then delete the first file:

```ruby
cmds = CompositeCommand.new

cmds.add_command(CreateFile.new('file1.txt', "hello world\n"))
cmds.add_command(CopyFile.new('file1.txt', 'file2.txt'))
cmds.add_command(DeleteFile.new('file1.txt'))
```

To actually execute all of these file comings and goings, we simply call `execute`:

```ruby
cmds.execute
```

The big win is that at any time—either after we execute the commands or before we do so—we can explain to the user what is happening. For example, the code

```ruby
puts(cmds.description)
```

produces

```
Create file: file1.txt
Copy file: file1.txt to file2.txt
Delete file: file1.txt
```

Being Undone by a Command

Enabling your client (either a real user or another program) to undo what has already been done is a common enough requirement. These days, undo is an absolute necessity for any decent editor or word processor, but it also shows up in other places. For example, most databases support rolling back transactions, which is just undo by another name. In fact, undo can show up as a requirement anywhere a fallible human or program invests substantial and perhaps misguided effort in a series of changes.

The naive way to implement an undo operation is to simply remember the state of things before you make the change and then restore the remembered state if the client wants to undo the change. The trouble with this approach is that text files and word-processing documents, not to mention databases, can be quite large. Making a complete copy of everything each time you make a change can get ugly, in a resource-intensive way, very quickly.

The Command pattern can help here, too. A command—being the encapsulation of how do some specific thing—can, with some enhancing surgery, also undo things. The idea is really quite simple: Every undo-able command that we create has two methods. Along with the usual execute method, which does the thing, we add an unexecute method, which undoes the same thing. As the user makes changes, we create command after command, executing each command immediately to effect the change. But we also store the commands, in order, in a list somewhere. If the user suddenly changes his or her mind and wants to undo a change, we find the last command on the list and unexecute it. And more than the last command can be undone—we can let the user march back in history as far as he or she likes by un-executing the previous command, and the one before that, and the one before that.

Redo—that is, the ability to unchange your mind and to reapply the change that you just undid—falls elegantly out of the same design. To redo something, we just start reexecuting the commands, starting with the last one that was undone.

Let's make this a little more concrete by going back to our installer example. Perhaps the requirement is not merely that we should be able to explain what we are doing to the user's system, but that we should be able to back out of the changes if the user decides that the installation is a bad idea. We start by adding an `unexecute` method to the `CreateFile` command:

```ruby
class CreateFile < Command
  def initialize(path, contents)
    super "Create file: #{path}"
    @path = path
    @contents = contents
  end

  def execute
    f = File.open(@path, "w")
    f.write(@contents)
    f.close
  end

  def unexecute
    File.delete(@path)
  end
end
```

The `unexecute` method does exactly what it name suggests: It deletes the file that the create command created. That which `execute` gives, `unexecute` takes away.

Things get a little more challenging with the `DeleteCommand`, because this command is inherently destructive: To undo a delete operation, we need to save the contents of the original file, *before we delete it*[1] In a real system, we would probably copy the contents of the file to some temporary directory, but for our example we will just read them into memory:

```ruby
class DeleteFile < Command
  def initialize(path)
    super "Delete file: #{path}"
    @path = path
  end
```

---

1. The astute reader (that would be you) will have realized that creating a file with `CreateFile` could be destructive, too: The file that we are trying to create might already exist and be overwritten as we create the new file. In a real system, we would need to deal with this possibility as well as with a host of issues related to file permissions and ownership. In the interest of keeping the examples simple, I will shunt all of those issues aside. Sometimes it is good to be just writing examples.

```
def execute
  if File.exists?(@path)
    @contents = File.read(@path)
  end
  f = File.delete(@path)
end

def unexecute
  if @contents
    f = File.open(@path,"w")
    f.write(@contents)
    f.close
  end
end
end
```

Adding unexecute to CopyFile would tangle you up in the same issues as DeleteFile: Before you do any copying in the execute method, you would need to check whether the target file exists and save its contents if it does. The unexecute method would need to restore the contents of the file if it did exist and simply delete it if it had not been there before.

Finally, we need to add an unexecute method to the CompositeCommand class:

```
class CompositeCommand < Command

  # ...

  def unexecute
    @commands.reverse.each { |cmd| cmd.unexecute }
  end

  # ...

end
```

Here, the unexecute method is pretty much the reverse of the execute method: We take the subcommands and unexecute them. Notice that we reverse the commands array before we iterate through it; we want to undo our actions by starting with the most recent command and working our way back to the most ancient command.

Queuing Up Commands

The Command pattern can also be useful in situations where you need to accumulate a number of operations over time, but want to execute them all at once. Installers do this all the time. In a typical installation program, you go through the wizard saying that *yes,* you want the basic program, and *yes,* you want the documentation, but *no,* you do not want the example files. As you progress through the installer, it memorizes a sort of to-do list: copy in the program, copy in the documentation, and so on. At the end of the wizard, you get one final chance to change your mind. Only when you actually click the Install button do things really start to happen. Clearly, the installer's to-do list can be a list of commands.

A similar situation arises when you need to perform a series of operations for which each operation has a substantial start-up cost when done alone. For example, it frequently takes a minor computer-time eternity to connect to a database. If you need to perform a number of database operations over time, you sometimes face the unpleasant choice of (1) leaving the connection open for the whole time, thereby wasting a scarce resource, or (2) wasting the time it takes to open and close the connection for each operation.

The Command pattern offers one way out of this kind of bind. Instead of performing each operation as a stand-alone task, you accumulate all of these commands in a list. Periodically, you can open a connection to the database, execute all of your commands, and flush out this list.

Using and Abusing the Command Pattern

There is something about the Command pattern seems to invite enthusiastic overuse. As concise as the Command pattern can be in Ruby,

```ruby
class FileDeleteCommand
  def initialize(path)
    @path = path
  end

  def execute
    File.delete(@path)
  end
end

fdc = FileDeleteCommand.new('foo.dat')
fdc.execute
```

there is nothing simpler than just getting on with it:

```
File.delete('foo.dat')
```

The key thing about the Command pattern is that it separates the thought from the deed. When you use this pattern, you are no longer simply saying, "Do this"; instead, you are saying, "Remember how to do this," and, sometime later, "Do that thing that I told you to remember." Even in the lightweight code block-based renditions of the Command pattern available in Ruby, the two-part aspect of this pattern adds some serious complexity to your code. Make sure that you really need that complexity before you pull the Command pattern out of your bag of tricks.

Assuming you really do need the Command pattern, to make it work you have to be sure that the initial thought is complete. You have to carefully think through the circumstances in which the command object will find itself when it is executed versus when it was created. Yes, this key file was open, and that vital object was initialized when I created the command. Will it all still be there for me when the command is executed?

Getting this "creation time versus execution time" stuff correct is usually not too difficult with a command that is simply do-able. Mostly you just need to save all of the arguments to the operation in the command object. It is the undo-able commands that require vigilance. Many operations are destructive—they wipe away existing data. If you plan to build an undo-able command, you have to somehow save the perishable data in the command object when you execute the command, so that you can put the data back if you need to unexecute the command.

The Command Pattern in the Wild

As you might expect from the discussion at the beginning of this chapter, the Command pattern pops up frequently in GUI frameworks. Both the TK and FXRuby GUI toolkits allow you to associate code block-style commands with GUI elements such as buttons and menu items. But the Command pattern also shows up in many other parts of the Ruby code base.

ActiveRecord Migrations

`ActiveRecord`[2] comes equipped with a classic example of an undo-able Command pattern implementation in the form of its migration facility. The `ActiveRecord` migration facility allows the programmer to define his or her database schema in a

---

2. `ActiveRecord`, you will recall, is the database interface that Rails uses.

database-vendor-independent way—in Ruby, of course. The thing that makes migrations relevant here that each bit of the schema definition is organized as a command. Here, for instance, is a migration that creates a new database table called books:

```ruby
class CreateBookTable < ActiveRecord::Migration
  def self.up
    create_table :books do |t|
      t.column :title, :string
      t.column :author, :string
    end
  end

  def self.down
    drop_table :books
  end
end
```

Notice that all of the actual creation code appears in the up method. The up method is the migration "execute" method—it does the dirty work of creating the books table. Our migration also features a down method, which drops the table created by the up method, thereby undoing the effect of the command, er, migration.

A typical Rails application will define an entire set of migration classes like the one above, adding new classes as the database expands or changes. The beauty of migrations lies in the fact that you can step your database schema forward or backward in time by either doing (up-ing?) or undoing (down-ing?) the migrations.

Madeleine

Another great example of the command pattern in real Ruby code comes from Madeleine. Madeleine is a Ruby implementation of Prevayler, a project that has its roots in the Java world but has since spread out to many different languages.

Madeleine is a transactional, high-performance, object persistence framework that does not need any object relational mapping for the simple reason that it does not use a relational database—or any other kind of database, for that matter. Instead, Madeleine relies on the Ruby Marshal package, a facility for converting live Ruby objects into bytes and for turning those bytes back into objects. Unfortunately, being able to marshal your objects to a file is not by itself a complete solution to application persistence. Imagine how slow your system would be if you had to write out a whole airport's worth of seat assignments every time someone changed his or her mind and wanted that aisle seat after all.

Things would go a lot more quickly if you could just save the changes—save the original state of your objects—and then subsequently just write out the changes. Wait, this sounds eerily familiar . . .

To get a feeling for Madeleine, let's build a simple personnel system with it. We start with the ubiquitous `Employee` class:

```ruby
require 'rubygems'
require 'madeleine'

class Employee
  attr_accessor :name, :number, :address

  def initialize(name, number, address)
    @name = name
    @number = number
    @address = address
  end

  def to_s
    "Employee: name: #{name} num: #{number} addr: #{address}"
  end
end
```

Next, we create a manager class for employees. This class manages a hash of employees, with the key being the employee number. The `EmployeeManager` class lets us add a new employee, delete an existing employee, change an employee's address, and find an employee by his or her employee number:

```ruby
class EmployeeManager
  def initialize
    @employees = {}
  end

  def add_employee(e)
    @employees[e.number] = e
  end
```

```
    def change_address(number, address)
      employee = @employees[number]
      raise "No such employee" if not employee
      employee.address = address
    end

    def delete_employee(number)
      @employees.remove(number)
    end

    def find_employee(number)
      @employees[number]
    end
  end
```

Nothing very exciting so far, but now the plot begins to thicken. We define a set of command objects, one for each of the operations supported by the EmployeeManager class. First, we have AddEmployee, which is the command for inserting a new Employee into the EmployeeManager hash. Like all of the other command classes, AddEmployee consists of an `initialize` method that simply stores enough information to be able to repeat the command and an `execute` method that actually does the command:

```
class AddEmployee
  def initialize(employee)
    @employee = employee
  end

  def execute(system)
    system.add_employee(@employee)
  end
end
```

The delete, change address, and find commands are very similar:

```
class DeleteEmployee
  def initialize(number)
    @number = number
  end
```

```
    def execute(system)
      system.add_employee(@number)
    end
  end

  class ChangeAddress
    def initialize(number, address)
      @number = number
      @address = address
    end

    def execute(system)
      system.change_address(@number, @address)
    end
  end

  class FindEmployee
    def initialize(number)
      @number = number
    end

    def execute(system)
      system.find_employee(@number)
    end
  end
```

Now we get to the interesting part—we create a new Madeleine object store by passing in the name of a directory where it will persist its data as well as a code block to create a new `EmployeeManager` instance:

```
store = SnapshotMadeleine.new('employees') {EmployeeManager.new}
```

We also need a thread that will save the state of the object store to disk every so often. Our thread simply tells Madeleine to save the current state of the system to disk every 20 seconds.

```
Thread.new do
  while true
    sleep(20)
    madeleine.take_snapshot
  end
end
```

With this thread running, we can start throwing commands at our personnel system:

```
tom = Employee.new('tom','1001','1 Division Street')
harry = Employee.new('harry','1002','3435 Sunnyside Ave')

store.execute_command(AddEmployee.new(tom))
store.execute_command(AddEmployee.new(harry))
```

With Tom and Harry safely in the Madeleine store, we can run some queries:

```
puts(store.execute_command(FindEmployee.new('1001')))
puts(store.execute_command(FindEmployee.new('1002')))
```

These queries will produce the following output:

```
Employee: name: tom num: 1001 addr: 1 Division Street
Employee: name: harry num: 1002 addr: 3435 Sunnyside Ave
```

We can even change Tom's address:

```
store.execute_command(ChangeAddress.new('1001', '555 Main Street'))
```

Madeleine is a great example of the Command pattern in action. As the commands arrive at Madeleine—add this employee or change this one address—Madeleine uses this pattern to modify its in-memory copy of the data. But Madeleine also writes the command out to a file. Should your system crash, Madeleine can restore its state back to the correct state by reading the last snapshot and applying all of the outstanding commands. Every so often—every 20 seconds in our example—we write the current data out to a new snapshot and clear out all of the commands that have accumulated on disk.

Wrapping Up

With the Command pattern, we construct objects that know how to perform some very specific actions. The key word here is "specific." A command instance in the Command pattern doesn't know how to change any employee's address; instead, it knows how to move one specific employee to his new house. Commands are useful for keeping a running list of things that your program needs to do, or for remembering what it has already done. You can also run your commands backward and undo the things that your program has done. Depending on the complexity of your commands, you can implement them either as a full-scale class or as a simple code block.

The Command pattern and the Observer pattern have a lot in common. Both patterns identify an object—the command in the former pattern and the observer in the latter pattern—that is called from the other participant in the pattern. Is that object that I pass to a GUI button a command, the thing that the button will do when it is pushed, or is it an observer, waiting to be notified when the button changes state? The answer is—well, it depends. A command object simply knows how to do something, but is not particularly interested in the state of the thing that executed it. Conversely, an observer is intensely interested in the state of the subject, the thing that called it.

CHAPTER 9

Filling in the Gaps with the Adapter

Like most people who like to tinker with electronics, I have a box in my basement that is overflowing with little electronic gizmos. Near the top of the box is always my trusty USB-to-PS2 converter that lets me plug my new USB keyboard into that battered old Pentium 250 that I keep around for some reason. A little deeper is a layer of serial-to-parallel converters. The bottom strata of my box consist of all those little black power supply things.

All of these gadgets have one thing in common: They let me connect two devices that really want to talk to each other but can't, because the pins do not line up or the sockets are the wrong size or the voltage coming from one is more than enough to send the other to gizmo heaven. In short, they are all adapters.

The software world needs adapters more than the hardware folks do. Software does not have physical form factors; software engineers do not specify that this pin must be exactly 1.5 mm from that other pin. But because software is made of ideas, because we can code interfaces just as fast as our little fingers can type, we developers have nearly limitless opportunities to construct incompatible objects—objects that want to talk to each other but cannot because their interfaces do not match.

In this chapter, we will explore adapters of the software kind. We will see how these software adapters allow us to bridge the gap between mismatching software interfaces. We will also see how we can use one of the most startling features of Ruby—the ability to modify objects and classes on the fly at runtime—to ease the burden of creating adapters.

Software Adapters

Let's start our look at software adapters by imagining that we have an existing class that encrypts a file:

```
class Encrypter
  def initialize(key)
    @key = key
  end

  def encrypt(reader, writer)
    key_index = 0
    while not reader.eof?
      clear_char = reader.getc
      encrypted_char = clear_char ^ @key[key_index]
      writer.putc(encrypted_char)
      key_index = (key_index + 1) % @key.size
    end
  end
end
```

The `encrypt` method of the `Encrypter` class takes two open files, one open for reading and the other open for writing, as well as a key. It writes an encrypted version of the input file to the output file, one byte at a time.[1]

Using the `Encrypter` class to encrypt an ordinary file is straightforward. You simply open the two files and call `encrypt` with the secret key of your choice:

```
reader = File.open('message.txt')
writer = File.open('message.encrypted','w')
encrypter = Encrypter.new('my secret key')
encrypter.encrypt(reader, writer)
```

Now comes the catch: What happens if the data we want to secure happen to be in a string, rather than in a file? In this case, we need an object that looks like an open

---

1. The `Encrypter` class uses a venerable encryption algorithm. To come up with the encrypted text, it computes the exclusive OR (sometimes known as XOR) of each character of the input text with the corresponding character of the key, repeating the key over and over as needed. The beauty of this algorithm is that it is its own inverse, so you can decrypt the text by simply running the encrypted text through—with the same key—a second time.

file—that supports the same interface as the Ruby IO object—on the outside, but actually gets its characters from the string on the inside. What we need is StringIOAdapter:

```ruby
class StringIOAdapter
  def initialize(string)
    @string = string
    @position = 0
  end

  def getc
    if @position >= @string.length
      raise EOFError
    end
    ch = @string[@position]
    @position += 1
    return ch
  end

  def eof?
    return @position >= @string.length
  end
end
```

Our StringIOAdapter class has two instance variables: a reference to the string and a position index. Each time getc is called, StringIOAdapter will return the character at the current position in the string, incrementing the position as it goes. The getc method will raise an exception if there are no more characters left in the string. The eof? method will return true if we have run out of characters and false otherwise.

To use Encrypter with StringIOAdapter, we just have to replace the input file with an adapter:

```ruby
encrypter = Encrypter.new('XYZZY')
reader= StringIOAdapter.new('We attack at dawn')
writer=File.open('out.txt', 'w')
encrypter.encrypt(reader, writer)
```

As you may have guessed from the name, StringIOAdapter class is an example of an adapter. An **adapter** is an object that crosses the chasm between the interface that you have and the interface that you need.

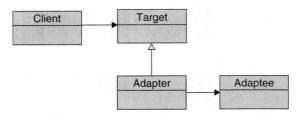

Figure 9-1 The Adapter pattern

The Class Diagram for adapters is usually drawn as shown in Figure 9-1. What this diagram is saying is that the client knows about some target class—as a client, I have a reference to my target object. The client expects the target to have a certain interface. But unknown to the client, the target object is really an adapter, and buried inside of the adapter is a reference to a second object, the adaptee, which actually performs the work. Perhaps in a perfect world all interfaces would line up perfectly and the client would talk directly to the adaptee. In the real world, however, we need to build adapters because the interface that the client is expecting is not the interface that the adaptee is offering.

Mapping this back to our example, `Encrypter` is our client object—it is looking for a reference to its target, which in our case is an `IO` instance. As shown in Figure 9-2, what the client *actually* has is a reference to the adapter, `StringIOAdapter`.

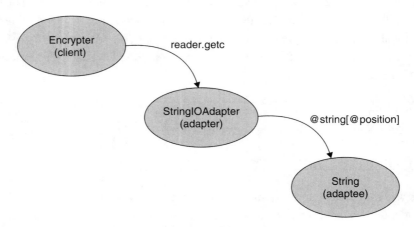

Figure 9-2   A StringIOAdapter object in action

The `StringIOAdapter` class looks like an ordinary `IO` object on the outside, but secretly it gets its characters from a string, which is the adaptee.

The Near Misses

Perhaps the most frustrating situations that seem to call for an adapter are those where the interface you have almost—but not quite—lines up with the interface that you need. For example, suppose we are writing a class to render text on the screen:

```ruby
class Renderer
  def render(text_object)
    text = text_object.text
    size = text_object.size_inches
    color = text_object.color

    # render the text ...
  end
end
```

Clearly, `Renderer` is looking to render objects that look something like this:

```ruby
class TextObject
  attr_reader :text, :size_inches, :color

  def initialize(text, size_inches, color)
    @text = text
    @size_inches = size_inches
    @color = color
  end
end
```

Unfortunately, we discover that some of the text that we need to render is contained in an object that looks more like this:

```ruby
class BritishTextObject
  attr_reader :string, :size_mm, :colour

  # ...

end
```

The good news is that `BritishTextObject` contains fundamentally everything we need to render the text. The bad news is that the text is stored in a field called `string`, not `text`; that the size of the text is in millimeters, not inches; and that the `colour` attribute has that bonus "u".

To fix these problems, we could certainly break out the Adapter pattern:

```ruby
class BritishTextObjectAdapter < TextObject
  def initialize(bto)
    @bto = bto
  end

  def text
    return @bto.string
  end

  def size_inches
    return @bto.size_mm / 25.4
  end

  def color
    return @bto.colour
  end
end
```

Maybe. Alternatively, we might choose to take advantage of Ruby's ability to modify a class on the fly.

An Adaptive Alternative?

If you are new to Ruby, you may have been thinking that the language is really pretty conventional: single inheritance, plus the usual built-in classes, methods, and `if` statements. Sure, the code blocks seem a little odd, but in the end they turn into `Proc` objects that behave in a fairly familiar way. Well, if that is what you are thinking, hold on to your keyboard: In Ruby, you can modify almost any class at any time.

To see what this means, imagine that we decide that we will not build an adapter to bridge the gap between the `BritishTextObject` instance that we have and the `TextObject` interface that we need. Instead, we'll just change the original `BritishTextObject` to look the way we need it to look. To do so, first we make sure that the original `BritishTextObject` class is loaded, and then we reopen the class and add some methods to it:

```
# Make sure the original class is loaded

require 'british_text_object'

# Now add some methods to the original class

class BritishTextObject
  def color
    return colour
  end

  def text
    return string
  end

  def size_inches
    return size_mm / 25.4
  end
end
```

The workings of this code are really quite simple. The `require` method at the top of the file loads the original `BritishTextObject` class. The `class BritishTextObject` statement after the `require` call does not create a new class, but rather reopens the existing class and adds some methods. There are really no limits as to what you can do when you modify a class. Not only can you add methods, but you can also change existing methods or delete them altogether. Perhaps most startling, you can do all of this to Ruby's built-in classes as well as the classes that you define. We could, for instance, vandalize the absolute value method in `Fixnum`:

```
# Don't do this!

class Fixnum
  def abs
    return 42
  end
end
```

With this "improved" version of abs, the absolute value of any Fixnum is now 42, so that both of the statements

```
puts(79.abs)
puts(-1234.abs)
```

will print

```
42
42
```

The ability to modify classes is one of the secrets behind Ruby's flexibility and power. But, as the preceding example illustrates, with great power comes great responsibility.

Modifying a Single Instance

If modifying an entire class on the fly seems a little extreme, Ruby provides another, perhaps less invasive alternative. Instead of modifying an entire class, you can modify the behavior of a single instance:

```
bto = BritishTextObject.new('hello', 50.8, :blue)

class << bto
  def color
    colour
  end

  def text
    string
  end

  def size_inches
    return size_mm/25.4
  end
end
```

The key bit of syntax in this code is this line:

```
class << bto
```

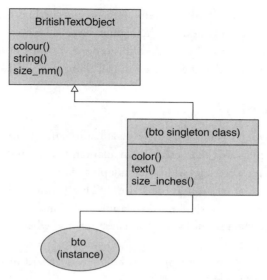

Figure 9-3   Singleton methods on a BritishTextObject instance

Essentially, this code is an instruction to modify the behavior of the `bto` object independently of its class. You can achieve the same effect with a different syntax by simply defining the methods on the instance:

```
def bto.color
    colour
end

def bto.text
    string
end

# ...
```

Ruby calls the methods that are unique to an object singleton methods.[2] It turns out that most Ruby objects,[3] along with their regular classes, have a second, more or less secret class. As shown in Figure 9-3, this second, **singleton class** is actually the first

---

2. The phrase *singleton method* is a reasonably unfortunate twist of terminology. Such methods really have nothing to do with the Singleton pattern that we will discuss in Chapter 12.
3. Immutable objects—instances of `Fixnum`, for example—will not cooperate with attempts to add singleton methods to them.

place where Ruby looks when you call a method, so any method defined in the single-ton class will override the methods in the regular class.[4] The preceding code modifies the singleton class of the `bto` object. All of this is done with the utmost discretion, and even after it has been modified the object will still claim to be of its old, original class.[5]

Adapt or Modify?

Undeniably, modifying a class or a single instance to support the interface that you need makes for simpler code than creating an adapter. If you modify the original class or object, you do not need the additional adapter class, nor do you need to worry about wrapping the adapter around the adaptee. Things just work. And yet the mod-ification technique involves serious encapsulation violations: You just dive in and start changing things. So when should you use an adapter, and when is it okay to rearrange the guts of a wayward class?

As usual, a pinch of pragmatism seems best. Lean toward modifying the class in the following circumstances:

- The modifications are simple and clear. The method aliasing we did earlier is a prime example of a simple, crystal-clear modification

- You understand the class you are modifying and the way in which it is used. Performing serious surgery on a class without taking a hard look at the class beforehand is probably going to lead to grief.

Lean toward an adapter solution in the following situations:

- The interface mismatch is extensive and complex. For example, you probably would not want to modify a string to look like a `Fixnum` object.

- You have no idea how this class works. Ignorance is always cause to tread lightly.

Engineering is all about trade-offs. Adapters preserve encapsulation at the cost of some complexity. Modifying a class may buy you some simplification, but at the cost of tinkering with the plumbing.

---

4. The singleton methods also override the methods in any module that happens to be included in the class, too.

5. Well, not too much discretion: You can query an object about its singleton methods with the `singleton_methods` method.

Using and Abusing the Adapter Pattern

One of the advantages that Ruby's duck typing gives to adapter writers is that it allows us to create adapters that support only that part of the target interface that the client will actually use. For example, `IO` objects sport a large number of methods—with a real `IO` object, you can read lines, search your file, and do lots of other file-related things. But the `StringIOAdapter` we created earlier implemented exactly two methods: `getc` and `eof?`. We got away with this because those were the only `IO` methods that the `Encrypter` class actually used. Partially implemented adapters are something of a double-edged sword: On the one hand, it is very convenient to implement only what you absolutely need; on the other hand, your program can come to grief if the client decides to call a method that you didn't think you needed.

Adapters in the Wild

You can find a classic application of the Adapter pattern buried in `ActiveRecord`, the object relational mapper used by Ruby on Rails. `ActiveRecord` has to deal with the fact that it needs to talk to a whole crowd of different database systems: MYSQL and Oracle and Postgres, not to mention SQLServer. All of these database systems provide a Ruby API—which is good. But all of the APIs are different—which is bad. For example, if you have a connection to a MYSQL database and you want to execute some SQL, you need to call the `query` method:

```
results = mysql_connection.query(sql)
```

But if you are talking to Sybase, you need to use the `sql` method:

```
results = sybase_connection.sql(sql)
```

Meanwhile, if you are dealing with Oracle, you call the `execute` method and get back a cursor to the results instead of the results themselves. It is almost as if the authors got together and conspired to ensure that there was no overlap.

`ActiveRecord` deals with all of these differences by defining a standardized interface, encapsulated in a class called `AbstractAdapter`. The `AbstractAdapter` class defines the interface to a database that is used throughout `ActiveRecord`. For example, `AbstractAdapter` defines a standard method to execute a SQL select statement and return the results, called `select_all`. A subclass of `AbstractAdapter` is available for each of the different flavors of databases—for example, there is a

MysqlAdapter and an OracleAdapter and a SybaseAdapter. Each individual adapter implements the select_all method in terms of the API of the underlying database system.

Finally, our StringIOAdapter example is inspired by the StringIO class, which comes with Ruby.

Wrapping Up

There really is no magic to adapters: They exist to soak up the differences between the interfaces that we need and the objects that we have. An adapter supports the interface that we need on the outside, but it implements that interface by making calls to an object hidden inside—an object that does everything we need it to do, but does it via the wrong interface.

Ruby also supports a second, albeit limited way to solve the "wrong interface" problem: We can simply modify the object with the wrong interface at runtime so that it has the right interface. In other words, we can beat the object into submission. The choice of using an adapter or modifying the object really comes down to how well you understand the class in question and the issue of encapsulation. If you know how the thing works and your interface changes are relatively minor, perhaps modifying the object is the way to go. If the object is complex or if you simply do not understand it fully, use a classic adapter.

The Adapter pattern is the first member of a family of patterns we will encounter—a family of patterns in which one object stands in for another object. This family of object-oriented impostors also includes proxies and decorators. In each case, an object acts more or less as the front man for another object. As you will see in subsequent chapters, in each of these patterns the code will look vaguely familiar. At the risk of repeating myself, keep in mind that a pattern is not just about code: Intent is critical. An adapter is an adapter only if you are stuck with objects that have the wrong interface and you are trying to keep the pain of dealing with these ill-fitting interfaces from spreading throughout your system.

CHAPTER 10

Getting in Front of Your Object with a Proxy

Software engineering is full of ironies. I can work day and night for months on the new `BankAccount` object, a technical masterpiece that allows clients to manage all their banking needs. Then I can labor for even more months to keep all but a very few (authorized) clients from getting anywhere near it.

But then my boss tells me that the authorized clients don't even want my `BankAccount` object. Well, at least they don't want it on their computers—it would be great if they could somehow use the `BankAccount` class while it is running on the server, but no way will the users install that thing on their computers.

Finally, as the all-but-impossible, *we got to have this code right now* deadline approaches, I get one more requirement: For performance reasons, please delay creating `BankAccount` objects at runtime until the last possible moment.

As disparate as these problems seem—controlling access to an object or providing a location-independent way of getting at the object or delaying its creation—all three actually have a common solution: the Proxy pattern.

In this chapter, we will look at the Proxy pattern, examine the traditional way of building a proxy, and see how we can use it to solve our trio of dilemmas. Finally, we will reach into our Ruby bag of tricks and pull out a technique that will make building a proxy as easy as writing a single method.

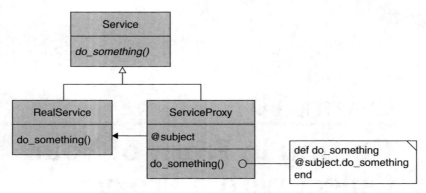

Figure 10-1   The Proxy pattern

Proxies to the Rescue

The Proxy pattern is essentially built around a little white lie. When the client asks us for an object—perhaps the bank account object mentioned earlier—we do indeed give the client back an object. However, the object that we give back is not quite the object that the client expected. What we hand to the client is an object that looks and acts like the object the client expected, but is actually an imposter. As you can see in Figure 10-1, the counterfeit object, called the **proxy** by the GoF, has a reference to the real object, the **subject,** hidden inside. Whenever the client code calls a method on the proxy, the proxy simply forwards the request to the real object.

To make the proxy idea a little more concrete, let's do some banking. The code below shows a simple class that keeps track of a bank account:

```ruby
class BankAccount
  attr_reader :balance

  def initialize(starting_balance=0)
    @balance = starting_balance
  end

  def deposit(amount)
    @balance += amount
  end

  def withdraw(amount)
    @balance -= amount
  end
end
```

Instances of `BankAccount` will be our real objects or subjects. Let's now move on to a proxy for `BankAccount`:

```ruby
class BankAccountProxy
  def initialize(real_object)
    @real_object = real_object
  end

  def balance
    @real_object.balance
  end

  def deposit(amount)
    @real_object.deposit(amount)
  end

  def withdraw(amount)
    @real_object.withdraw(amount)
  end
end
```

We can now create a bank account and a proxy for the bank account and use them more or less interchangeably:

```ruby
account = BankAccount.new(100)
account.deposit(50)
account.withdraw(10)

proxy = BankAccountProxy.new(account)
proxy.deposit(50)
proxy.withdraw(10)
```

There really is nothing very exciting going on in `BankAccountProxy`. The `BankAccountProxy` presents exactly the same interface as its subject, the `BankAccount` object. But the proxy doesn't really know a thing about high finance—whenever someone calls a method on it, the `BankAccountProxy` turns to the real `BankAccount` object, delegating the method call to the subject.

Of course, if our proxy did nothing more than echo every call blindly down to the subject, we will not have accomplished much except create a sink for those extra

CPU cycles as the method calls arrive at the proxy, only to be immediately bounced off to the subject. But once we have a proxy, we have a place to stand squarely between the client and the real object. If we want to manage who does what to the bank account, the proxy provides the ideal pinch point to exert control.

The Protection Proxy

Let's take our generic, do-nothing `BankAccountProxy` and turn it into a **protection proxy,** a proxy that controls access to the subject. To do so, we need simply add a check at the start of each method:

```ruby
require 'etc'

class AccountProtectionProxy
  def initialize(real_account, owner_name)
    @subject = real_account
    @owner_name = owner_name
  end

  def deposit(amount)
    check_access
    return @subject.deposit(amount)
  end

  def withdraw(amount)
    check_access
    return @subject.withdraw(amount)
  end

  def balance
    check_access
    return @subject.balance
  end

  def check_access
    if Etc.getlogin != @owner_name
      raise "Illegal access: #{Etc.getlogin} cannot access account."
    end
  end
end
```

Each operation on the account is protected by a call to the check_access method. The check_access method does what its name implies: It makes sure that the current user is allowed to access the account. The example version of check_access uses the Etc[1] module to get the name of the current user; it then compares this name to the name of the account owner, which is passed in to the constructor.

Clearly, we could have included the checking code in the BankAccount object itself. The advantage of using a proxy for protection is that it gives us a nice separation of concerns: The proxy worries about who is or is not allowed to do what. The only thing that the real bank account object need be concerned with is, well, the bank account. By implementing the security in a proxy, we make it easy to swap in a different security scheme (just wrap the subject in a different proxy) or eliminate the security all together (just drop the proxy). For that matter, we can also change the implementation of the BankAccount object without messing with our security scheme.

Protection proxies have another advantage over the naive "implement all of the security and functionality in one class" approach. By splitting the protection cleanly off from the workings of the real object, we can minimize the chance that any important information will inadvertently leak out through our protective shield.

Remote Proxies

Perhaps security is not really your problem; perhaps location is the real issue. Maybe you have a program on some client machine and it would like to use the BankAccount object. The trouble is that the BankAccount object lives on a server machine that is way, way across the network. Now you could make the client program work really hard—have it cook up packets and submit them to the network and deal with all of the complexities of holding a conversation over a (possibly unreliable) network. Alternatively, you could hide the complexity behind a remote proxy, an object that lives on the client machine and looks, to the client code, just like the real BankAccount object. When a request comes in, the remote proxy goes through all the horror of packaging up the request, sending it over the network, waiting for a response, unpacking the response, and returning the answer to the unsuspecting client.

---

1. The Etc module is kind of, sort of, pretty much standard with Ruby. It is part of the standard Ruby distribution for UNIX and UNIX-like systems. There is also an optional—albeit widely available—Windows version. The Windows version comes packaged with the one-click Ruby Windows installer, so I will just assume that you have it.

From the client's point of view, it called a method on what it thought was the real `BankAccount` object and sometime later—perhaps an unusually long time later—the answer came back. This is how virtually all **remote procedure call (RPC)** systems work.

As a quick example of a remote proxy, the following code uses Ruby's own SOAP client mechanism to create a proxy for a public SOAP service that provides weather information:[2]

```
require 'soap/wsdlDriver'

wsdl_url = 'http://www.webservicex.net/WeatherForecast.asmx?WSDL'

proxy = SOAP::WSDLDriverFactory.new( wsdl_url ).create_rpc_driver
weather_info = proxy.GetWeatherByZipCode('ZipCode'=>'19128')
```

Once the proxy object is set up, the client code no longer has to worry about the fact that the service actually lives at `www.webservicex.net`. Instead, it simply calls `GetWeatherByZipCode` and leaves all of the network details to the proxy.

Remote proxies offer many of the same advantages as protection proxies. In particular, the remote proxy enables a nice separation of concerns: One object, the subject, can focus on forecasting the weather or whatever domain-specific thing that it is doing while the other object, the proxy, can concentrate on shipping the bytes across the network. Changing protocols (perhaps from SOAP to XMLRPC) is as easy as swapping out the proxy.

Virtual Proxies Make You Lazy

Finally, we can use a proxy to delay creating expensive objects until we really need them. This is exactly what we need to deal with the final twist of fate in the little parable that opened this chapter. Recall that the last requirement for our banking project was to delay the creation of `BankAccount` instances for as long as possible. We do not want to create the real `BankAccount` until the user is ready to do something with it, such as making a deposit. But we also do not want to spread the complexity of that delayed creation out over all the client code. The answer is to use yet another flavor of proxy, the **virtual proxy.**

---

2. If you decide to try out this example, please keep in mind that public Web services seem to have approximately the same life expectancy as a day-old mayfly, so the specific service shown in the example may not be around when you try to access it.

In a sense, the virtual proxy is the biggest liar of the bunch. It pretends to be the real object, but it does not even have a reference to the real object until the client code calls a method. Only when the client actually calls a method does the virtual proxy scurry off and create or otherwise get access to the real object.

Implementing the virtual proxy is very simple:

```ruby
class VirtualAccountProxy
  def initialize(starting_balance=0)
    @starting_balance=starting_balance
  end

  def deposit(amount)
    s = subject
    return s.deposit(amount)
  end

  def withdraw(amount)
    s = subject
    return s.withdraw(amount)
  end

  def balance
    s = subject
    return s.balance
  end

  def subject
    @subject || (@subject = BankAccount.new(@starting_balance))
  end
end
```

The heart of our `VirtualAccountProxy` is the `subject` method. The `subject` method checks whether the `BankAccount` object has already been created and, if not, creates a new one. The `subject` method uses a very common, if slightly strange-looking Ruby idiom to get the job done:

```ruby
@subject || (@subject = BankAccount.new(@starting_balance))
```

This line of code is really just one big OR expression. The first term of the OR expression is `@subject`. If `@subject` is not `nil`, the expression evaluates to that non-nil value (it this case, our bank account object) and we are done. If `@subject` is `nil`, Ruby will evaluate the right side of the OR expression, which creates the new bank account; thus the value of the expression is the new bank account.

One drawback of the `VirtualAccountProxy` implementation shown above is that the proxy is responsible for creating the bank account object. That approach tangles the proxy and the subject up a little more than we might like. We can improve on this strategy by applying a little of that Ruby code block magic:

```ruby
class VirtualAccountProxy
  def initialize(&creation_block)
    @creation_block = creation_block
  end

  # Other methods omitted ...

  def subject
    @subject || (@subject = @creation_block.call)
  end
end
```

In this new implementation, the code that creates the proxy passes in a block that is responsible for creating the bank account when the time comes:

```ruby
account = VirtualAccountProxy.new { BankAccount.new(10) }
```

Like the other two flavors of proxies, the virtual proxy provides us with a good separation of concerns: The real `BankAccount` object deals with deposits and withdrawals, while the `VirtualAccountProxy` deals with the issue of when to create the `BankAccount` instance.

Eliminating That Proxy Drudgery

One annoying characteristic that all of our proxies so far have shared is the need to write all of those boring, repetitive proxied methods. For example, our bank account proxies all needed to implement proxy methods for `deposit`, `withdrawal`, and `balance` methods. Of course, three methods is by no means the limit, or even typical. Ruby's `Array` class has 118 methods, while `String` has 142. Writing 142 dumb methods is not merely pure drudgery; it is also a rich source of opportunities for screwing up.

Can we avoid writing all these boring methods? It turns out that Ruby does have a way—a way that is rooted in something you learned very early in your object-oriented programming career and have probably long since forgotten.

Message Passing and Methods

If your introduction to object-oriented programming was like mine, somewhere early on day 1 you learned about "message passing." You were told that doing something like

```
account.deposit(50)
```

meant that you were sending the deposit message to the account object. Of course, if you were learning about a statically typed language, you soon figured out that `account.deposit(50)` was synonymous with calling the `deposit` method on the account object. The whole static typing system was there to make sure that the `deposit` method was there and was called. So by the end of day 1 of object-oriented programming, we all stopped talking about passing messages and started talking about calling methods.

The concept of message passing would make more sense if we could say `account.deposit(50)`, and the `BankAccount` class was then free to do something else with the message besides simply calling the `deposit` method. Perhaps the `BankAccount` class could call some method other than `deposit`, or perhaps it could decide to do nothing. It turns out that this is all possible in Ruby.

The Ruby meaning of `account.deposit(50)` is much closer to true message passing than the "we all know this is a straight method call" model of most statically typed languages. When you invoke `account.deposit(50)`, Ruby will initially do exactly what you expect: It will look for the `deposit` method first in `BankAccount`'s class, then in its superclass, and so on, until it either finds the method or runs out of superclasses. If Ruby finds the method, we get the behavior that we have long come to expect: `deposit` is called and you are $50 richer.

But what if there is no `deposit` method? In this case, Ruby does something a little unexpected: Behind the scenes it calls another method. This fallback method is named `method_missing`. Again Ruby will look in the `BankAccount` class, this time for `method_missing`. If there is no `method_missing` in `BankAccount`, Ruby will again climb up the inheritance tree from class to superclass until it either finds a `method_missing` or hits `Object`. The search will stop at `Object` because the `Object` class comes equipped with a `method_missing` method. Its implementation of `method_missing` simply raises the usual `NoMethodError` exception.

The net effect of all of this is that if you do not define a `method_missing` method in your class (or in a superclass), things work as we have come to expect: You call a bad method and Ruby raises an exception. The beauty of the `method_missing` method is that by implementing it in your class, you can build classes that can catch any arbitrary method—or, should I say, message—that comes down the road and do whatever seems correct in that situation.[3] This is message passing.

The method_missing Method

The `method_missing` method is one of those variable argument methods that we glimpsed briefly in Chapter 2. The first argument is always a symbol—the name of the nonexistent method. It is followed by all of the arguments from the original call.

Let's look at a simple example, a class that whines in its own special way whenever a nonexistent method is called. Try running the following code:

```ruby
class TestMethodMissing
  def hello
    puts("Hello from a real method")
  end

  def method_missing(name, *args)
    puts("Warning, warning, unknown method called: #{name}")
    puts("Arguments: #{args.join(' ')}")
  end
end
```

If we send a message to an instance of `TestMethodMissing` that does correspond to a real method,

```ruby
tmm=TestMethodMissing.new
tmm.hello
```

we get the behavior that we have long expected:

```
Hello from a real method
```

---

3. The Smalltalk programming language behaves pretty much the same way as Ruby does when someone calls a nonexistent method, but in Smalltalk the name of the catch-all method is the much more descriptive `doesNotUnderstand`.

But if we throw something unexpected at `TestMethodMissing`, then `method_missing` is called:

```
tmm.goodbye('cruel', 'world')
Warning, warning, unknown method called: goodbye
Arguments: cruel world
```

Sending Messages

The idea of message passing is so thoroughly integrated into Ruby that you can not only catch unexpected messages with `method_missing`, but also explicitly send messages to objects with the `send` method. For example, sending the messages

```
tmm.send(:hello)
tmm.send(:goodbye, 'cruel', 'world')
```

gives the same output as calling `hello` and `goodbye` in the normal way:

```
Hello from a real method
Warning, warning, unknown method called: goodbye
Arguments: cruel world
```

The arguments to `send` are identical to the arguments to `method_missing`. The first argument is the name of the message, which is followed by any arguments that go along with the message.

So what, you may be wondering, is all the excitement about? Yes, you can catch unexpected method calls with `method_missing`. And yes, you can explicitly send messages. But why would you ever bother with `account.send(:deposit, 50)` when `account.deposit(50)` is not only shorter but also more familiar? It turns out that this message-passing nonsense actually makes building proxies and a number of other patterns much easier.

Proxies without the Tears

Recall that just before we went off on our message-passing tangent, we were lamenting the fact that building proxies involved painfully repeating in the proxy all of the methods of the subject class that we wanted to proxy. But what if we did not repeat these methods? What if we built our proxy class and simply did not define any of the methods we intended to proxy? We might end up with something like this:

```
class AccountProxy
  def initialize(real_account)
    @subject = real_account
  end
end
```

As it stands, our `AccountProxy` class is quite useless. If we create this class and call any of the methods from `BankAccount` on it,

```
ap = AccountProxy.new( BankAccount.new(100) )
ap.deposit(25)
```

all we get is a blank stare:

```
proxy1.rb:32: undefined method 'deposit'
  for #<AccountProxy:0x401bd408>(NoMethodError)
```

Based on our discussion in the previous section, we know what is happening behind the scenes here. First Ruby will look for the `deposit` method and will fail to find it. Having failed to find the deposit method, Ruby will look for the `method_missing` method, which it will find in the `Object` class. It is this `Object` method that raises the `NoMethodError` exception.

Now here comes the key insight: If we add a `method_missing` method to our proxy class, the proxy can catch any method call that comes its way. Using the `send` method, the proxy can also forward the message—the message that the proxy has no idea how to handle—to the real account object! Here is the new and improved `AccountProxy`:

```
class AccountProxy
  def initialize(real_account)
    @subject = real_account
  end

  def method_missing(name, *args)
    puts("Delegating #{name} message to subject.")
    @subject.send(name, *args)
  end
end
```

We can now throw any `BankAccount` message we want at the proxy, serene in the knowledge that any message that `AccountProxy` does not understand will be bounced to `method_missing`, which will send the message on to the real account object. Let's create one of these new account proxies and start using it:

```
ap = AccountProxy.new( BankAccount.new(100) )
ap.deposit(25)
ap.withdraw(50)
puts("account balance is now: #{ap.balance}")
```

We will get the following outcome:

```
delegating deposit method to subject.
delegating withdraw method to subject.
delegating balance method to subject.
account balance is now: 75
```

What we have here is a very painless method of delegation, which is exactly what we need to take the sting out of building proxies. Let's rewrite our `AccountProtectionProxy` using the `method_missing` technique:

```
class AccountProtectionProxy
  def initialize(real_account, owner_name)
    @subject = real_account
    @owner_name = owner_name
  end


  def method_missing(name, *args)
    check_access
    @subject.send( name, *args )
  end

  def check_access
    if Etc.getlogin != @owner_name
      raise "Illegal access: #{Etc.getlogin} cannot access account."
    end
  end
end
```

There are two interesting things to note about our new `AccountProtection` `Proxy`, one obvious and one a little more subtle. The obvious thing is that `AccountProtectionProxy` is 15 lines long—and it will stay 15 lines long, no matter how many methods we need to delegate to the real account object. Less obvious is the fact that there is nothing `BankAccount`-specific about `AccountProtectionProxy`. `AccountProtectionProxy` will cheerfully proxy (and protect) any object that you throw at it, applying the same access policy to all comers.

To try a silly example, suppose we use `AccountProtectionProxy` to defend an ordinary string. If we wrap the string with a proxy with the correct user (me!), things work just fine:

```
s = AccountProtectionProxy.new( "a simple string", 'russ' )
puts("The length of the string is #{s.length}")
```

But if the string belongs to Fred,

```
s = AccountProtectionProxy.new( "a simple string", 'fred' )
puts("The length of the string is #{s.length}")
```

then I will not get anywhere near it:

```
string_permission.rb:17.in `check_access':
  Illegal access: russ cannot access account.
```

We can just as easily build a virtual proxy with our `method_missing` technique:

```
class VirtualProxy
  def initialize(&creation_block)
    @creation_block = creation_block
  end

  def method_missing(name, *args)
    s = subject
    s.send( name, *args )
  end
```

```
    def subject
      @subject = @creation_block.call unless @subject
      @subject
    end
  end
```

Like our new `method_missing`-based protection proxy, this second virtual proxy is pretty universal. We can, for instance, use it to delay the creation of an array:

```
array = VirtualProxy.new { Array.new }

array << 'hello'
array << 'out'
array << 'there'
```

As we will see in the pages to come, `method_missing` is useful in many situations that require delegation.

Using and Abusing Proxies

An easy trap to fall into when building a proxy, especially when you are using the `method_missing` technique, is to forget that every object starts out with a minimal set of methods—those that it inherits from `Object`. For example, every object inherits a method called `to_s` from `Object`. Call `to_s` on most any object, and you will get back a string containing some kind of description of the object. A proxy is supposed to pretend to be its subject, but if you call `to_s` on any of the proxies that we have built so far, the illusion quickly breaks down:

```
account = VirtualProxy.new { BankAccount.new }
puts(account)

#<VirtualProxy:0x40293b48>
```

What is happening here is that we are calling the `VirtualProxy` `to_s` method, not the `BankAccount` `to_s` method. This may or may not be the behavior we are looking for; the point is that you need to think about those often-forgotten `Object` methods as you build your proxies.

The `method_missing` technique extolled in this chapter also has some downsides. For example, using `method_missing` involves a bit of a performance hit. If you compare a class with a straightforward method

```
class DirectCall
  def add(a, b)
    a+b
  end
end
```

with a class that uses the `method_missing` method

```
class MethodMissingCall
  def method_missing(name, a, b)
    a+b
  end
end
```

the `method_missing` version will run somewhat more slowly. On my machine, the first, traditionally written class runs about 10 percent faster than calling `add` on the second version and letting the unknown method fall through to `method_missing`.

More importantly, overusing `method_missing`, like overusing inheritance, is a great way to obscure your code. When you use the `method_missing` technique, you are creating objects whose messages are handled more or less magically. Anyone reading the code for our banking system, for example, will start by looking for the `deposit` and `withdraw` methods in the proxy classes. The Ruby-savvy reader will rapidly make the mental jump and recognize the `method_missing` technique. But your code should not require any more metal athletics than necessary—make sure you have a good reason to put the next coder who comes along through all of that.

Proxies in the Wild

By far, the most popular use of the Proxy pattern in Ruby today takes the form of a remote proxy. Aside from the Ruby SOAP client that we saw earlier, the Distributed Ruby package (drb) is also available; it allows you to build distributed Ruby applications that are bound together by a TCP/IP network. The drb package is really easy to use: Just about any plain old Ruby object (a PORO perhaps?) can act as a drb service. Let's build a stupendously dumb one:

```ruby
class MathService
  def add(a, b)
    return a + b
  end
end
```

To expose this object as a drb service requires only a few lines of code:

```ruby
require 'drb/drb'

math_service=MathService.new
DRb.start_service("druby://localhost:3030", math_service)
DRb.thread.join
```

Essentially, we create a `MathService` object and then mumble the correct drb incantation to advertise the new object on port 3030. To get things going, we would start up the math service program on some computer and then let it sit there in the background, ready to handle incoming requests.

To generate a request, we will need a client program. Move to another window or even another computer on your network and crank up the following code. First we need to initialize the drb client side:

```ruby
require 'drb/drb'
DRb.start_service
```

Now we can connect to the remote math service:

```ruby
math_service = DRbObject.new_with_uri("druby://localhost:3030")
```

Of course, if you are running the service on a different computer or port, you will need to change the URL accordingly. Running the client program allows us to exercise the stupendous math server:

```ruby
sum=math_service.add(2,2)
```

This is all relevant to the Proxy pattern because the client-side `math_service` is actually a remote proxy to the real math service, which is running inside the server-side Ruby interpreter. If you poke around inside the drb innards, you will find the same `method_missing` technique that we have discussed in this chapter.

Wrapping Up

In this chapter, we looked at three different problems: protecting an object from unauthorized access, hiding the fact that this object really lives somewhere else on the network, and delaying the creation of an expensive object until the last possible instant. Remarkably, all of these problems find a common solution in the Proxy pattern. Proxies are the con artists of the programming world: They pretend to be some other object when they are not, in fact, that object. Inside the proxy is hidden a reference to the other, real object—an object that the GoF referred to as the subject.

Nevertheless, the proxy does not just act as a method call conduit for the subject. Instead, it serves as a pinch point between the client and the subject. "Is this operation authorized?" asks the protection proxy. "Does the subject actually live on this other machine?" asks the remote proxy. "Have I actually created the subject yet?" asks the virtual proxy. In short, the proxy controls access to the subject. We also saw in this chapter how using the `method_missing` technique can substantially reduce the coding burden of building proxies.

The Proxy pattern is the second pattern we have encountered in which one object stands in for another. In Chapter 9, we considered the adapter, which wraps one object with another to transform the interface of the first object. Superficially, the proxy is very similar to the adapter: One object stands in for another. But the proxy does not change the interface; the interface of the proxy is exactly the same as the interface of its subject. Instead of trying to transform the interface of that inner object in the same way that an adapter does, the proxy tries to control access to it.

It turns out that the "object within an object," Russian-doll kind of construction that we have seen in the Adapter and Proxy patterns is so useful that we will see it a one more time before this book ends. In particular, it is likely to pop up again in the very next chapter . . .

CHAPTER 11

Improving Your Objects with a Decorator

Among the most basic questions of software engineering is this: How do you add features to your program without turning the whole thing into a huge, unmanageable mess? So far, you have seen how to split the internal workings of your objects up among a family of classes with the Template Method pattern and how to use the Strategy pattern to split off whole chunks of algorithms. You have also seen how to react to requests coming into your objects with the Command pattern and how to keep up with changes made to other objects with the Observer pattern. Composites and iterators each help in their own way in dealing with collections of objects.

But what if you simply need to vary the responsibilities of an object? What do you do when sometimes your object needs to do a little more, but sometimes a little less? In this chapter we will look at the Decorator pattern, which enables you to easily add an enhancement to an existing object. The Decorator pattern also allows you to layer features atop one another so that you can construct objects that have exactly the right set of capabilities that you need for any given situation. As usual, we will take a look at a very Ruby-flavored alternative to the Decorator pattern. Finally, we will see why highly decorated objects are not always everyone's idea of a hero.

Decorators: The Cure for Ugly Code

Imagine that you have some text that needs to be written to a file. Sounds simple enough, but in your system sometimes you want to write out just the plain, unadorned text, while at other times you want to number each line as it gets written out.

Sometimes you want to add a time stamp to each line as it goes out into the file. Sometimes you need a checksum from the text so that later on you can ensure that it was written and stored properly.

To handle these demands, you might just start out with an object that wraps a Ruby IO object and has several methods, one for each output variation:

```ruby
class EnhancedWriter
  attr_reader :check_sum

  def initialize(path)
    @file = File.open(path, "w")
    @check_sum = 0
    @line_number = 1
  end

  def write_line(line)
    @file.print(line)
    @file.print("\n")
  end

  def checksumming_write_line(data)
    data.each_byte {|byte| @check_sum = (@check_sum + byte) % 256 }
    @check_sum += "\n"[0] % 256
    write_line(data)
  end

  def timestamping_write_line(data)
    write_line("#{Time.new}: #{data}")
  end

  def numbering_write_line(data)
    write_line("%{@line_number}: #{data}")
    @line_number += 1
  end

  def close
    @file.close
  end
end
```

You can then use `EnhancedWriter` to write out ordinary text:

```
writer = EnhancedWriter.new('out.txt')
writer.write_line("A plain line")
```

Or a line that gets included in the checksum:

```
writer.checksumming_write_line('A line with checksum')
puts("Checksum is #{writer.check_sum}")
```

Or a time-stamped line or a numbered one:

```
writer.timestamping_write_line('with time stamp')
writer.numbering_write_line('with line number')
```

There is only one thing wrong with this approach: everything. First, every client that uses `EnhancedWriter` will need to know whether it is writing out numbered, checksummed, or time-stamped text. And the clients do not need to know this just once, perhaps to set things up—no, they need to know it continuously, with every line of data that they write out. If a client gets things wrong just once—for example, if it uses `timestamping_write_line` when it meant to use `numbering_write_line` or if it uses plain old `write_line` when it meant to use `checksumming_write_line`— then the name of the class, `EnhancedIO`, is going to seem more than a little ironic.

An only slightly less obvious problem with this "throw it all in one class" approach is, well, that everything is thrown together in a one class. There is all of the line numbering code sitting alongside the checksum code, which is nestled up against the time stamp code, and all of them are locked together in the same class, used or not, just looking for trouble.

You might be able to separate out all of these text writing concerns by creating a base class and subclasses—in other words, use our old friend inheritance—along the lines shown in the UML diagram in Figure 11-1.

But what if you want a checksum of your numbered output? What if you want to put line numbers on your output, but only after you add time stamps to it? You can still do it, but the number of classes does seem to be getting out of hand, as is painfully clear in Figure 11-2.

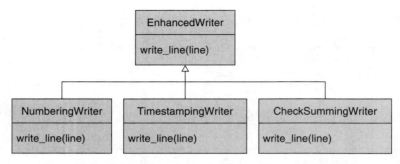

Figure 11-1   Solving the enhanced writer problem with inheritance

Now consider that even with the forest of classes shown in Figure 11-2, we still can't get a checksum of that time-stamped text after we have line-numbered it. The trouble is that the inheritance-based approach requires you to come up with all possible combinations of features up-front, at design time. Chances are, you are not really going to need every single combination—you are just going to need the combinations that you need.

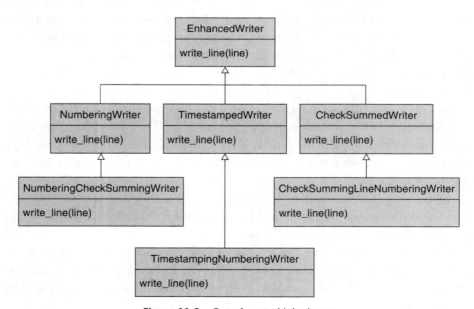

Figure 11-2   Out-of-control inheritance

A better solution would allow you to assemble the combination of features that you really need, dynamically, at runtime. Let's start over with a very dumb object that just knows how to write the plain, unadorned text and do a few other file-related operations:

```ruby
class SimpleWriter
  def initialize(path)
    @file = File.open(path, 'w')
  end

  def write_line(line)
    @file.print(line)
    @file.print("\n")
  end

  def pos
    @file.pos
  end

  def rewind
    @file.rewind
  end

  def close
    @file.close
  end
end
```

If you want your lines numbered, insert an object (perhaps one called NumberingWriter) between your SimpleWriter and the client, an object that adds a number to each line and forwards the whole thing on to the basic SimpleWriter, which then writes it to disk. NumberingWriter adds its own contribution to the abilities of SimpleWriter—in a sense, it **decorates** SimpleWriter; hence the name of the pattern. We plan to write a bunch of these decorator objects, so let's factor out the generic code into a common base class:

```ruby
class WriterDecorator
  def initialize(real_writer)
    @real_writer = real_writer
  end
```

```ruby
  def write_line(line)
    @real_writer.write_line(line)
  end

  def pos
    @real_writer.pos
  end

  def rewind
    @real_writer.rewind
  end

  def close
    @real_writer.close
  end
end

class NumberingWriter < WriterDecorator
  def initialize(real_writer)
    super(real_writer)
    @line_number = 1
  end

  def write_line(line)
    @real_writer.write_line("#{@line_number}: #{line}")
    @line_number += 1
  end
end
```

Because the NumberingWriter class presents the same core interface as the plain old writer, the client does not really have to worry about the fact that it is talking to a NumberingWriter instead of a plain old SimpleWriter. At their most basic, both flavors of writer look exactly the same.

To get our lines numbered, we just encase our SimpleWriter in a Numbering-Writer:

```ruby
writer = NumberingWriter.new(SimpleWriter.new('final.txt'))
writer.write_line('Hello out there')
```

We can follow the same pattern to build a decorator that computes checksums. That is, another object will sit between the client and the SimpleWriter, this time summing up all of the bytes before it sends them off to the `SimpleWriter` for writing:

```ruby
class CheckSummingWriter < WriterDecorator
  attr_reader :check_sum

  def initialize(real_writer)
    @real_writer = real_writer
    @check_sum = 0
  end

  def write_line(line)
    line.each_byte {|byte| @check_sum = (@check_sum + byte) % 256 }
    @check_sum += "\n"[0] % 256
    @real_writer.write_line(line)
  end
end
```

The `CheckSummingWriter` is a little different from our first decorator in that it has an enhanced interface. In addition to the usual methods found on all of the writers, `CheckSummingWriter` sports the `check_sum` method.[1]

Finally, we can write a class that adds time stamps to the data as it goes by:

```ruby
class TimeStampingWriter < WriterDecorator
  def write_line(line)
    @real_writer.write_line("#{Time.new}: #{line}")
  end
end
```

Now here is the punchline: Because all of the decorator objects support the same basic interface as the original, the "real" object that we supply to any one of the decorators does not actually have to be an instance of `SimpleWriter`—it can, in fact, be any other decorator. This means that we can build arbitrarily long chains of decorators, with each one adding its own secret ingredient to the whole. We can, for example, finally get that checksum of that time-stamped text, after we have line-numbered it:

```ruby
writer = CheckSummingWriter.new(TimeStampingWriter.new(
           NumberingWriter.new(SimpleWriter.new('final.txt'))))

writer.write_line('Hello out there')
```

---

1. Of course, the `check_sum` method was generated for us by `attr_reader`.

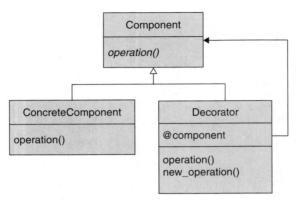

Figure 11-3   The Decorator pattern

Formal Decoration

All of the players in the Decorator pattern, as shown in Figure 11-3, implement the component interface.

The **ConcreteComponent** is the "real" object, the object that implements the basic component functionality. In the writer example, the `SimpleWriter` is the ConcreteComponent. The **Decorator** class has a reference to a **Component**—the next Component in the decorator chain—and it implements all of the methods of the Component type. Our example has three different Decorator classes: one for line numbering, one for checksumming, and one for time stamping. Each Decorator layers its own special magic onto the workings of the base component, adding its own talent to at least one of the methods. Decorators can also add new methods—that is, operations that are not defined in the Component interface—although this behavior is optional. In our example, only the decorator that computes the checksum adds a new method.

Easing the Delegation Blues

The Decorator pattern takes one bit of GoF advice to heart: It incorporates a lot of delegation. We can see this in the `WriterDecorator` class, which consists almost entirely of boilerplate methods that do nothing except delegate to the next writer down the line.

We could eliminate all of this boring code with a variation on the `method_missing` technique that we learned in Chapter 10, but the `forwardable` module is probably a better fit. The `forwardable` module will automatically generate all of those dull delegating methods for us with very little effort. Here is our `WriterDecorator` class rewritten to take advantage of `forwardable`:

```ruby
require 'forwardable'

class WriterDecorator
  extend Forwardable

  def_delegators :@real_writer, :write_line, :rewind, :pos, :close

  def initialize(real_writer)
    @real_writer = real_writer
  end

end
```

The `forwardable` module supplies the `def_delegators` class method,[2] which takes two or more arguments. The first argument is the name of an instance attribute.[3] It is followed by the name of one or more methods. The `def_delegators` method will add all of the named methods to your class, and each of those new methods in turn delegates to the object referred to by the attribute. Thus the `WriterDecorator` class will end up with `write`, `rewind`, `pos`, and `close` methods, all of which delegate to `@component`.

The `forwardable` module is more of a precision weapon than the `method_missing` technique. With `forwardable`, you have control over which methods you delegate. Although you could certainly put logic in `method_missing` to pick and choose which methods to delegate, the `method_missing` technique really shines when you want to delegate large numbers of calls.

Dynamic Alternatives to the Decorator Pattern

The runtime flexibility of Ruby presents some interesting alternatives to the GoF Decorator pattern. In particular, we can obtain most of that decorator goodness either by dynamically wrapping methods or via module decorations.

---

2. You may have noticed that we `extend` the `Forwardable` module in `WriterDecorator` instead of `include`-ing it. The difference is subtle–the `Forwardable` module wants to add class-level methods, not instance methods.

3. Oddly, complete with the `@`.

Wrapping Methods

We have already seen that Ruby allows us to modify the behavior of single instances or whole classes pretty much anytime. Armed with this flexibility, plus some knowledge of the `alias` keyword, we can turn a plain-vanilla writer into a time-stamping writer:

```
w = SimpleWriter.new('out')

class << w

  alias old_write_line write_line

  def write_line(line)
    old_write_line("#{Time.new}: #{line}")
  end

end
```

The `alias` keyword creates a new name for an existing method. In the preceding code, we start by creating an alias for the original `write` method, so that we can refer to it as either `write` or `old_write`. Then we redefine the `write` method, but—critically—`old_write` continues to point to the original definition. It's all downhill from there: The new method time-stamps each line and then calls the original method (now known only as `old_write_line`) to write the time-stamped text out.

Luckily for all you would-be decorators, the "wrap the method" technique is a bit limited. It suffers from the danger of method name collisions. For example, as our code stands right now, if we tried to add two sets of line numbers to our output, we would lose our reference to the original `write` method because we do the alias twice. You could probably come up with a clever scheme to avoid name collisions, but as your decorations become more complicated they just cry out to live in their own classes. Nevertheless, for smaller-scale problems, the method-wrapping technique is useful enough that it should be in every Ruby programmer's toolkit.

Decorating with Modules

Another way to add capabilities to a Ruby object is to dynamically mix in modules with the `extend` method. To use this technique, we need to refactor our decorating classes into modules:

```
module TimeStampingWriter
  def write_line(line)
    super("#{Time.new}: #{line}")
  end
end

module NumberingWriter
  attr_reader :line_number

  def write_line(line)
    @line_number = 1 unless @line_number
    super("#{@line_number}: #{line}")
    @line_number += 1
  end
end

class Writer
  define write(line)
    @f.write(line)
  end
end
```

The extend method essentially inserts a module into an object's inheritance tree before its regular class. We can, therefore, start with an ordinary writer and then simply add in the functionality that we need:

```
w = SimpleWriter.new('out')
w.extend(NumberingWriter)
w.extend(TimeStampingWriter)

w.write_line('hello')
```

The last module added will be the first one called. Thus, in the preceding example, the processing would run from client to TimeStampingWriter to NumberingWriter to Writer.

While either of the dynamic techniques work—and they are, in fact, the runaway choice in existing Ruby code—they do have one disadvantage: With both of these techniques, it is hard to undo the decoration. Unwrapping an aliased method is likely to be tedious, and you simply cannot un-include a module.

Using and Abusing the Decorator Pattern

The classic Decorator pattern is loved more by the folks who build the thing than by those who use it. As we have seen, the Decorator pattern helps the person who is trying to build all of this functionality neatly separate out the various concerns—line numbering in this class, checksumming over in this other class, time stamping in a third. The irritating moment comes when someone tries to assemble all of these little building block classes into a working whole. Instead of being able to instantiate a single object, perhaps with `EnhancedWriter.new(path)`, the client has to put all of the pieces together itself. Of course, there are things that the author of a decorator implementation can do to ease the assembly burden. If there are common chains of decorators that your clients will need, by all means provide a utility (perhaps a Builder?[4]) to get that assembly done.

One thing to keep in mind when implementing the Decorator pattern is that you need to keep the component interface simple. You want to avoid making the component interface overly complex, because a complex interface will make it that much harder to get each decorator right.

Another potential drawback of the Decorator pattern is the performance overhead associated with a long chain of decorators. When you trade in that single, monolithic `ChecksummingNumberingTimestampingWriter` class for a chain of decorators, you are gaining a lot of programming compartmentalization and code clarity. Of course, the price you pay is that you are multiplying the number of objects floating around in your program. This may not be much of a concern if, as in our writer example, you are dealing with a handful of open files. It becomes much more problematic if we are talking about every employee in a very large company. Remember, too, that besides the number of objects involved, any data that you send through a chain of N decorators will change hands N times as the first decorator hands it off to the second decorator, which hands it off to the third decorator, and so on.

Finally, one drawback of the method-aliasing technique for decorating objects is that it tends to make your code harder to debug. Think about it: Your methods will show up in the stack trace with different names than they have in the code stored in your source files. This is not a fatal difficulty, just one more thing to keep in mind.

---

4. See Chapter 14.

Decorators in the Wild

A good example of the method-aliasing style of decorating objects can be found `ActiveSupport`, the package of support utilities used by Rails. `ActiveSupport` adds a method to all objects called `alias_method_chain`. The `alias_method_chain` method allows you to decorate your methods with any number of features. To use `alias_method_chain`, you start with a plain-vanilla method in your class, such as `write_line`:

```
def write_line(line)
  puts(line)
end
```

You then add in another method that adds some decoration to the original method:

```
def write_line_with_timestamp(line)
  write_line_without_timestamp("#{Time.new}: #{line}")
end
```

Finally, you call `alias_method_chain`:

```
alias_method_chain :write_line, :timestamp
```

The `alias_method_chain` method will rename the original `write_line` method to `write_line_without_timestamp` and rename `write_line_with_timestamp` to plain old `write_line`, essentially creating a chain of methods. The nice thing about `alias_method_chain` is that, as its name suggests, you can chain together a number of enhancing methods. For example, we could add on a line-numbering method:

```
def write_line_with_numbering(line)
  @number = 1 unless @number
  write_line_without_numbering("#{@number}: #{line}")
  @number += 1
end

alias_method_chain :write_line, :numbering
```

Wrapping Up

The Decorator pattern is a straightforward technique that you can use to assemble exactly the functionality that you need at runtime. It offers an alternative to creating a monolithic "kitchen sink" object that supports every possible feature or a whole forest of classes and subclasses to cover every possible combination of features. Instead, with the Decorator pattern, you create one class that covers the basic functionality and a set of decorators to go with it. Each decorator supports the same core interface, but adds its own twist on that interface. The key implementation idea of the Decorator pattern is that the decorators are essentially shells: Each takes in a method call, adds its own special twist, and passes the call on to the next component in line. That next component may be another decorator, which adds yet another twist, or it may be the final, real object, which actually completes the basic request.

The Decorator pattern lets you start with some basic functionality and layer on extra features, one decorator at a time. Because the Decorator pattern builds these layers at runtime, you are free to construct whatever combination you need, at runtime.

The Decorator pattern is the last of the "one object stands in for another" patterns that we will consider in this book. The first was the Adapter pattern; it hides the fact that some object has the wrong interface by wrapping it with an object that has the right interface. The second was the Proxy pattern. A proxy also wraps another object, but not with the intent of changing the interface. Instead, the proxy has the same interface as the object that it is wrapping. The proxy isn't there to translate; it is there to control. Proxies are good for tasks such as enforcing security, hiding the fact that an object really lives across the network, and delaying the creation of the real object until the last possible moment. And then we have the subject of this chapter, the decorator, which enables you to layer features on to a basic object.

CHAPTER **12**

Making Sure There Is Only One with the Singleton

Pity the poor Singleton pattern. Even coders who do not know very much about patterns know about the singleton. Mainly they know one thing: Singletons are Bad, with a capital "B". And yet we cannot seem to live without the things. Singletons are everywhere. In the Java world, singletons show up in some of the most widely used software around—you will find them in tomcat, in ant, and in JDOM. On the Ruby side, we can find singletons lurking in `Webrick`, in rake, and even in Rails, just to name a few.

What is it about the Singleton pattern that makes it so indispensable and yet so widely detested? In the pages that follow we will look at why you might need a singleton, how you would go about building singletons and singleton-like things in Ruby, why singletons cause trouble, and what you can do to ease some of this pain.

One Object, Global Access

The motivation behind the Singleton pattern is very simple: There are some things that are unique. Programs frequently have a single configuration file. It is not unusual for a program to let you know how it is doing via a single log file. GUI applications frequently have a one main window, and they typically take input from exactly one keyboard. Many applications need to talk to exactly one database. If you only ever have one instance of a class and a lot of code that needs access to that instance, it seems silly to pass the object from one method to another. In this kind of situation, the GoF suggest that you build a **singleton**—a class that can have only one instance and that provides global access to that one instance.

There are a number of different ways that you can get some or all of the singleton behavior in Ruby, but we will start with the method that is closest to the one recommended by the GoF: Let the class of the singleton object manage the creation and access to its sole instance. To do so, we need to look first at class variables and class methods in Ruby.

Class Variables and Methods

So far, all of the code that we have written in this book has involved *instance* methods and variables—that is, code and data that are attached to individual instances of a class. Ruby, like most object-oriented languages, also supports *class* variables and methods, which are attached to a class.[1]

Class Variables

As we have seen, a class variable is a variable that is attached to a class[2] instead of to an instance of the class. Creating a class variable is very straightforward: You simply add another at sign (@) to the variable name. Here, for example, is a class that counts the number of times the increment method is called in two different variables—once in an instance variable and once in a class variable:

```ruby
class ClassVariableTester
  @@class_count = 0

  def initialize
    @instance_count = 0
  end

  def increment
    @@class_count = @@class_count + 1
    @instance_count = @instance_count + 1
  end

  def to_s
    "class_count: #{@@class_count} instance_count: #{@instance_count}"
  end
end
```

---

1. Many other languages—most notably, C++ and Java—refer to class-level methods and variables as *static* methods and variables. The terminology is different, but the idea is more or less the same.

2. Actually, in Ruby, class variables are attached to the whole inheritance hierarchy. Thus a class shares a common set of class variables with its superclass and all of its subclasses. Most Ruby programmers regard this behavior as an unfortunate quirk of the language, and there is talk of changing it.

Now let's create an instance named `ClassVariableTester` and call its `increment` method a couple of times:

```
c1 = ClassVariableTester.new
c1.increment
c1.increment
puts("c1: #{c1}")
```

Not surprisingly, both counts end up being 2:

```
c1: class_count: 2 instance_count: 2
```

Things get more interesting when you create a second instance of the class:

```
c2 = ClassVariableTester.new
puts("c2: #{c2}")
```

This produces

```
c2: class_count: 2 instance_count: 0
```

What is happening here is that the instance counter was reset to zero for the second `ClassVariableTester` instance, whereas the class counter, which is shared by both instances, keeps right on counting.

Class Methods

Creating class-level methods in Ruby is a bit more challenging, but only a bit. We cannot just open a class and define a method:

```
class SomeClass
  def a_method
    puts('hello from a method')
  end
end
```

As we have already seen, if we do that we end up with an instance method:

```
SomeClass.a_method
instance.rb:11: undefined method 'a_method' for SomeClass:Class
```

The secret to creating a class method is knowing that when you are inside a class definition—but outside a method definition—the `self` variable is the class you are defining. You do not have to take my word for it, however. Suppose you run this class definition:

```
class SomeClass
  puts("Inside a class def, self is #{self}")
end
```

You will see the following output:

```
Inside a class def, self is SomeClass
```

With this useful bit of information in hand, we can define a method on the class:

```
class SomeClass
  def self.class_level_method
    puts('hello from the class method')
  end
end
```

We can now call `class_level_method` exactly as its name suggests, at the class level:

```
SomeClass.class_level_method
```

If you do not like the `self.method_name` syntax, Ruby offers another option. You can just define the class method by calling out the name explicitly:

```
class SomeClass
  def SomeClass.class_level_method
    puts('hello from the class method')
  end
end
```

Ruby programmers seem evenly split on this syntactical conundrum: Some like `self`, and some like the explicit class name. Personally, I like the `self` format, because you have less to change if you rename the class or transplant code to another class.

A First Try at a Ruby Singleton

Now that we know how to create class variables and methods, we have all the tools we need to create a singleton. Let's start with an ordinary, non-singleton class (a multiton?) and transform it into a singleton. Perhaps you have a logging class, a little facility for keeping track of the comings and goings of your program. Your ordinary, non-singleton version of the logging class might look something like this:

```ruby
class SimpleLogger
  attr_accessor :level

  ERROR = 1
  WARNING = 2
  INFO = 3

  def initialize
    @log = File.open("log.txt", "w")
    @level =  WARNING
  end

  def error(msg)
    @log.puts(msg)
    @log.flush
  end

  def warning(msg)
    @log.puts(msg) if @level >= WARNING
    @log.flush
  end

  def info(msg)
    @log.puts(msg) if @level >= INFO
    @log.flush
  end
end
```

You might use this version of the logger by creating a new one and passing it around:

```
logger = SimpleLogger.new
logger.level = SimpleLogger::INFO

logger.info('Doing the first thing')
# Do the first thing...
logger.info('Now doing the second thing')
# Do the second thing...
```

Managing the Single Instance

The whole point of the Singleton pattern is to avoid passing an object like the logger all over the place. Instead, you want to make the SimpleLogger class responsible for managing its single instance. So how would you turn SimpleLogger into a singleton?

First, you add a class variable to hold the one and only instance of your class. You will also need a class method to return the singleton instance.

```
class SimpleLogger

  # Lots of code deleted...

  @@instance = SimpleLogger.new

  def self.instance
    return @@instance
  end
end
```

We can now call the instance method of the SimpleLogger class any number of times and always get back the same logger object:

```
logger1 = SimpleLogger.instance    # Returns the logger
logger2 = SimpleLogger.instance    # Returns exactly the same logger
```

More practically, we can get at the singleton logger from anywhere in our code and use it to write out messages:

```
SimpleLogger.instance.info('Computer wins chess game.')
SimpleLogger.instance.warning('AE-35 hardware failure predicted.')
SimpleLogger.instance.error(
    'HAL-9000 malfunction, take emergency action!')
```

Making Sure There Is Only One

Our singleton is now sort of functional, but it is not really complete. Remember, one requirement of the singleton is to ensure that the one and only singleton is the sole instance of the singleton class. So far we have ignored this requirement. As things stand right now, any program can call `SimpleLogger.new` to make a second instance of our allegedly singleton class. So how do we go about securing `SimpleLogger` against promiscuous instantiation?

We do so by making the `new` method on `SimpleLogger` private:

```
class SimpleLogger

  # Lots of code deleted...

  @@instance = SimpleLogger.new

  def self.instance
    return @@instance
  end

  private_class_method :new
end
```

There are two ideas to take away from this code fragment, one a detail and the other a bit more profound. The detail is that by adding the `private_class_method` call, we have done exactly what the name suggests: We made the new class method private, preventing any other class from creating new instances of our logger. The broader issue is that new is just another class-level method. Yes, the new method does perform some special behind-the-scenes magic in allocating a new object, but in the end it is just another class-level method.

The Singleton Module

Our singleton implementation is now complete, in that we have all of the ingredients required of a full-fledged GoF singleton. Our class creates exactly one instance of itself, any code that is interested can access the single instance, and no one can ever create a second instance.

Our singleton implementation does appear to have one problem, however. What if we want to build a second singleton class, perhaps for our configuration data? It seems that we will need to go through the whole exercise again: create a class variable for the singleton instance along with a class method to access it. Oh, and don't forget to make the new method private. If we need a third instance, we need to do it all again a third time. This seems like a lot of duplicated effort.

Fortunately, we can avoid working so hard. Instead of going through all of the pain of turning our classes into singletons by hand, we can just include the Singleton module:

```ruby
require 'singleton'

class SimpleLogger
  include Singleton

  # Lots of code deleted...

end
```

The Singleton module does all of the heavy lifting of creating the class variable and initializing it with the singleton instance, creating the class-level instance method, and making new private. All we need to do is include the module. From the outside, this new Singleton module-based logger looks exactly like our previous hand-built implementations: Just call SimpleLogger.instance to retrieve the instance and off you go.

Lazy and Eager Singletons

There is one significant difference between the singleton implementation that we constructed and the one provided by the Singleton module. Recall that our implementation created the singleton instance as the class was being defined:

```
class SimpleLogger

  # Lots of code deleted...

  @@instance = SimpleLogger.new

  # Lots of code deleted...

end
```

As a consequence, our singleton instance is created before any client code ever gets a chance to call `SimpleLogger.instance`. Creating the singleton instance before you actually need it is called **eager instantiation**—we just can't wait to make the thing. The `Singleton` module, by contrast, waits until someone calls `instance` before it actually creates its singleton. This technique is known as **lazy instantiation.**

Alternatives to the Classic Singleton

While the class-managed technique for building singletons that we have introduced here closely follows the implementation recommended in *Design Patterns,* it by no means exhausts the possibilities for realizing some or all of the singleton behavior. There are a number of other alternatives that we might use to achieve the same effect.

Global Variables as Singletons

We might, for example, use a global variable as a singleton. I will pause here while the screams of horror die down. In Ruby, any variable whose name begins with a dollar sign—`$logger`, for example—is global. Global variables certainly have the global access part of the singleton routine down pat: You can access `$logger` in any context, in any class, module, or method, and it will always be the same `$logger`. Because there is only one instance of any given global variable and because that variable is available everywhere (it being global and all), global variables seem like they might be a good platform for implementing singletons.

Sadly, no. Global variables lack some of the fundamental moving parts of a singleton. While `$logger` always refers to exactly one object at any given time, there is no way to control the value of a global variable. While we might start off with our global pseudo-singleton carefully set to the right thing:

```
$logger = SimpleLogger.new
```

But there is absolutely nothing to prevent some misguided code from changing it:

```
$logger = LoggerThatDoesSomethingBad.new
```

If change is the problem, then maybe we should turn to a flavor of Ruby variable that not only has global scope but also resists change: the constant. Recall that a Ruby constant is a variable whose name starts with an uppercase letter and has the nice property that, once set, its value is not supposed to change:

```
Logger = SimpleLogger.new
```

Recall from Chapter 2 that Ruby will complain if we change the value of a constant, which is at least an improvement in attitude over the "anything goes" philosophy of global variables. So is this the simple solution to the singleton?

Not really. Both global variables and constants share a number of deficiencies as singletons. First, if you use a global variable or a constant for this purpose, there is no way to delay the creation of the singleton object until you need it. The global variable or constant is there from the moment we first set it. Second, neither of these techniques does anything to prevent someone from creating a second or third instance of your supposedly singleton class. You could, of course, deal with that issue separately. For example, you might create the singleton instance and then change the class so that it will refuse to create any more instances—but all of this is beginning to feel rather ad hoc and messy.

Given that global variables and constants seem to fall short, are there any other ways to do the singleton thing?

Classes as Singletons

As we have seen, we can define methods and variables directly on a class object. In fact, our original singleton implementation used class methods and variables to manage the singleton instance. But given that we can have methods and variables on a class, why not just use the class itself as a container for the singleton functionality? Each class is unique—there can be only one `SimpleLogger` class loaded at any one time—so we might just define our singleton functionality as class methods and variables on a class object:

```
class ClassBasedLogger
  ERROR = 1
  WARNING = 2
  INFO = 3
```

```ruby
  @@log = File.open('log.txt', 'w')
  @@level = WARNING

  def self.error(msg)
    @@log.puts(msg)
    @@log.flush
  end

  def self.warning(msg)
    @@log.puts(msg) if @@level >=  WARNING
    @@log.flush
  end

  def self.info(msg)
    @@log.puts(msg) if @@level >=  INFO
    @@log.flush
  end

  def self.level=(new_level)
    @@level = new_level
  end

  def self.level
    @@level
  end
end
```

Using the class-based singleton is not hard:

```ruby
ClassBasedLogger.level = ClassBasedLogger::INFO

ClassBasedLogger.info('Computer wins chess game.')
ClassBasedLogger.warning('AE-35 hardware failure predicted.')
ClassBasedLogger.error('HAL-9000 malfunction, take emergency action!')
```

The "class as singleton" technique has a key advantage over the global variable and constant methods: You are sure that no one will create a second instance of your singleton. Lazy initialization remains a problem with this technique, however. Specifically, your class is initialized when it gets loaded (typically when someone requires the file that the class lives in), and you do not have a lot of control over the timing of this initialization. Another disadvantage of using a class as a singleton is that programming class methods and variables is just not as easy as coding garden-variety instance methods and variables; all of those `self.methods` and `@@variables` have a strange feel to them.

Modules as Singletons

Another possibility is to use a module as the container for your singleton behavior. As noted earlier in this chapter, modules have a lot in common with classes. In fact, modules are so much like classes that you can define module-level methods and variables in exactly the same way that you define class methods and variables. Except for changing `class` to `module`, the module-based implementation is exactly the same as the class-based one:

```
module ModuleBasedLogger
  ERROR = 1
  WARNING = 2
  INFO = 3

  @@log = File.open("log.txt", "w")
  @@level = WARNING

  def self.error(msg)
    @@log.puts(msg)
    @@log.flush
  end


  # Lots of code, exactly like the
  # ClassBasedSingleton deleted...

end
```

You can use module methods from just about anywhere, just like class methods:

```
ModuleBasedLogger.info('Computer wins chess game.')
```

The "module as singleton" technique does have one notable advantage over the "class as singleton" technique. Because you cannot instantiate a module (that is the key difference between a module and a class), the intent of a module-based singleton is probably a bit clearer from the code: Here is a bucket of methods meant to be called and not something you can instantiate.

A Safety Harness or a Straitjacket?

The discussion of the alternative ways of implementing the Singleton pattern raises the question of language-based safety features, and what such features can mean in a language as flexible as Ruby. To reach for a handy example, we have seen that one of the effects of including the `Singleton` module is to make the `new` method private. This, of course, prevents anyone from making a second or third instance of the singleton class. If our singleton class is defined as

```ruby
require 'singleton'

class Manager
  include Singleton

  def manage_resources
    puts("I am managing my resources")
  end
end
```

I cannot make another instance of `Manager`. For example, if I try

```ruby
m = Manager.new
```

I will get

```
private method 'new' called for Manager:Class
```

Actually, the `Singleton` module cannot really prevent anything. All I need is a little insight into how `Singleton` works and a bit of knowledge about `public_class_method` (the evil twin of `private_class_method`), and it becomes very easy to circumvent all of that prevention:

```ruby
class Manager
  public_class_method :new
end

m = Manager.new
```

In the same spirit, we noted earlier that one advantage of the class- or module-based singleton is that no one can make a second instance of your singleton. Well, not by accident, they can't. But no matter whether you are using `ClassBasedLogger` or its cousin `ModuleBasedLogger`, your logger is in the end an object, and all objects in Ruby inherit the `clone` method. The `clone` method is wonderful utility for short-circuiting that singleton-ness that we have been working so hard to establish:

```
a_second_logger = ClassBasedLogger.clone
a_second_logger.error('using a second logger')
```

We might, of course, override the `clone` method in `ClassBasedLogger` to prevent unauthorized cloning. Of course, the determined cloner could just reopen your class to un-override the method . . .

The point is not that this kind of thing is a good idea, but rather that in a language where virtually everything done at runtime can be undone a little later in runtime, very few decisions are irreversible. The Ruby philosophy is that if you decide to circumvent the very clear intent of the author of the `ClassBasedLogger` class by cloning it, the language is there to help you out. You are in the driver's seat, not the language. By keeping almost everything open to modification, Ruby allows you to do the things that you say you want to do—but it is up to you to say the right things.

Using and Abusing the Singleton Pattern

Now that we know how to build a singleton, let's figure out why this is perhaps the most hated of all patterns.

They Are Really Just Global Variables, Right?

Let's start with the most obvious problem first: A singleton bears a very strong family resemblance to its outlaw cousin, the global variable. No matter whether you implement your singleton with the GoF class-managed technique or as a bunch of class- or module-level methods and variables, you are creating a single object with global scope. Create a singleton, and you have just made it possible for widely separated bits of your program to use that singleton as a secret channel to communicate with each other and, in the process, tightly couple themselves to each other. The horrible consequences of this coupling are why software engineering got out of the global variable business in the first place.

There is only one solution to this problem: *Don't do that*. Properly applied, singletons are not global variables. Rather, they are meant to model things that occur exactly once. Yes, because it occurs only once, you can use a singleton as a unique communications conduit between bits of your program. But *don't do that*. Singletons are like every other pattern and programming technique—which means you can really screw things up if you abuse them. I can only repeat: *Don't do that*.

Just How Many of These Singletons Do You Have?

Which brings us to another obvious-sounding, but all-too-common way to come to grief with the Singleton pattern: to lose count. As you are considering applying the Singleton pattern, ask yourself this question: Am I sure that there is only one of these things? The Singleton pattern gives us a way to model a single instance of something, but this modeling also just happens to come with a nice coding feature that makes that single instance very easily accessible—just call `SimpleLogger.instance`. That easy access can have a hypnotic allure: "My code will be so much simpler if this thing is a singleton." Don't listen to the siren song of that easy access. Instead, focus on the question of how many of these things exist and treat the easy access as a bonus.

Singletons on a Need-to-Know Basis

Another mistake that many people make is to spread the knowledge of a class's singleton-ness far and wide. You can look at the fact that a class is a singleton as something of an implementation detail: Once you get hold of the configuration file, exactly how you got hold of it is not really important. Remember that you can always grab the singleton object in one or a few places and then pass it around from there.

This technique comes in handy when your application needs to use the singleton in a few widely scattered clusters of code. For example, you might have an application structured like the one shown in Figure 12-1.

Imagine that the `PreferenceManager` class and the classes that it uses need access to a database connection, as does the `DataPersistence` class and its friends.

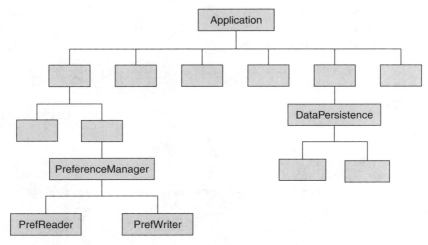

Figure 12-1   An application with widely scattered uses of a singleton

Further imagine that the entire application uses a single instance of the class
`DatabaseConnectionManager` for all of its connection management needs.
Recognizing this, you make `DatabaseConnectionManager` a singleton:

```
require 'singleton'

class DatabaseConnectionManager
  include Singleton

  def get_connection
    # Return the database connection...
  end
end
```

Now here's the question: Which classes are actually aware that `Database-`
`ConnectionManager` is a singleton? We could spread this information far and wide,
perhaps among the preference readers and writers:

```
class PreferenceManager
  def initialize
    @reader = PrefReader.new
    @writer = PrefWriter.new
    @preferences = { :display_splash=>false, :background_color=>:blue }
  end

  def save_preferences
    preferences = {}
    # Preference are in
    @writer.write(@preferences)
  end

  def get_preferences
    @preferences = @reader.read
  end
end

class PrefWriter
  def write(preferences)
    connection = DatabaseConnectionManager.instance.get_connection
    # Write the preferences out
  end
end
```

```
class PrefReader
  def read
    connection = DatabaseConnectionManager.instance.get_connection
    # Read the preferences and return them...
  end
end
```

A better approach might be to concentrate the knowledge that Database-ConnectionManager is a singleton in the PreferenceManager class and simply pass it into the preference reader and writer:

```
class PreferenceManager
  def initialize
    @reader = PrefReader.new
    @writer = PrefWriter.new
    @preferences = { :display_splash=>false, :background_color=>:blue }
  end

  def save_preferences
    preferences = {}
    # Preference are in
    @writer.write(DatabaseConnectionManager.instance, @preferences)
  end

  def get_preferences
    @preferences = @reader.read(DatabaseConnectionManager.instance)
  end
end
```

This little refactoring decreases the amount of code that needs to know that DatabaseConnectionManager is a singleton. There are two advantages to doing this. First, there is less code to fix if it turns out that your singleton is not, in fact, quite so alone. Second, by excising the singleton from the PrefReader and PrefWriter classes, you have made those classes much more easily testable.

Curing the Testing Blues

This last point brings us to testing. One exceedingly nasty thing about the Singleton pattern is the way that it interferes with unit testing. A good unit test needs to start with a known state. After all, your test results are unlikely to be worth much if you aren't sure how things were set up when you started the test. A good unit test also needs to be independent of any other test, so that test 3 should give you exactly the same results no matter whether you run it between tests 2 and 4, after test 20, or all by itself. The problem, of course, is that if tests 1 through 20 are testing a singleton, each test is liable to modify the one and only singleton instance in some unpredictable way. So much for test independence.

One way to deal with this problem is to create two classes: an ordinary (i.e., non-singleton) class that contains all of the code, and a subclass of the first class that is a singleton. Something like this:

```
require 'singleton'

class SimpleLogger
  # All of the logging functionality in this class...
end


class SingletonLogger < SimpleLogger
  include Singleton
end
```

The actual application code uses the `SingletonLogger`, while the tests can use the plain old, non-singleton `Logger` class.

Singletons in the Wild

You can find a good example of the use of the Singleton pattern in real life in `ActiveSupport`, which is a library of utility classes used by Rails. Rails relies heavily on the use of conventions, and many of the Rails conventions involve working out the plurals of singular words and the singulars of plural words. To do so, `ActiveSupport` maintains a list of rules, which encapsulate facts like "The plural of *employee* is *employees,* but the plural of *criterion* is *criteria.*" But since the rules are, well, the rules, you really need to keep only one copy of them around. So the `Inflections` class is a singleton, which saves space and ensures that the same inflection rules are available everywhere.

Ruby's build utility, rake, also uses a singleton. As it runs, rake—like most build tools—reads in information about what it needs to do: which directories to create, which files to copy, and so on.[3] All of this information needs to be available to all of the moving parts of rake, so rake stores it all in a single object (the `Rake::Application` object, to be precise) that is available as a singleton to the entire rake program.

Wrapping Up

In this chapter, we looked at the somewhat checkered career of the Singleton pattern. The Singleton pattern can help us deal with the cases where there is only one of something. There are two characteristics that make a singleton a singleton: A singleton class has exactly one instance, and access to that one instance is available globally. Using class methods and variables, we can easily build the "classic" implementation of the singleton, the one recommended by the GoF.

We can also build singletons (or at least near-singletons) using a variety of other methods. For example, we could get some of the singleton behavior from global variables or constants, although these elements lack the uniqueness characteristic that makes a real singleton a singleton. In addition, we can build singletons from class- or module-level methods and variables.

We spent a fair bit of time in this chapter looking at the landmines scattered around Singleton-land. We saw that the singleton presents rich opportunities for coupling your code to itself in very unfortunate ways. We also saw that you might want to limit the amount of code that is aware of an object's singleton-ness, and we looked at one way to ease the burden that singletons place on testing.

The Singleton pattern is a bit like that ancient table saw that my dad used to have. That saw was incredibly effective at cutting lumber, but, since it had very few safety features, it was equally adept at slicing an unwary hand in two.

---

3. The rake utility actually uses the Internal DSL pattern (discussed in Chapter 16) to do most of this reading.

CHAPTER 13

Picking the Right Class with a Factory

My high school physics teacher was one of those extraordinary educators who could make even the driest of subjects come alive. It seemed that by about the second month of the school year, all of us in his Introduction to Physics class had forgotten about getting a decent grade and had moved on to a higher goal: We all wanted to do good physics. "Doing good physics" involved a lot of things—I recall careful experiments and a lot of thinking were involved—but there was one thing that a good physics student needed to avoid at all costs. There was to be no "hand waving." Hand waving, as it was defined in my class, involved glossing over some key detail, fudging some equation, or simply assuming some fact that was not supported by experiment.

And now I have a confession to make: I have done a bit of hand waving in this book. The key detail that I have been glossing over until now is the one where your code magically knows which class to pick at some critical point. Picking the right class usually requires very little brain power: If I need a `String` or a `Date` or even a `PersonnelRecord`, I generally just call `new` on the `String` or `Date` or `PersonnelRecord` class and I am done. But sometimes the choice of which class to use is a critical decision. Examples of this kind of situation are easy to come by. For example, think about the Template Method pattern. When you use the Template Method pattern, you need to pick one of the subclasses—and the subclass that you pick determines which variation of the algorithm you will end up using. Will you be using a `PlainReport` or an `HTMLReport` today? Similarly, with the Strategy pattern, you must pick the correct strategy to feed to your context object: Do you need the `VirginiaTaxCalculator` or the `NewJerseyTaxCalculator`? Likewise, if you plan to proxy an object, you need to select the proxy class that does what you want.

There are a number of ways to deal with the problem of picking the right class for the circumstances, including two of the original GoF patterns. In this chapter, we will look at both of these GoF patterns: the Factory Method pattern and the Abstract Factory pattern. We will also shine our light on some dynamic Ruby techniques that will help us build factories more effectively.

So let's get started before I incur the wrath of Mr. Malone, physics teacher extra-ordinaire.

A Different Kind of Duck Typing

To start our exploration of factories, let's begin with a programming problem. Imagine that you are asked to build a simulation of life in a pond. In particular, you need to model the comings and goings of the ducks. So you sit down and write a class to model the ducks:

```ruby
class Duck
  def initialize(name)
    @name = name
  end

  def eat
    puts("Duck #{@name} is eating.")
  end

  def speak
    puts("Duck #{@name} says Quack!")
  end

  def sleep
    puts("Duck #{@name} sleeps quietly.")
  end
end
```

As you can see from this code, ducks—like most animals—eat, sleep, and make noise. But ducks also need a place to live, and for that you build a `Pond` class:

```ruby
class Pond
  def initialize(number_ducks)
    @ducks = []
    number_ducks.times do |i|
      duck = Duck.new("Duck#{i}")
      @ducks << duck
    end
  end

  def simulate_one_day
    @ducks.each {|duck| duck.speak}
    @ducks.each {|duck| duck.eat}
    @ducks.each {|duck| duck.sleep}
  end
end
```

Running the pond simulation is not much of a challenge:

```ruby
pond = Pond.new(3)
pond.simulate_one_day
```

The preceding code simulates one day in the life of a three-duck pond, and it produces the following output:

```
Duck Duck0 says Quack!
Duck Duck1 says Quack!
Duck Duck2 says Quack!
Duck Duck0 is eating.
Duck Duck1 is eating.
Duck Duck2 is eating.
Duck Duck0 sleeps quietly.
Duck Duck1 sleeps quietly.
Duck Duck2 sleeps quietly.
```

Life on the pond continues idyllically until one dark day when you get a request to model a different denizen of the puddle: the frog. Now it is easy enough to create a `Frog` class that sports exactly the same interface as the ducks:

```
class Frog
  def initialize(name)
    @name = name
  end

  def eat
    puts("Frog #{@name} is eating.")
  end

  def speak
    puts("Frog #{@name} says Crooooaaaak!")
  end

  def sleep
    puts("Frog #{@name} doesn't sleep; he croaks all night!")
  end
end
```

But there *is* a problem with the `Pond` class—right there in the `initialize` method you are explicitly creating ducks:

```
def initialize(number_ducks)
  @ducks = []
  number_ducks.times do |i|
    duck = Duck.new("Duck#{i}")
    @ducks << duck
  end
end
```

The trouble is that you need to separate out something that is changing—the specific creatures that inhabit the pond (duck or frog)—from something that is staying the same—the other workings of the `Pond` class. If only you could somehow excise that `Duck.new` from the `Pond` class, then the `Pond` class could support both ducks and frogs. This dilemma brings us to the central question of this chapter: Which class do you use?

The Template Method Strikes Again

One way to deal with the "which class" problem is to push the question down onto a subclass. We start by building a generic base class, a class that is generic in the sense that it does not make the "which class" decision. Instead, whenever the base class needs a new object, it calls a method that is defined in a subclass. For example, we could recast our Pond class as shown below so that it relies on a method called new_animal to produce the inhabitants of the pond:

```ruby
class Pond
  def initialize(number_animals)
    @animals = []
    number_animals.times do |i|
      animal = new_animal("Animal#{i}")
      @animals << animal
    end
  end

  def simulate_one_day
    @animals.each {|animal| animal.speak}
    @animals.each {|animal| animal.eat}
    @animals.each {|animal| animal.sleep}
  end
end
```

Next we can build two subclasses of Pond—one for a pond full of ducks and the other for a pond hopping with frogs:

```ruby
class DuckPond < Pond
  def new_animal(name)
    Duck.new(name)
  end
end

class FrogPond < Pond
  def new_animal(name)
    Frog.new(name)
  end
end
```

Now we need simply choose the right kind of pond, and it will be full of the right kind of creatures:

```
pond = FrogPond.new(3)
pond.simulate_one_day
```

And we get all sorts of slimy green goings on:

```
Frog Animal0 says Crooooaaaak!
Frog Animal1 says Crooooaaaak!
Frog Animal2 says Crooooaaaak!
Frog Animal0 is eating.
Frog Animal1 is eating.
...
```

Although I won't show it here, we could also create a subclass of Pond whose new_animal method produces a mix of both ducks and frogs without much trouble.

The GoF called this technique of pushing the "which class" decision down on a subclass the **Factory Method** pattern. Figure 13-1 shows the UML diagram for this pattern, which includes two separate class hierarchies. On the one hand, we have the **creators,** the base and concrete classes that contain the factory methods. On the other hand, we have the **products,** the objects that are being created. In our pond example, the creator is the Pond class, and the specific types of ponds (like DuckPond and

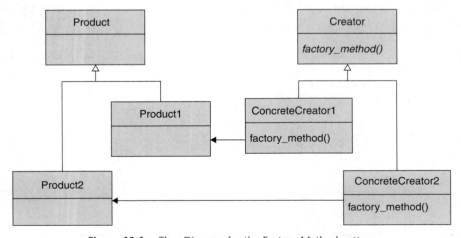

Figure 13-1　Class Diagram for the Factory Method pattern

FrogPond) are the concrete creators; the products are the Duck and Frog classes. While Figure 13-1 shows the two products sharing a common base class (Product), our Duck and Frog are not actually blood relatives: They simply share a common type because they implement a common set of methods.

If you stare at Figure 13-1 long enough, you may discover that the Factory Method pattern is not really a new pattern at all. At its heart, this pattern is really just the Template Method pattern (remember Chapter 3?) applied to the problem of creating new objects. In both the Factory Method pattern and the Template Method pattern, a generic part of the algorithm (in our pond example, its day-to-day aquatic existence) is coded in the generic base class, and subclasses fill in the blanks left in the base class. With the factory method, those filled-in blanks determine the class of objects that will be living in the pond.

Parameterized Factory Methods

One problem with successful programs is that they tend to attract an ever-increasing pile of requirements. Suppose your pond simulation is so popular that your users start asking you to simulate plants as well as animals. So you wave your magic code wand and come up with a couple of plant classes:

```ruby
class Algae
  def initialize(name)
    @name = name
  end

  def grow
    puts("The Algae #{@name} soaks up the sun and grows")
  end
end

class WaterLily
  def initialize(name)
    @name = name
  end

  def grow
    puts("The water lily #{@name} floats, soaks up the sun, and
grows")
  end
end
```

You also modify the Pond class to deal with plants, like this:

```ruby
class Pond
  def initialize(number_animals, number_plants)
    @animals = []
    number_animals.times do |i|
      animal = new_animal("Animal#{i}")
      @animals << animal
    end

    @plants = []
    number_plants.times do |i|
      plant = new_plant("Plant#{i}")
      @plants << plant
    end
  end

  def simulate_one_day
    @plants.each {|plant| plant.grow }
    @animals.each {|animal| animal.speak}
    @animals.each {|animal| animal.eat}
    @animals.each {|animal| animal.sleep}
  end
end
```

You will also need to modify the subclasses to create some flora:

```ruby
class DuckWaterLilyPond < Pond
  def new_animal(name)
    Duck.new(name)
  end

  def new_plant(name)
    WaterLily.new(name)
  end
end

class FrogAlgaePond < Pond
  def new_animal(name)
    Frog.new(name)
  end
```

```
    def new_plant(name)
      Algae.new(name)
    end
  end
```

An awkward aspect of this implementation is that we need a separate method for each type of object we are producing: We have the new_animal method to make frogs and ducks and the new_plant method to create lilies and algae. Having a separate method for each type of object that you need to produce is not too much of a burden if you are dealing with only two types, as in our pond example. But what if you have five or ten different types? Coding all those methods can be, well, tedious.

A different and perhaps cleaner way to go is to have a single factory method that takes a parameter, a parameter that tells the method which kind of object to create. The following code shows yet another version of our Pond class, this time sporting a **parameterized factory method**—a method that can produce either a plant or an animal, depending on the symbol that is passed in:

```
class Pond
  def initialize(number_animals, number_plants)
    @animals = []
    number_animals.times do |i|
      animal = new_organism(:animal, "Animal#{i}")
      @animals << animal
    end

    @plants = []
    number_plants.times do |i|
      plant = new_organism(:plant, "Plant#{i}")
      @plants << plant
    end
  end

  # ...
end

class DuckWaterLilyPond < Pond
  def new_organism(type, name)
    if type == :animal
      Duck.new(name)
    elsif type == :plant
      WaterLily.new(name)
```

```
      else
        raise "Unknown organism type: #{type}"
      end
    end
  end
```

Parameterized factory methods tend to slim down the code, because each subclass needs to define only one factory method. They also make the whole thing a bit easier to extend. Suppose you need to define a new kind of product, perhaps fish to go in your pond. In that case, you need to modify only a single method in the subclasses instead of adding a whole new method—another example of the virtues of separating the things that change from those that don't.

Classes Are Just Objects, Too

A more significant objection to the Factory Method pattern as we have written it so far is that this pattern requires a separate subclass for each specific type of object that needs to be manufactured. This is reflected in the names of the subclasses in the last version—we have `DuckWaterLilyPond` and `FrogAlgaePond`, but we could have just as easily needed a `DuckAlgaePond` or a `FrogWaterLilyPond`. Add a few more types of animals and plants, and the number of possible subclasses becomes truly scary. But the only difference between the various flavors of ponds is the class of objects produced by the factory method: In the one case it produces lilies and ducks, and in the other it makes algae and frogs.

The thing to realize is that the `Frog`, `Duck`, `WaterLily`, and `Algae` classes are just objects—objects that make their living by producing other objects, but objects nevertheless. We can get rid of this whole hierarchy of `Pond` subclasses by storing the classes of the objects that we want to create in instance variables:

```
class Pond
  def initialize(number_animals, animal_class,
                 number_plants, plant_class)
    @animal_class = animal_class
    @plant_class = plant_class

    @animals = []
    number_animals.times do |i|
      animal = new_organism(:animal, "Animal#{i}")
      @animals << animal
    end
```

```
    @plants = []
    number_plants.times do |i|
      plant = new_organism(:plant, "Plant#{i}")
      @plants << plant
    end
  end

  def simulate_one_day
    @plants.each {|plant| plant.grow}
    @animals.each {|animal| animal.speak}
    @animals.each {|animal| animal.eat}
    @animals.each {|animal| animal.sleep}
  end

  def new_organism(type, name)
    if type == :animal
      @animal_class.new(name)
    elsif type == :plant
      @plant_class.new(name)
    else
      raise "Unknown organism type: #{type}"
    end
  end
end
```

Using the new Pond class is not really any more complex than using the old one. We just pass the plant and animal classes into the constructor:

```
pond = Pond.new(3, Duck, 2, WaterLily)
pond.simulate_one_day
```

By storing the animal and plant classes in Pond, we have knocked the number of classes that we need to write down to one. That's a good thing, considering that we have not really added any additional complexity to Pond.

Bad News: Your Program Hits the Big Time

Suppose even more success has befallen your pond simulator, and new requirements are pouring in faster than ever. The most pressing request is to extend this program to model other types of habitats besides ponds. In fact, a jungle simulation seems to be the next order of business.

Clearly, this change calls for major surgery on the code. You obviously will need classes for the jungle animals (perhaps tigers) and the jungle plants (mainly trees):

```
class Tree
  def initialize(name)
    @name = name
  end

  def grow
    puts("The tree #{@name} grows tall")
  end
end

class Tiger
  def initialize(name)
    @name = name
  end

  def eat
    puts("Tiger #{@name} eats anything it wants.")
  end

  def speak
    puts("Tiger #{@name} Roars!")
  end

  def sleep
    puts("Tiger #{@name} sleeps anywhere it wants.")
  end
end
```

You also need to change your `Pond` class's name to something more appropriate for jungles as well as ponds. `Habitat` seems like a good choice:

```
jungle = Habitat.new(1, Tiger, 4, Tree)
jungle.simulate_one_day

pond = Habitat.new( 2, Duck, 4, WaterLily)
pond.simulate_one_day
```

Other than the name change, `Habitat` is exactly the same as our last `Pond` implementation (the one with the plant and animal classes). We can create new habitats in exactly the same way that we did ponds.

Bundles of Object Creation

One problem with our new `Habitat` class is that it is possible to create incoherent (not to mention ecologically unsound) combinations of fauna and flora. For instance, nothing in our current habitat implementation tells us that tigers and lily pads do not go together:

```
unstable = Habitat.new( 2, Tiger, 4, WaterLily)
```

This may not seem like much of a problem when you are dealing with just two kinds of things (plants and animals, in this case), but what if our simulation was much more detailed, extending to insects and birds and mollusks and fungi? We certainly don't want any mushrooms growing on our lily pads or fish floundering away in the boughs of some jungle tree.

We can deal with this problem by changing the way we specify which creatures live in the habitat. Instead of passing the individual plant and animal classes to `Habitat`, we can pass a single object that knows how to create a consistent set of products. We will have one version of this object for ponds, a version that will create frogs and lily pads. We will have a second version of this object that will create the tigers and trees that are appropriate to a jungle. An object dedicated to creating a compatible set of objects is called an **abstract factory.** In fact, the Abstract Factory pattern is yet another of those patterns made famous by the GoF. The code below shows two abstract factories for our habitat simulation, one for the jungle and one for the pond:

```
class PondOrganismFactory
  def new_animal(name)
    Frog.new(name)
  end

  def new_plant(name)
    Algae.new(name)
  end
end
```

```
class JungleOrganismFactory
  def new_animal(name)
    Tiger.new(name)
  end

  def new_plant(name)
    Tree.new(name)
  end
end
```

After a few simple modifications, our `Habitat initialize` method is ready to begin using the abstract factory:

```
class Habitat
  def initialize(number_animals, number_plants, organism_factory)
    @organism_factory = organism_factory

    @animals = []
    number_animals.times do |i|
      animal = @organism_factory.new_animal("Animal#{i}")
      @animals << animal
    end

    @plants = []
    number_plants.times do |i|
      plant  = @organism_factory.new_plant("Plant#{i}")
      @plants << plant
    end
  end

  # Rest of the class...
```

We can now feed different abstract factories to our habitat, serene in the knowledge that there will be no unholy mixing of pond creatures with jungle denizens:

```
jungle = Habitat.new(1, 4, JungleOrganismFactory.new)
jungle.simulate_one_day

pond = Habitat.new( 2, 4, PondOrganismFactory.new)
pond.simulate_one_day
```

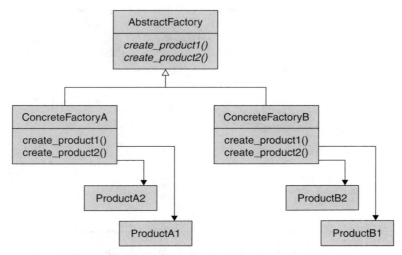

Figure 13-2   The Abstract Factory pattern

Figure 13-2 shows the UML diagram for the Abstract Factory pattern. Here we have two concrete factories, each of which produces its own set of compatible products.

The Abstract Factory pattern really boils down to a problem and a solution. The problem is that you need to create sets of compatible objects. The solution is that you write a separate class to handle that creation. In the same way that the Factory Method pattern is really the Template Method pattern applied to object creation, so the Abstract Factory pattern is simply the Strategy pattern applied to the same problem.

Classes Are Just Objects (Again)

One way to look at the abstract factory is to view it as a sort of super-duper-class object. While ordinary class objects know how to create only one type of object (i.e., instances of themselves), the abstract factory knows how to create several different types of objects (i.e., its products). This suggests a way to simplify our Abstract Factory pattern implementation: We can make it a bundle of class objects, with one class for each product. This is exactly the same "classes are just objects" insight that helped us simplify the Factory Method pattern.

The code below shows a class-based abstract factory. Instead of having several different abstract factory classes, one class for each set of things that the factory needs to produce, we can have just one factory class that stores the class objects of the things that it needs to produce:

```ruby
class OrganismFactory
  def initialize(plant_class, animal_class)
    @plant_class = plant_class
    @animal_class = animal_class
  end

  def new_animal(name)
    @animal_class.new(name)
  end

  def new_plant(name)
    @plant_class.new(name)
  end
end
```

With this class-based abstract factory, we can create a new instance of the factory for each compatible set of objects that we need:

```ruby
jungle_organism_factory = OrganismFactory.new(Tree, Tiger)
pond_organism_factory = OrganismFactory.new(WaterLily, Frog)

jungle = Habitat.new(1, 4, jungle_organism_factory)
jungle.simulate_one_day

pond = Habitat.new( 2, 4, pond_organism_factory)
pond.simulate_one_day
```

This all may seem a bit circular. After all, didn't we originally create the abstract factory to avoid specifying the individual classes? And with our latest abstract factory implementation, aren't we right back to being able to create a pond full of tigers or a jungle overrun by algae? Not really. The important thing about the abstract factory is that it encapsulates the knowledge of which product types go together. You can express that encapsulation with classes and subclasses, or you can get to it by storing the class objects as we did in the code above. Either way, you end up with an object that knows which kind of things belong together.

Leveraging the Name

Another way that we can simplify the implementation of abstract factories is to rely on a consistent naming convention for the product classes. This approach won't work for our habitat example, which is populated with things like tigers and frogs that have unique names, but imagine you need to produce an abstract factory for objects that know how to read and write a variety of file formats, such as PDF, HTML, and PostScript files. Certainly we could implement `IOFactory` using any of the techniques that we have discussed so far. But if the reader and writer class names follow some regular pattern, something like `HTMLReader` and `HTMLWriter` for HTML and `PDFReader` and `PDFWriter` for PDF, we can simply derive the class name from the name of the format. That's exactly what the following code does:

```ruby
class IOFactory
  def initialize(format)
    @reader_class = self.class.const_get("#{format}Reader")
    @writer_class = self.class.const_get("#{format}Writer")
  end

  def new_reader
    @reader_class.new
  end

  def new_writer
    @writer_class.new
  end
end

html_factory = IOFactory.new('HTML')
html_reader = html_factory.new_reader

pdf_factory = IOFactory.new('PDF')
pdf_writer = pdf_factory.new_writer
```

The `const_get` method used in `IOFactory` takes a string (or a symbol) containing the name of a constant[1] and returns the value of that constant. For example, if you pass `const_get` the string `"PDFWriter"`, you will get back the class object of that name, which is exactly what we want in this case.[2]

---

1. Recall that in Ruby all class names are constants.
2. Of course, if there is no `PDFWriter` class, `const_get` will throw an exception, which in this case is also exactly what we want to happen.

Using and Abusing the Factory Patterns

The best way to go wrong with any of the object creation techniques that we have examined in this chapter is to use them when you don't need them. Not every object needs to be produced by a factory. In fact, most of the time you will want to create most of your objects with a simple call to `MyClass.new`. Use the techniques discussed in this chapter when you have a choice of several different, related classes and you need to choose among them.

Remember, chances are You Ain't Gonna Need It. The YAGNI principle applies with a vengeance to factories. Perhaps I am dealing with only ducks and lilies at the moment, but maybe in the future I might need to cope with tigers and trees. Should I build a factory now to get ready? Probably not. You have to balance the cost of the additional, currently useless factory infrastructure against the likelihood that you will actually need the factory. Factor in the price of back-fitting a factory in later. The answer depends on the details, but engineers do have a tendency to build the *Queen Mary* (or perhaps the *Titanic?*) when a canoe will suffice. If you have a choice of exactly one class at the moment, put off adding in a factory.

Factory Patterns in the Wild

It is actually fairly difficult to find the classic inheritance-based versions of either factory pattern in the Ruby code base. Ruby programmers have resoundingly voted with their keyboards for the more dynamic versions of the factories, the ones based on the class objects or on various class naming schemes. For example, the SOAP library that came with your Ruby interpreter goes from XML strings to Ruby objects by leveraging the names. Similarly, the XMLRPC[3] implementation that is included in the Ruby standard library supports several XML parsing options. Each of these methods of parsing XML has an associated parser class; there is one class for parsing the XML as a stream and another for parsing it as a DOM tree. But there is no separate subclass of some XMLRPC class for each parsing technique. Instead, the XMLRPC code simply holds on to the class of the chosen XML parser and manufactures new instances of the parser from the class object as required.

A fairly exotic version of a factory method lives in `ActiveRecord`. As we saw in Chapter 9, `ActiveRecord` has an adapter class for each different kind of database that

---

3. XMLRPC, if you have not come across it before, is an XML-based remote procedure call mechanism, along the lines of SOAP. Unlike SOAP, XMLRPC really does strive for simplicity.

it talks to—there is a MySQL adapter, an Oracle adapter, and so on. When you ask `ActiveRecord` to set up a connection to a database, you need to specify—along with the user name, password, and port—a string containing the name of the adapter that `ActiveRecord` should use. So you supply `"mysql"` if you want `ActiveRecord` to talk to a MySQL database or `"oracle"` if it is to communicate with Oracle. But how does `ActiveRecord` go from that adapter name to an instance of the adapter?

It turns out that `ActiveRecord` uses a fairly interesting technique to come up with an adapter instance, all of it centered on the `Base`[4] class. `Base` starts out completely ignorant of any specific database adapters:

```
class Base
  # Lots of non-adapter-related code removed...
end
```

However, each database adapter contains code that modifies `Base` in a particular way; that is, each adapter adds a method that creates its specific flavor of connection to the `Base` class. For example, the MySQL adapter contains code more or less like this:

```
class Base
  def self.mysql_connection(config)
    # Create and return a new MySQL connection, using
    # the user name, password, etc. stored in the
    # config hash...
  end
end
```

Similarly, the Oracle adapter contains code that looks like this:

```
class Base
  def self.oracle_connection(config)
    # Create a new Oracle connection...
  end
end
```

---

4. Actually, the `Base` class is defined inside the `ActiveRecord` module, so its name is usually written as `ActiveRecord::Base`. In the interest of simplicity, I have stripped the module as well as many other irrelevant details from the code in this section.

After all of the adapters are finished with it, the `Base` class has a method called `<<db_type>>_connection` for each of the different types of databases it can accommodate.

To create an actual connection from the name of the adapter, `Base` constructs the name of the database-specific method as a string. It works something like this:

```
adapter = "mysql"
method_name = "#{adapter}_connection"
Base.send(method_name, config)
```

The last line of this method effectively calls the database-specific method, passing along the database connection configuration (things like the database, user name, and password) as a parameter. Voila—instant connection.

Wrapping Up

In this chapter, we looked at the two GoF factory patterns, both of which are techniques for answering the question "Which class?"

The Factory Method pattern involves the application of the Template Method pattern to object creation. True to its Template Method roots, this pattern says to just leave the "which class" question to be answered by a subclass. We saw that we could use this pattern to build a generic `Pond` class that knows all about environmental simulations but leaves the choice of the specific plant and animal classes to its subclass. We therefore create subclasses with names like `DuckWaterLilyPond` and `FrogAlgaePond`, which in turn fill in the factory methods with implementations that create the appropriate kinds of objects.

The Abstract Factory pattern comes into play when you want to create compatible sets of objects. If you want to ensure that your frogs and algae don't end up in the same habitat as your tigers and trees, then create an abstract factory for each valid combination.

The key thing that we discovered in this chapter is how both of these patterns morphed in Ruby's dynamic environment—specifically, how they became much simpler. While the GoF concentrated on inheritance-based implementations of their factories, we can get the same results with much less code by taking advantage of the fact that in Ruby, classes are just objects. In Ruby we can look up classes by name, pass them around, and store them away for future use.

Looking ahead, the next pattern that we will examine is the Builder pattern, which also produces new objects but is much more tightly focused on constructing complex objects than on picking the right class. But we are by no means finished with the question of how to produce the right objects for the problem at hand. In Chapter 17, we will look at meta-programming, a technique for customizing your classes and objects at runtime.

## CHAPTER 14

Easier Object Construction with the Builder

I remember the day we bought my son his first bike. The morning went well enough—the drive to the store, finding the right size, and the lengthy but critical process of selecting the right color. Then there was the middle phase of getting the bike home and getting everything out of the box. Of course, some assembly was required. Perhaps more than some. What followed our happy arrival home was the third phase, the phase that took all afternoon and involved a descent into frustration and multiple skinned knuckles. I spent hours trying to pull together a minor junkyard of parts according to instructions that would have baffled the entire National Security Agency. As it turned out, picking that bike was the easy part; putting it together was the real challenge.

Objects can be like that, too. Chapter 13 was all about using factories to lay your hands on the right kind of object. But sometimes getting hold of the right object is not the main problem. No, sometimes the problem is in configuring the object.

In this chapter, we will look at the Builder pattern, a pattern designed to help you configure those complex objects. We will see that, as you might expect, there is a fair bit of overlap between builders and factories. We will also look at magic methods, a Ruby technique that can make your builders even easier to use. In addition, we will consider the issues that arise in reusing a builder. Finally, we will see how the Builder pattern can help you avoid accidentally creating invalid objects and perhaps even help you create valid ones.

Building Computers

Imagine that you are writing a system that will support a small computer manufacturing business. Each machine is custom made to order, so you need to keep track of the components that will go into each machine. To keep things simple, suppose each computer is made up of a display, a motherboard, and some drives:

```ruby
class Computer
  attr_accessor :display
  attr_accessor :motherboard
  attr_reader   :drives

  def initialize(display=:crt, motherboard=Motherboard.new, drives=[])
    @motherboard = motherboard
    @drives = drives
    @display = display
  end
end
```

The display is easy; it is either a :crt or an :lcd. The motherboard is a whole object in itself; it has a certain amount of memory and holds either an ordinary CPU or a superfast turbo processor:

```ruby
class CPU
  # Common CPU stuff...
end

class BasicCPU < CPU
  # Lots of not very fast CPU-related stuff...
end

class TurboCPU < CPU
  # Lots of very fast CPU stuff...
end

class Motherboard
  attr_accessor :cpu
  attr_accessor :memory_size
```

```
    def initialize(cpu=BasicCPU.new, memory_size=1000)
      @cpu = cpu
      @memory_size = memory_size
    end
  end
```

The drives, which come in three flavors (hard drive, CD, and DVD) are modeled by the `Drive` class:

```
class Drive
  attr_reader :type # either :hard_disk, :cd or :dvd
  attr_reader :size # in MB
  attr_reader :writable # true if this drive is writable

  def initialize(type, size, writable)
    @type = type
    @size = size
    @writable = writable
  end
end
```

Even with this somewhat simplified model of, constructing a new instance of `Computer` is painfully tedious:

```
# Build a fast computer with lots of memory...

motherboard = Motherboard.new(TurboCPU.new, 4000)

# ...and a hard drive, a CD writer, and a DVD

drives = []
drives << Drive.new(:hard_drive, 200000, true)
drives << Drive.new(:cd, 760, true)
drives << Drive.new(:dvd, 4700, false)

computer = Computer.new(:lcd, motherboard, drives)
```

The very simple idea behind the Builder pattern is that you take this kind of construction logic and encapsulate it in a class all of its own. The **builder** class takes charge of assembling all of the components of a complex object. Each builder has an interface that lets you specify the configuration of your new object step by step. In a sense, a builder is sort of like a multipart new method, where objects are created in an extended process instead of all in one shot. A builder for our computers might look something like this:

```ruby
class ComputerBuilder
  attr_reader :computer

  def initialize
    @computer = Computer.new
  end

  def turbo(has_turbo_cpu=true)
    @computer.motherboard.cpu = TurboCPU.new
  end

  def display=(display)
    @computer.display=display
  end

  def memory_size=(size_in_mb)
    @computer.motherboard.memory_size = size_in_mb
  end

  def add_cd(writer=false)
    @computer.drives << Drive.new(:cd, 760, writer)
  end

  def add_dvd(writer=false)
    @computer.drives << Drive.new(:dvd, 4000, writer)
  end

  def add_hard_disk(size_in_mb)
    @computer.drives << Drive.new(:hard_disk, size_in_mb, true)
  end
end
```

The ComputerBuilder class factors out all of the details involved in creating an instance of Computer. To use it, you simply make a new instance of the builder

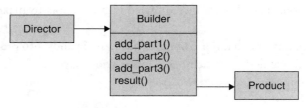

Figure 14-1   A Builder

and step through the process of specifying all the options that you need on your computer:

```
builder = ComputerBuilder.new
builder.turbo
builder.add_cd(true)
builder.add_dvd
builder.add_hard_disk(100000)
```

Finally, you get the shiny new `Computer` instance from the builder:

```
computer = builder.computer
```

Figure 14-1 shows the UML diagram for our basic builder.

The GOF called the client of the builder object the **director** because it directs the builder in the construction of the new object (called the **product**). Builders not only ease the burden of creating complex objects, but also hide the implementation details. The director does not have to know the specifics of what goes into creating the new object. When we use the `ComputerBuilder` class, we can stay blissfully ignorant of which classes represent the DVDs or the hard disks; we just ask for the computer configuration that we need.

Polymorphic Builders

This chapter began by contrasting the Builder pattern with factories and saying that builders are less concerned about picking the right class and more focused on helping you configure your object. Factoring out all of that nasty construction code is the main motivation behind builders. Nevertheless, given that builders are involved in object construction, they also are incredibly convenient spots to make those "which class" decisions.

For example, imagine that our computer business expands into producing laptops along with traditional desktop machines. Thus we now have two basic kinds of products: desktop computers and laptops.

```ruby
class DesktopComputer < Computer
  # Lots of interesting desktop details omitted...
end

class LaptopComputer < Computer
  def initialize( motherboard=Motherboard.new,  drives=[] )
    super(:lcd, motherboard, drives)
  end

  # Lots of interesting laptop details omitted...

end
```

Of course, the components of a laptop computer are not the same as the ones you find in a desktop computer. Fortunately, we can refactor our builder into a base class and two subclasses to take care of these differences. The abstract base builder deals with all of the details that are common to the two kinds of computers:

```ruby
class ComputerBuilder
  attr_reader :computer

  def turbo(has_turbo_cpu=true)
    @computer.motherboard.cpu = TurboCPU.new
  end

  def memory_size=(size_in_mb)
    @computer.motherboard.memory_size = size_in_mb
  end
end
```

The `DesktopBuilder` knows how to build desktop computers. In particular, it knows to create instances of the `DesktopComputer` class and it is aware that desktop computers use ordinary drives:

```ruby
class DesktopBuilder < ComputerBuilder
  def initialize
    @computer = DesktopComputer.new
  end

  def display=(display)
    @display = display
  end

  def add_cd(writer=false)
    @computer.drives << Drive.new(:cd, 760, writer)
  end

  def add_dvd(writer=false)
    @computer.drives << Drive.new(:dvd, 4000, writer)
  end

  def add_hard_disk(size_in_mb)
    @computer.drives << Drive.new(:hard_disk, size_in_mb, true)
  end
end
```

By contrast, the laptop builder knows to create instances of LaptopComputer and to populate that object with instances of the special LaptopDrive:

```ruby
class LaptopBuilder < ComputerBuilder
  def initialize
    @computer = LaptopComputer.new
  end

  def display=(display)
    raise "Laptop display must be lcd" unless display == :lcd
  end

  def add_cd(writer=false)
    @computer.drives << LaptopDrive.new(:cd, 760, writer)
  end

  def add_dvd(writer=false)
    @computer.drives << LaptopDrive.new(:dvd, 4000, writer)
  end

  def add_hard_disk(size_in_mb)
    @computer.drives << LaptopDrive.new(:hard_disk, size_in_mb, true)
  end
end
```

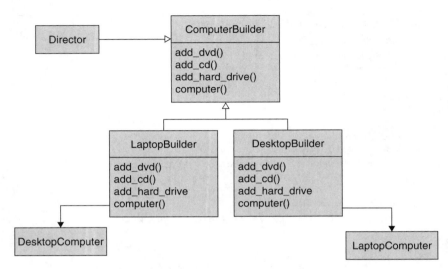

Figure 14-2   A polymorphic builder implementation

Figure 14-2 shows the UML diagram for our new, polymorphic builder. If you compare Figure 14-2 with the UML diagram for the abstract factory (Figure 13-2), you will see that the two patterns share a certainly family resemblance.

Alternatively, we could have written a single builder class that creates either a laptop or a desktop system depending on the value of a parameter.

Builders Can Ensure Sane Objects

In addition to making object construction easier, builders can make object construction safer. That final "give me my object" method makes an ideal place to check that the configuration requested by the client really makes sense and that it adheres to the appropriate business rules. For example, we might enhance our `computer` method to make sure that it has a sane hardware configuration:

```
def computer
  raise "Not enough memory" if @computer.motherboard.memory_size < 250
  raise "Too many drives" if @computer.drives.size > 4
  hard_disk = @computer.drives.find {|drive| drive.type == :hard_disk}
  raise "No hard disk." unless hard_disk
  @computer
end
```

Nor do we have to simply throw up our hands and raise an exception in the face of an incomplete configuration:

```
# ...
if ! hard_disk
  raise "No room to add hard disk." if @computer.drives.size >= 4
  add_hard_disk(100000)
end
# ...
```

The preceding code simply adds in a hard drive if there is room for one and the client did not specify one.

Reusable Builders

An important issue to consider when writing and using builders is whether you can use a single builder instance to create multiple objects. For example, you might quite reasonably expect that you could use a `LaptopBuilder` to create a couple of identical computers in one go:

```
builder = LaptopBuilder.new
builder.add_hard_disk(100000)
builder.turbo

computer1 = builder.computer
computer2 = builder.computer
```

The trouble is, because the `computer` method always returns the same computer, both `computer1` and `computer2` end up being references to the same computer, which is probably not what you expected here. One way to deal with this issue is to equip your builder with a reset method, which reinitializes the object under construction:

```
class LaptopBuilder

  # Lots of code omitted...

  def reset
    @computer = LaptopComputer.new
  end

end
```

The reset method will let you reuse the builder instance, but it also means that you have to start the configuration process all over again for each computer. If you want to perform the configuration once and then have the builder produce any number of objects based on that configuration, you need to store all of the configuration information in instance attributes and create the actual product only when the client asks for it.

Better Builders with Magic Methods

Our computer builder is certainly an improvement over spreading all of that object creation, configuration, and validation code throughout your application. Unfortunately, even with the builder, the process of fitting out a new computer is less than elegant. As we have seen, you still have to create the builder and then call any number of methods to configure the new computer. The question is, can we make the process of configuring the new computer a bit terser and perhaps a shade more elegant?

One way we might do this is by creating a **magic method.** The idea behind a magic method is to let the caller make up a method name according to a specific pattern. For example, we might configure a new laptop with

```
builder.add_dvd_and_harddisk
```

or perhaps even

```
builder.add_turbo_and_dvd_and_harddisk
```

Magic methods are very easy to implement using the `method_missing` technique that we first met back when we were talking about proxies (in Chapter 10). To use a magic method, you simply catch all unexpected methods calls with `method_missing` and parse the method name to see if it matches the pattern of your magic method name:

```
def method_missing(name, *args)
  words = name.to_s.split("_")
  return super(name, *args) unless words.shift == 'add'
  words.each do |word|
    next if word == 'and'
    add_cd if word == 'cd'
    add_dvd if word == 'dvd'
    add_hard_disk(100000) if word == 'harddisk'
    turbo if word == 'turbo'
  end
end
```

This code breaks the method name up along the underscores and tries to make sense of it as a request to add various options to the computer.

The magic method technique is certainly not limited to builders. You can use it in any situation where you want to let client code specify multiple options succinctly.

Using and Abusing the Builder Pattern

The need for the Builder pattern sometimes creeps up on you as your application becomes increasingly complex. For example, in its early days your `Computer` class may have just tracked the CPU type and memory size. Using a builder for so simple a class would clearly be overdoing things. But as you enhanced the `Computer` class to model the drives, the number of options and the interdependences between those options suddenly explodes—and a build starts to make more sense. It is usually fairly easy to spot code that is missing a builder: You can find the same object creation logic scattered all over the place. Another hint that you need a builder is when your code starts producing invalid objects: "Oops, I checked the number of drives when I create a new `Computer` over here, but not over there."

As with factories, the main way that you can abuse the Builder pattern is by using it when you don't need it. I don't think it is a good idea to anticipate the need for a builder. Instead, let `MyClass.new` be your default way of creating new objects. Add in a builder only when cruel fate, or ever-escalating requirements, force your hand.

Builders in the Wild

One of the more interesting builders that you will find in the Ruby code base claims that it is not a builder at all. Despite its name, `MailFactory`[1] is a really nice builder that helps you create e-mail messages. Although e-mail messages are, at their heart, just chunks of plain text, anyone who has ever tried to construct a message with multipart MIME attachments knows that even plain text can be very complicated.

`MailFactory` propels you past all of this complication by providing a nice builder-style interface to create your message:

```
require 'rubygems'
require 'mailfactory'

mail_builder = MailFactory.new
mail_builder.to ='russ@russolsen.com'
```

---

1. The `MailFactory` package was written by David Powers.

```
mail_builder.from = 'russ@russolsen.com'
mail_builder.subject = 'The document'
mail_builder.text = 'Here is that document you wanted'
mail_builder.attach('book.doc')
```

Once you have told `MailFactory` (builder!) all about your e-mail message, you can get the text of the message—the thing that you can ship off to an SMTP server—by calling the `to_s` method:

```
puts mail_builder.to_s
to: russ@russolsen.com
from: russ@russolsen.com
subject: Here is that document you wanted
Date: Wed, 16 May 2007 14:02:32 -0400
MIME-Version: 1.0
Content-Type: multipart/mixed;
boundary="—=_NextPart_3rj.Kbd9.t9JpHIc663P_4mq6"
Message-ID: <1179338750.3053.1000.-606657668@russolsen.com>

This is a multi-part message in MIME format.
...
```

The most prominent examples of magic methods are the finder methods in `ActiveRecord`. In exactly the same way that our last computer builder allowed us to specify computer configurations with the name of the method we call, `ActiveRecord` allows us to encode database queries. You might, for instance, find all of the employees in the `Employee` table by Social Security number:

```
Employee.find_by_ssn('123-45-6789')
```

Or you could search by first and last names:

```
Employee.find_by_firstname_and_lastname('John', 'Smith')
```

Wrapping Up

The idea behind the Builder pattern is that if your object is hard to build, if you have to write a lot of code to configure each object, then you should factor all of that creation code into a separate class, the builder.

The Builder pattern suggests that you provide an object—the builder—that takes a multipart specification of your new object and deals with all the complexity and drudgery of creating that object. Builders, because they are in control of configuring your object, can also prevent you from constructing an invalid object. The builder is uniquely positioned to look over the client's shoulder and say, "No, I think a fifth wheel on that car may be a bit too much . . ."

With a little ingenuity, you can create magic methods to facilitate the building. To build a magic method, you catch arbitrary method calls to your object with method_missing, parse the names of those nonexistent methods, and build the right thing based on the name. Magic methods tend to take speedy object construction to the next level by allowing the client to specify a number of configuration options with a single method call.

When you create a builder, and especially when you use one, you need to be aware of the reusability issue. Can you use a single instance of a builder to create multiple instances of the product? It is certainly easier to write one-shot builders, or builders that need to be reset before reuse, than it is to create completely reusable builders. The question is this: Which kind of builder are you creating or using?

The Builder pattern is the last of the patterns that we will examine that is concerned with object creation.[2] In the next chapter, we will stop talking about creating new objects and go back to talking about doing something interesting with all those brand-new objects: create an interpreter.

---

2. Or in the case of the Singleton pattern, preventing object creation.

CHAPTER 15

Assembling Your System with the Interpreter

In the late 1980s, a much earlier edition of Russ Olsen the software engineer—perhaps the beta version of the professional me, certainly not the release candidate—worked on a Geographical Information System (GIS). One of the key goals of that GIS system was easy adaptability. Customers' maps were all different, and each customer wanted to have its maps look just the way that customer wanted them to look. Also, each customer wanted to use its maps in some unique way, and we naturally wanted our system to zig with every customer's zag.

Unfortunately, we were writing this system in the C programming language. While C has a lot of points to recommend it, easy adaptability is not one of them. Writing C is hard—you need to pay close attention to all of that pointer arithmetic or your program is very likely to suffer an early demise. What was worse, C lived on the wrong conceptual level for our system. When you write a C program you are dealing with ints and floats and pointers to structs, but we wanted to spend our time dealing with the valleys and rivers and political borders that make up a map.

The architects of that GIS system (an elite group that emphatically did not include me) solved the easy-adaptability problem with one dramatic decision: They ruled that most of the system was not to be written in C after all. Instead, perhaps 80 percent of the application was coded in a specialized language that knew all about geographic things like latitudes and longitudes. This language sported a sophisticated query syntax that made it easy to move all of the medium-sized trees to the north by 500 meters.

The map language was not exactly what you would hear when two cartographers get together for lunch, but it was much closer to that than any C program ever written.

As I say, about 80 percent of the code was this specialized, map-oriented stuff. And what of the other 20 percent? That was written in C, but the interesting part was what it did: That C code implemented an interpreter, an interpreter for the other 80 percent of the code, the stuff written in the specialized, map-oriented language. In short, that old GIS system was a massive implementation of the Interpreter pattern.

In this chapter, we will look at the Interpreter pattern, which suggests that sometimes the best way to solve a problem is to invent a new language for just that purpose. We will explore how a typical interpreter is assembled and consider some ways of dealing with the tedious task of parsing. We will also find out that interpreters are perhaps not the best-performing beasts in the programming zoo, but that for their performance price they do offer a lot of flexibility and extensibility.

The Right Language for the Job

The Interpreter pattern is built around a very simple idea: Some programming problems are best solved by creating a specialized language and expressing the solution in that language. What kind of problems are good candidates for the Interpreter pattern? As a general rule, problems well suited to the Interpreter pattern tend to be self-contained, with crisp boundaries around them. For example, if you are writing code that searches for specific objects based on some specification, you might consider creating a query language.[1] Conversely, if you are faced with the task of creating complex object configurations, you might think about building a configuration language.

Another clue that your problem might be right for the Interpreter pattern is that you find yourself creating lots of discrete chunks of code, chunks that seem easy enough to write in themselves, but which you find yourself combining in an ever-expanding array of combinations. Perhaps a simple interpreter could do all of the combining work for you.

Building an Interpreter

Interpreters typically work in two phases. First, the parser reads in the program text and produces a data structure, called an **abstract syntax tree (AST).** The AST represents the same information as the original program, but transformed into a tree of

---

1. This is, of course, what the folks behind SQL did for databases.

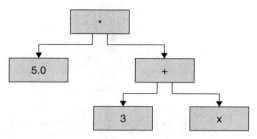

Figure 15-1   Abstract syntax tree for a simple arithmetic expression

objects that, unlike the original program text, can be executed with reasonable efficiency. Second, the AST is evaluated against some set of external conditions, or context, to produce the desired computation.

For example, we might build an interpreter to evaluate very simple arithmetic expressions like this one:

```
5.0*(3+x)
```

First, we need to parse this expression. Our parser would start out by tackling the first character of the expression—the numeral 5—and then move on to the decimal point and the zero, working out along the way that it is dealing with a floating-point number. Having finished with the 5.0, the parser would move on to process the rest of the expression, eventually producing a data structure that looks something like Figure 15-1.

The data structure shown in Figure 15-1 is our AST. The leaf nodes of the AST— that is, the 5.0, the 3, and the x—are called **terminals,** and represent the most basic building blocks of the language. The nonleaf nodes—in this example, the + and the *— are called (logically enough) **nonterminals.** The nonterminals represent the higher-order concepts in the language.

As you can see from the UML diagram in Figure 15-2, the nonterminals have a reference to one or more subexpressions, which allows us to build arbitrarily complex trees.[2]

Although the GoF called the key method in the Interpreter pattern interpret, names such as evaluate or execute also make sense and show up in code frequently.

---

2. Yes, you have seen this diagram before. ASTs are, in fact, specialized examples of the Composite pattern, with the nonterminal expressions playing the parts of the composites.

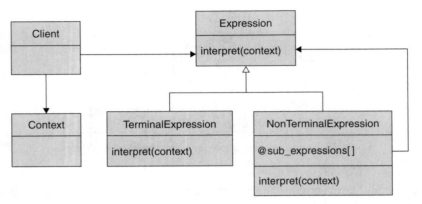

Figure 15-2　Class Diagram for the Interpreter pattern

With the AST in hand, we are almost ready to evaluate our expression, save for one small detail: What is the value of x? To evaluate our expression, we need to supply a value for x. Is x equal to 1 or 167 or –279? The GoF called such values or conditions supplied at the time the AST is interpreted the **context.** Returning to our example, if we interpret our AST with a context where x is set to 1, we will get a result of 20.0; if we interpret it a second time with x set to 4, we will get a result of 35.0.

Whatever the values in the context, the AST evaluates itself by recursively descending down the tree. We ask the root node of the tree (in this case, the node representing the multiplication) to evaluate itself. It, in turn, recursively tries to evaluate its two factors. The 5.0 is easy, but the other factor, the addition, must evaluate its terms (the 3 and x). We finally hit bottom here and the results come bubbling back up through the recursion.

We can learn two things from this simple arithmetic expression example. First, the Interpreter pattern has a lot of moving parts. Think of all the different classes that make up the AST and then add in the parser. The sheer number of components is why the Interpreter pattern is in practice limited to relatively simple languages: We are presumably trying to solve some real business problem and not engage in programming language research. The second thing that we can take away from the example is that the Interpreter pattern is unlikely to be fast. Aside from the parsing overhead, traversing the AST will inevitably exact some speed penalty of its own.

We do get a couple of things back in return for the interpreter's complexity and speed penalty. First, we get flexibility. Once you have an interpreter, it is usually very easy to add new operations to it. Certainly we can imagine that once we have built an interpreter for our little arithmetic expressions that it would be easy to add subtraction and multiplication nodes to the AST. Second, we get the AST itself. An AST is a data structure that represents some specific bit of programming logic. While we originally built the AST to evaluate it, we can manipulate it so that it does other things, too. We might, for example, have the AST print out a description of itself:

```
Multiply 5.0 by the sum of 3 and x, where x is 1.
```

A File-Finding Interpreter

Enough theory—let's create an interpreter in Ruby. The last thing the world needs is another arithmetic expression interpreter, so we will do something a little different here. Imagine that we are writing a program that manages files, lots of files of many different formats and sizes. We will frequently need to search for files with particular characteristics, such as all the MP3 files or all the writable files. Not only that, but we will also need to find files that share a specific combination of characteristics, such as all the big MP3 files or all the JPEG files that are read only.

Finding All the Files

This sounds like a problem that could be solved with a simple query language. We can imagine that each expression in our language will specify the kind of files that we are looking for. Let's start with the classes that will make up the AST and put off the parser until later.

The most basic kind of file search simply returns *all* of the files, so we build a class to do that:

```ruby
require 'find'

class Expression
  # Common expression code will go here soon...
end

class All < Expression
 def evaluate(dir)
   results= []
   Find.find(dir) do |p|
     next unless File.file?(p)
     results << p
   end
   results
 end
end
```

There is not a lot going on here. The key method of our interpreter is called evaluate; the evaluate method in All simply uses the Ruby standard library Find class to gather up all the files that live under a given directory. If you pass Find.find a directory name and a block, it will call the block once for everything that it finds under that directory. And I mean everything: Because Find works recursively, our block will be called not only for all of the files in the directory but also for all of the subdirectories, all of the files in the subdirectories, and so on. Of course, we are only interested in files, so we need to do a bit of filtering. The line

```
next unless File.file?(p)
```

will skip anything that is not a file.

Oh, and don't fret too much about that empty Expression superclass. We will fill it in with some useful code a little later on.

Finding Files by Name

The next most obvious thing is to create a class that will return all files whose names match a given pattern:

```
class FileName < Expression
  def initialize(pattern)
    @pattern = pattern
  end

  def evaluate(dir)
    results= []
    Find.find(dir) do |p|
      next unless File.file?(p)
      name = File.basename(p)
      results << p if File.fnmatch(@pattern, name)
    end
    results
  end
end
```

FileName is only slightly more complicated than All. This class employs a couple of very useful methods from the Ruby File class. The File.basename method returns just the filename part of a path—give it "/home/russ/chapter1.doc" and you will get back "chapter1.doc". The File.fnmatch method returns true only if the filename pattern specified in the first parameter (something like `"*.doc"`) matches the filename in the second parameter (something like `"chapter1.doc"`).

Using our file-finding classes is very straightforward. If my `test_dir` directory contains two MP3 files and an image, I can find all three files with this code:

```
expr_all = All.new
files = expr_all.evaluate('test_dir')
```

But if I am just interested in the MP3s, I can say this:

```
expr_mp3 = FileName.new('*.mp3')
mp3s = expr_mp3.evaluate('test_dir')
```

In the preceding examples, the directory name that we pass into the `evaluate` method plays the part of the context—some set of externally supplied parameters that we evaluate the expression against. We can evaluate the same expression against different contexts and produce different results. I might, for example, want to find all of the MP3 files in my music directory:

```
other_mp3s = expr_mp3.evaluate('music_dir')
```

Big Files and Writable Files

Of course, finding all the files, or finding all the files with a certain style of name, in no way exhausts the possibilities. We might, for example, want to look for files that are bigger than some specified size:

```
class Bigger < Expression
 def initialize(size)
   @size = size
 end

 def evaluate(dir)
   results = []
   Find.find(dir) do |p|
     next unless File.file?(p)
     results << p if( File.size(p) > @size)
   end
   results
 end
end
```

Or we might go looking for files that are writable:

```
class Writable < Expression
  def evaluate(dir)
    results = []
    Find.find(dir) do |p|
      next unless File.file?(p)
      results << p if( File.writable?(p) )
    end
    results
  end
end
```

More Complex Searches with Not, And, and Or

Now that we have some basic file-searching classes—these will become the terminals in our AST—let's move on to something more interesting. What if we want to find all of the files that are *not writable?* Clearly, we could build yet another class along the lines of the ones we created earlier. But let's do something different; let's build our first nonterminal, Not:

```
class Not < Expression
  def initialize(expression)
    @expression = expression
  end

  def evaluate(dir)
    All.new.evaluate(dir) - @expression.evaluate(dir)
  end
end
```

The constructor of the Not class takes another file-finding expression, which represents the expression we want to negate. When evaluate is called, it starts with all of the paths (as conveniently determined by the All class) and, using the Array subtraction operator, removes all of the paths returned by the expression. What is left is every path that is *not* returned by the expression. Thus, to find all of the files that are not writable, you would say:

```
expr_not_writable = Not.new( Writable.new )
readonly_files = expr_not_writable.evaluate('test_dir')
```

The beauty of the Not class is that it is not just applicable to Writable. We might, for instance, use Not to find all of the files smaller than 1KB:

```
small_expr = Not.new( Bigger.new(1024) )
small_files = small_expr.evaluate('test_dir')
```

Or we might look for all files that are not MP3s:

```
not_mp3_expr = Not.new( FileName.new('*.mp3') )
not_mp3s = not_mp3_expr.evaluate('test_dir')
```

We can also create a nonterminal that combines the results of two file-searching expressions:

```
class Or < Expression
  def initialize(expression1, expression2)
    @expression1 = expression1
    @expression2 = expression2
  end

  def evaluate(dir)
    result1 = @expression1.evaluate(dir)
    result2 = @expression2.evaluate(dir)
    (result1 + result2).sort.uniq
  end
end
```

With Or, we can find all of the files that are either MP3s *or* writable in one shot:

```
big_or_mp3_expr = Or.new( Bigger.new(1024), FileName.new('*.mp3') )
big_or_mp3s = big_or_mp3_expr.evaluate('test_dir')
```

And where there is an Or, can And be far behind?

```
class And < Expression
  def initialize(expression1, expression2)
    @expression1 = expression1
    @expression2 = expression2
  end
```

```
  def evaluate(dir)
    result1 = @expression1.evaluate(dir)
    result2 = @expression2.evaluate(dir)
    (result1 & result2)
  end
end
```

We now have everything we need to specify some truly complex file searches. How about all of the big MP3 files that are not writable?

```
complex_expression = And.new(
                     And.new(Bigger.new(1024),
                            FileName.new('*.mp3')),
                     Not.new(Writable.new ))
```

This complex expression gives us a glimpse into another nice property of the Interpreter pattern. Once we have created a complex AST like the one above, we can use it over and over with different contexts:

```
complex_expression.evaluate('test_dir')
complex_expression.evaluate('/tmp')
```

Done correctly, the Interpreter pattern gives you a lot of mileage for your effort. In our example, it took us only seven classes to get to a reasonably flexible file-searching AST.

Creating the AST

Surprisingly, the Interpreter pattern as defined by the GoF is silent on the origins of the AST. The pattern simply assumes that you have somehow gotten your hands on an AST and works from there. Of course, the AST has to come from somewhere. In practice, there are a surprising number of alternative ways to create an AST.

A Simple Parser

Perhaps the most obvious way of coming up with an AST is to build a parser. Building a parser for our little file-searching language is not especially difficult. Suppose we define the syntax to look something like this:

```
and (and(bigger 1024)(filename *.mp3)) writable
```

Then the following code does a passable job of parsing, all in about 50 lines:

```ruby
class Parser
  def initialize(text)
    @tokens = text.scan(/\(|\)|[\w\.\*]+/)
  end

  def next_token
    @tokens.shift
  end

  def expression
    token = next_token

    if token == nil
      return nil

    elsif token == '('
      result = expression
      raise 'Expected )' unless next_token == ')'
      result

    elsif token == 'all'
      return All.new

    elsif token == 'writable'
      return Writable.new

    elsif token == 'bigger'
      return Bigger.new(next_token.to_i)

    elsif token == 'filename'
      return FileName.new(next_token)

    elsif token == 'not'
      return Not.new(expression)

    elsif token == 'and'
      return And.new(expression, expression)

    elsif token == 'or'
      return Or.new(expression, expression)
```

```
    else
      raise "Unexpected token: #{token}"
    end
  end
end
```

To use the parser, pass the file-finding expression into the constructor and then call the `parse` method. The `parse` method returns the corresponding AST, all ready to be evaluated:

```
parser = Parser.new "and (and(bigger 1024)(filename *.mp3)) writable"
ast = parser.expression
```

The `Parser` class uses the `scan` method from the `String` class to break up the expression into convenient tokens:

```
@tokens = text.scan(/\(|\)|[\w\.\*]+/)
```

Using a little regular-expression magic,[3] this code breaks the string contained in `text` into an array of substrings or tokens, where each token is either a left or right parenthesis or a discrete chunk of the expression like "filename" or "*.mp3".[4]

The bulk of the parser is taken up by the `expression` method, which looks at the tokens one at a time, building up the AST as it goes.

A Parser-less Interpreter?

Although the parser that we built was not really all that difficult to create, it did take some effort and raises a somewhat subversive-sounding question: Do we really need a parser at all? The file-searching classes that we have built so far would, all by themselves, make a fine internal programmer-oriented API. If we just need a good way to specify file searches from code, then perhaps we can just create the file-searching AST

---

3. If you are not very familiar with regular expressions, take a look at Appendix B, Digging Deeper. Regular expressions are well worth the effort that it takes to figure them out.

4. If you *are* familiar with regular expressions, no doubt you have spotted the fact that my parser will not handle filenames with spaces in them. Let me again plead the need for simple examples—not to mention the fact that I think that filenames with embedded spaces are a serious breach of ethics.

in code in exactly the same way we did in the examples in the previous section. In this way, we can still get all of the flexibility and extensibility benefits of the Interpreter pattern without the bother of dealing with parsing.

If you do decide to go with a parser-less interpreter, it is frequently worth the trouble of adding some shortcuts to make life easier for your users. For example, we could extend our file-searching interpreter by defining some operators in the Expression class that will create And and Or expressions with a little less syntax:[5]

```
class Expression
  def |(other)
    Or.new(self, other)
  end

  def &(other)
    And.new(self, other)
  end
end
```

You knew I was going to come up with a use for the Expression class! With these new operators defined, complex file-searching expressions flow a little more easily off the keyboard. Instead of

```
Or.new(
  And.new(Bigger.new(2000), Not.new(Writable.new)),
  FileName.new('*.mp3'))
```

we can now say

```
(Bigger.new(2000) & Not.new(Writable.new)) | FileName.new("*.mp3")
```

We can even take this syntactic sugaring one step further by defining some convenience methods to create the terminals:

```
def all
  All.new
end
```

---

5. While in principle there is nothing wrong with defining operators for your classes, it is something that is best done in moderation. Zealous overuse of operators tends to make code hard to understand.

```
def bigger(size)
  Bigger.new(size)
end

def name(pattern)
  FileName.new(pattern)
end

def except(expression)
  Not.new(expression)
end

def writable
  Writable.new
end
```

The new convenience methods reduce the file-searching expression above to something even more succinct:

```
(bigger(2000) & except(writable) )  | file_name('*.mp3')
```

The only caveat here is that we can't use the name not for the Not.new convenience method because this name collides with the Ruby not operator.

Let XML or YAML Do the Parsing?

If you do decide that you need a parser, a tempting alternative to building your own is to define your new language in XML or even YAML.[6] If you do this, then you can use the built-in XML or YAML parsing libraries that come with your Ruby installation to handle the parsing. On the surface, this sounds like a great idea—you get to enjoy all of the flexibility and extensibility of a full interpreter and you don't have to mess with the details of a parser. Who could complain?

Unfortunately, your users might well complain. While XML and YAML are great choices for representing data, neither is really ideal for expressing programs. Keep in mind that the main motivation behind building an interpreter is to give your users a natural way to express the kind of processing that needs to be done. If the ideas

---

6. YAML, which stands for "YAML Ain't Markup Language," is a plain text file format used, like XML, to store hierarchical data. Unlike XML, YAML is very human-friendly and is popular with the Ruby community.

embodied in your interpreter can be naturally expressed in XML or YAML, then go ahead and use that format and take full advantage of the built-in parser for that format. But if your language does not fit—and I would venture to guess that most Interpreter pattern languages will not—then don't try to jam your language into the wrong format just to save a bit of coding.

Racc for More Complex Parsers

If your language is fairly complex and neither XML nor YAML seems appropriate, you might consider using a parser generator such Racc. Racc is modeled (and named) after the venerable UNIX YACC utility. Racc takes as input a description of the grammar for your language and spits out a parser, written in Ruby for that language. While Racc is a fine tool, it is not for the faint of heart—learning how to use a parser generator entails a fairly long walk up a steep learning curve.

Let Ruby Do the Parsing?

There is one other answer to the parser question. Perhaps, just perhaps, you could implement your Interpreter pattern in such a way that users could write their programs in actual Ruby code. Maybe you could design your AST API in such a way that the code flows so naturally that your users might be unaware that they are, in fact, writing Ruby code. This is such an intriguing idea that I will leave it for now and devote the next chapter to it.

Using and Abusing the Interpreter Pattern

In my mind, the Interpreter pattern is unique among the GoF patterns that we will look at in this book in that it tends to be underused. Over the years I have seen a number of systems that could have benefited from the Interpreter pattern, systems that laboriously solved their problems with other, less appropriate designs. For example, back in the stone age of databases, a query was a *program* that some database expert laboriously coded. This kind of thing went on for a very long time until the advent of (mostly interpreted) query languages like SQL. Similarly, for many years the construction of even very simple GUIs required the services of a software engineer, who would take days or weeks to spew out page after page of code. Now every middle school kid with access to a keyboard can create reasonably elaborate GUIs, all thanks to the introduction of an interpreted language; we call it HTML.

Why is the Interpreter pattern so widely neglected? Most software engineers who spend their days solving business problems may be expert in things like database design and Web application development, but they may not have thought about ASTs and parsers since that second-year CIS 253 course, if at all. That's too bad. As we have seen, when properly applied, the Interpreter pattern adds a unique flexibility to your system.

We have already touched on the main technical drawbacks of interpreters. First, there is the complexity issue. When you are considering the Interpreter pattern, and especially if you are going to build a parser, think about how complex your language will be. The simpler, the better. Also, think about who will be writing programs in your new language. Will these programmers be experienced software engineers, who will be able to get along with minimal error messages, or will your users be less technical civilians, who may need more elaborate diagnostics?

Second, there is the issue of program efficiency. Remember, it is going to be darned hard to make

```
Add.new(Constant.new(2), Constant.new(2)).interpret
```

run as quickly as

```
2 + 2
```

For all of its flexibility and power, the Interpreter pattern is not a good choice for the 2 percent of your code that really is performance sensitive. Of course, that does leave the remaining 98 percent wide open . . .

Interpreters in the Wild

Interpreters are easy to find in the Ruby world. In fact, we need look no farther than Ruby itself. Ruby is, of course, an interpreted language, albeit a slightly more complex one than is envisioned by the Interpreter pattern.

Similarly, regular expressions—those marvelous pattern-matching beasts that were so helpful when we needed to code our little parser—are themselves implemented as an interpreted language. When you write a regular expression like /[rR]uss/, behind the scenes it gets translated into an AST that matches a couple of variations of my first name.

There is also **Runt,**[7] a library that provides a simple language for expressing things like date and time ranges and schedules. Using Runt, you can write **temporal expressions** that will, for example, match only certain days of the week:

---

7. The Runt library was written by Matthew Lipper and is based on the idea of temporal expressions from Martin Fowler.

```
require 'rubygems'
require 'runt'

mondays = Runt::DIWeek.new(Runt::Monday)
wednesdays = Runt::DIWeek.new(Runt::Wednesday)
fridays = Runt::DIWeek.new(Runt::Friday)
```

With the three objects above, we can discover that Christmas will fall on a Friday in 2015, since

```
fridays.include?(Date.new(2015,12,25))
```

will return `true`, while

```
mondays.include?(Date.new(2015,12,25))
wednesdays.include?(Date.new(2015,12,25))
```

will both return `false`.

As usual with the Interpreter pattern, the real power of Runt shines through when you start combining expressions. Here is a Runt expression that will match the dreaded "all morning long" class schedule that I used to suffer through in my college days:

```
nine_to_twelve = Runt::REDay.new(9,0,12,0)
class_times = (mondays | wednesdays | fridays) & nine_to_twelve
```

Runt is a good example of a parser-less interpreter: It is intended to be a simple, easy-to-use library of classes for Ruby programmers.

Wrapping Up

In this chapter, we looked at the Interpreter pattern. This pattern suggests that sometimes a simple interpreter is the best way to solve a problem. The Interpreter pattern is good at solving well-bounded problems such as query or configuration languages and is a good option for combining chunks of existing functionality together.

The heart of the Interpreter pattern is the abstract syntax tree. You think of your new little language as a series of expressions, and decompose those expressions into a tree structure. How you perform that decomposition is up to you: You can supply your clients with an API for building up the tree in code, or you can write a parser that takes strings and turns them into the AST. Either way, once you have the AST, you can use it to evaluate itself and come up with the solution.

The Interpreter pattern brings with it the advantages of flexibility and extensibility. By building different ASTs, you can get the same Interpreter classes to do different things. It is usually straightforward to extend your language by adding new kinds of nodes to your AST. These benefits carry a cost, however, in terms of performance and complexity. Interpreters do tend to be slow and making them run fast is difficult, so it is probably best to limit your use of the Interpreter pattern to areas that do not demand high performance. The complexity comes from the simple fact that the Interpreter pattern requires a fair bit of infrastructure: You need all of the classes that go into building the AST, and maybe a parser to boot.

In the next chapter, we will look at domain-specific languages (DSLs), a pattern that is closely related to the Interpreter pattern. In particular, we will spend a lot of time examining internal DSLs, an elegant alternative to the sometimes painful job of coming up with a parser for your interpreter.

PART III

Patterns for Ruby

CHAPTER 16

Opening Up Your System with Domain-Specific Languages

In Chapter 15, we looked at the process of creating interpreters to solve certain kinds of problems. The Interpreter pattern is all about using an abstract syntax tree (AST) to obtain the answer or perform the action that you are looking for. As we saw in that chapter, the Interpreter pattern is not really concerned with where the AST comes from; it just assumes that you have one and focuses on how the AST should operate. In this chapter, we will explore the Domain-Specific Language (DSL) pattern, which looks at the world from the other end of the telescope. The DSL pattern suggests that you should focus on the *language* itself, not on the interpreter. It says that sometimes you can make problems easier to solve by giving the user a convenient syntax for expressing the problem in the first place.

You won't find the DSL pattern in your copy of *Design Patterns.* Nevertheless, as we will see in this chapter, Ruby's flexible syntax makes building a particular style of DSL very easy.

The Domain of Specific Languages

Like most of the patterns that we have looked at in this book, the basic idea behind the DSL pattern is not very complicated. You can understand DSLs by stepping back and asking exactly what we are trying to do when we write programs. The answer is (I hope) that we are trying to make our users happy. A user is interested in getting the computer to do something—balance the accounts or steer a space probe to Mars. In short, the user wants the computer to satisfy some requirement. Given that, we might naively ask, why does the user need us? Why can't we just hand the user the Ruby interpreter with a hearty "Good luck!" This is a silly idea because, in general, users do not understand programming and computers; they don't usually know any more about bits and bytes than we know about accounting or celestial mechanics. The user understands his or her one area, his or her *domain*, but not the domain of programming.

What if we could create a programming language that, instead of expressing computer-related ideas, allowed the user say things about his or her domain of interest directly? What if we created a language that allows accountants to say accounting things and rocket scientists to say space probe things? Then that silly idea of just handing the user the language and saying, "Have at it," doesn't seem so bad after all.

Now we could certainly build such a language using all the techniques that we saw in Chapter 15. That is, we could sharpen up our pencil and write a parser for an accounting language or use Racc to create a celestial navigation language. Martin Fowler calls these more or less traditional approaches *external* DSLs. External DSLs are external in the sense that there is a parser and an interpreter for the DSL, and there are the programs written in the DSL, and the two are completely distinct. For example, if we created a specialized accounting DSL and wrote a parser and interpreter for it in Ruby, we would end up with two entirely separate things: the accounting DSL and an interpreter program for it.

Given the existence of external DSLs, we might wonder whether there are also internal DSLs and how they might differ from the external kind. An *internal* DSL, again according to Fowler, is one in which we start with some implementation language, perhaps Ruby, and we simply bend that one language into being our DSL. If we are using Ruby to implement our DSL—and if you have looked at the title of this book, you know we are—then anyone who writes a program in our little language is actually, and perhaps unknowingly, writing a Ruby program.

A File Backup DSL

It turns out that it is actually fairly easy to build internal DSLs in Ruby. Imagine that we want to build a backup program, something that will wake up every so often and copy our valuable files off to some (presumably safe) directory. We decide to do this by creating a DSL, a language called PackRat, that will allow users to talk purely in terms of which files that they want to back up and when. Something like this would do fine:

```
backup '/home/russ/documents'

backup '/home/russ/music', file_name('*.mp3') & file_name('*.wav')

backup '/home/russ/images', except(file_name('*.tmp'))

to '/external_drive/backups'

interval 60
```

What this little PackRat program says is that we have three directories full of stuff that we want copied to the /external_drive/backups directory once an hour (i.e., every 60 minutes). While we want everything from the documents directory backed up, as well as everything except the temporary files from the images directory, we want only the audio files from the music directory. Because we are never in the mood to reinvent things that already exist, PackRat makes use of the handy file-finding expressions that we built in Chapter 15.

It's a Data File—No, It's a Program!

Now we might decide to pull out our regular expressions or parser generator and write a traditional parser for the PackRat program above: We first read a word that should be "backup," then we look for a quote, and then . . . But there must be an easier way. Looking over the backup instructions, we realize that they could almost be Ruby method calls. Wait! They could *be* Ruby method calls. If backup, to, and interval are all names of Ruby methods, then what we have is perfectly valid Ruby program— that is, a series of calls to backup, to, and interval, each with one or two parameters. There are no parentheses around the arguments to those method calls, but of course that is perfectly valid in Ruby.

Just to get things started, let's see if we can't write a little Ruby program that does nothing except read in the backup.pr file. Here is the start of our DSL interpreter, a little program called packrat.rb:

```
require 'finder'

def backup(dir, find_expression=All.new)
  puts "Backup called, source dir=#{dir} find expr=#{find_expression}"
end
```

```
def to(backup_directory)
  puts "To called, backup dir=#{backup_directory}"
end

def interval(minutes)
  puts "Interval called, interval = #{minutes} minutes"
end

eval(File.read('backup.pr'))
```

It doesn't look like much, but this code captures a lot of the ideas that you need to implement an internal DSL in Ruby. First, we have the three methods `backup`, `to`, and `interval`. The key bit of code for our DSL is the last statement:

```
eval(File.read('backup.pr'))
```

This statement says to read in the contents of the file `backup.pr` and run those contents *as Ruby program text*.[1] This means that the `interval` and `to` methods and all those `backup` statements in `backup.pr`—in other words, the things that *looked* like Ruby method calls—will actually be sucked into our program and interpreted *as Ruby method calls*. When we run `packrat.rb`, we get the output of all those method calls:

```
Backup called, source
                dir=/home/russ/documents find expr=#<All:0xb7d84c14>
Backup called, source dir=/home/russ/music find expr=#<And:0xb7d84b74>
Backup called, source dir=/home/russ/images find expr=#<Not:0xb7d84afc>
To called, backup dir=/external_drive/backups
Interval called, interval = 60 minutes
```

It is this idea of sucking in the DSL and interpreting it as Ruby that puts the "internal" into an internal DSL. With that `eval` statement, the interpreter and the PackRat program merge. It is very B-movie science fiction.

---

1. Ruby also features a `load` method that will evaluate the contents of a file as Ruby code in one step, but for the purposes of a DSL the two-step `read` and `eval` method just seems clearer.

Building PackRat

Now that we have our user unknowingly writing Ruby method calls, what should we really do inside those methods? That is, what should `interval`, `to`, and `backup` actually do? The answer is that they should remember that they were called; in other words, they should set up some data structures. To get started, let's create a class that represents the whole backup request. Let's call it `Backup`:

```ruby
class Backup
  include Singleton

  attr_accessor :backup_directory, :interval
  attr_reader :data_sources

  def initialize
    @data_sources = []
    @backup_directory = '/backup'
    @interval = 60
  end

  def backup_files
    this_backup_dir = Time.new.ctime.tr(' :','_')
    this_backup_path = File.join(backup_directory, this_backup_dir)
    @data_sources.each {|source| source.backup(this_backup_path)}
  end

  def run
    while true
      backup_files
      sleep(@interval*60)
    end
  end
end
```

The `Backup` class is really just a container for the information stored in the `backup.pr` file. It has attributes for the interval and the backup directory plus an array in which to store all of the directories to be backed up. The only slightly complex aspect of `Backup` is the `run` method, which actually performs the periodic backups by copying all of the source data to the backup directory (actually a time-stamped subdirectory under the backup directory) and then sleeping until it is time for the next backup. We have made the `Backup` class a singleton given that our little utility will only ever have one.

Next we need a class to represent the directories that are to be backed up:

```ruby
class DataSource
  attr_reader :directory, :finder_expression

  def initialize(directory, finder_expression)
    @directory = directory
    @finder_expression = finder_expression
  end

  def backup(backup_directory)
    files=@finder_expression.evaluate(@directory)
    files.each do |file|
      backup_file( file, backup_directory)
    end
  end

  def backup_file( path, backup_directory)
    copy_path = File.join(backup_directory, path)
    FileUtils.mkdir_p( File.dirname(copy_path) )
    FileUtils.cp( path, copy_path)
  end
end
```

A DataSource is just a container for a path to a directory and a file-finder expression AST. DataSource also has much of the code to do the actual file copying.

Pulling Our DSL Together

Now that we have built all of our supporting code, making the PackRat DSL actually work is easy. Let's rewrite our original backup, to, and interval methods to use the classes we just wrote:

```ruby
def backup(dir, find_expression=All.new)
  Backup.instance.data_sources << DataSource.new(dir, find_expression)
end

def to(backup_directory)
  Backup.instance.backup_directory = backup_directory
end
```

```
def interval(minutes)
  Backup.instance.interval = minutes
end

eval(File.read('backup.pr'))
Backup.instance.run
```

We'll look at this code this one method at a time. The `backup` method just grabs the `Backup` singleton instance and adds a data source to it. Similarly, the `interval` method collects the backup interval and sets the right field on the `Backup` singleton. The `to` method does the same with the backup directory path.

Finally, we have the last two lines of our PackRat interpreter:

```
eval(File.read('backup.pr'))
Backup.instance.run
```

The `eval` statement we have seen before: It just pulls in our PackRat file and evaluates it as Ruby code. The very last line of the program finally starts the backup cycle going.

The structure of the PackRat interpreter is pretty typical of this style of internal DSL. Start by defining your data structures—in our case, the `Backup` class and its friends. Next, set up some top-level methods that will support the actual DSL language—in PackRat, the `interval`, `to`, and `backup` methods. Then, suck in the DSL text with an `eval(File.read(...))` statement. Typically, the effect of pulling in the DSL text is to fill in your data structures; in our case, we ended up with a fully configured Backup instance. Finally, do whatever it is that the user asked you to do. How do you know what to do? Why, by looking in those freshly populated data structures.

Taking Stock of PackRat

The internal DSL technique certainly has some advantages: We managed to create the whole backup DSL in less than 70 lines of code, and most of those are devoted to the `Backup/Source` infrastructure that we probably would have needed no matter how we implemented the program. In addition, with a Ruby-based internal DSL, you get the entire language infrastructure for free. If you had a directory name with a single quote in it,[2] you could escape that quote in the usual Ruby way:

```
backup '/home/russ/bob\'s_documents'
```

---

2. In my view, such a name would be evidence that you had taken leave of your senses, but opinions do differ.

In fact, since this is Ruby, you could also do it like this:

```
backup "/home/russ/bob's_documents"
```

If we were writing our own parser in the traditional way, we would probably need to write some code to deal with that embedded quote. Not so here, because we just inherit it from Ruby. Likewise, we get comments for free:

```
#
# Back up Bob's directory
#
backup "/home/russ/bob's_documents"
```

Our users can also take advantage of the full programming capabilities of Ruby if they want:

```
#
# A file-finding expression for music files
#
music_files = file_name('*.mp3') | file_name('*.wav')

#
# Back up my two music directories
#
backup '/home/russ/oldies', music_files
backup '/home/russ/newies', music_files

to '/tmp/backup'

interval 60
```

The preceding code creates a file-finding expression ahead of time and uses it in two backup statements.

Improving PackRat

Although our PackRat implementation is functional, it is a bit limited, in that we can specify only one backup configuration at a time. If we want to use two or three backup directories, or if we want to back up some files on a different schedule than other files, we are out of luck with our current implementation. Another problem is that PackRat is a bit messy: It relies on the `interval`, `to`, and `backup` top-level methods.

A way around this is to redo the syntax for our `packrat.pr` file so that the user is actually creating and configuring multiple instances of `Backup`:

```
Backup.new do |b|
  b.backup '/home/russ/oldies', file_name('*.mp3') | file_name('*.wav')
  b.to '/tmp/backup'
  b.interval 60
end

Backup.new do |b|
  b.backup '/home/russ/newies', file_name('*.mp3') | file_name('*.wav')
  b.to '/tmp/backup'
  b.interval 60
end
```

Let's see how we can get this to work, starting with the `Backup` class itself:

```
class Backup
  attr_accessor :backup_directory, :interval
  attr_reader :data_sources

  def initialize
    @data_sources = []
    @backup_directory = '/backup'
    @interval = 60
    yield(self) if block_given?
    PackRat.instance.register_backup(self)
  end

  def backup(dir, find_expression=All.new)
    @data_sources << DataSource.new(dir, find_expression)
  end

  def to(backup_directory)
    @backup_directory = backup_directory
  end

  def interval(minutes)
    @interval = minutes
  end
```

```
  def run
    while true
      this_backup_dir = Time.new.ctime.tr(" :","_")
      this_backup_path = File.join(backup_directory, this_backup_dir)
      @data_sources.each {|source| source.backup(this_backup_path)}
      sleep @interval*60
    end
  end
end
```

Because the user will be creating any number of instances, the Backup class is no longer a singleton. We have also moved the backup, to, and interval methods inside the Backup class. The remaining two changes both appear in the initialize method. The Backup class's initialize method calls yield with itself as the only parameter. This allows the user to configure the Backup instance in a code block passed into new:

```
Backup.new do |b|
  # Configure the new Backup instance
end
```

The other change to the Backup initialize method is that the new version registers itself with the new PackRat class:

```
class PackRat
  include Singleton

  def initialize
    @backups = []
  end

  def register_backup(backup)
    @backups << backup
  end

  def run
    threads = []
    @backups.each do |backup|
      threads << Thread.new {backup.run}
    end
```

```
        threads.each {|t| t.join}
    end

  end

  eval(File.read('backup.pr'))
  PackRat.instance.run
```

The `PackRat` class maintains a list of `Backup` instances and starts each one up in its own thread when its `run` method is called.

Using and Abusing Internal DSLs

As we have seen, internal DSLs allow you to apply a unique kind of leverage to certain kinds of problems. But like all tools, they are not without their limitations. As free flowing as Ruby syntax is, you are limited to what you can parse with a Ruby-based internal DSL. For example, you probably could not write an internal DSL in Ruby that could directly parse raw HTML.

Another issue is error messages. Unless you are very careful, errors in the DSL program can produce some pretty strange messages. For example, what if your hapless user accidentally typed x when he or she meant b in the `backup.pr` file:

```
Backup.new do |b|
  b.backup '/home/russ/newies', name('*.mp3') | name('*.wav')
  b.to '/tmp/backup'
  x.interval 60
end
```

The result would be the following error message:

```
./ex6_multi_backup.rb:86: undefined local variable or method 'x' ...
```

To a user who is just trying to specify some files to back up and who knows nothing about Ruby, this error message is, well, less than friendly. With careful coding and judicious use of exception catching, you can frequently mitigate this problem. Nevertheless, these kinds of non sequitur error messages are a constant problem in internal DSLs.

Finally, if security is an issue, stay away from internal DSLs—far, far away. After all, the whole point of an internal DSL is that you take some arbitrary code that someone else wrote and suck it into your program. That requires a toothbrush-sharing level of trust.

Internal DSLs in the Wild

The most prominent example of a pure internal DSL in the Ruby world is probably rake, Ruby's answer to ant or make. The rake DSL syntax is similar to the second version of the PackRat syntax, which allowed for multiple backups.

The rake utility lets you specify the steps that make up your build process as a series of tasks. Tasks can depend on one another. Thus, if task B depends on task A, then rake will run task A before it runs task B. As a simple example, the following rake file backs up my music directories:

```ruby
#
# Directories for my collection of music
#
OldiesDir = '/home/russ/oldies'
NewiesDir = '/home/russ/newies'

#
# Backup directory
#
BackupDir = '/tmp/backup'

#
# Unique directory name for this copy
#
timestamp=Time.new.to_s.tr(" :", "_")

#
# rake tasks
#
task :default => [:backup_oldies, :backup_newies]

task :backup_oldies do
  backup_dir = File.join(BackupDir, timestamp, OldiesDir)
  mkdir_p File.dirname(backup_dir)
  cp_r OldiesDir, backup_dir
end

task :backup_newies do
  backup_dir = File.join(BackupDir, timestamp, NewiesDir)
  mkdir_p File.dirname(backup_dir)
  cp_r NewiesDir, backup_dir
end
```

This rake file defines three tasks. The `backup_oldies` and `backup_newies` tasks do precisely what their names suggest. The third task, `default`, depends on the other two. Thus, when rake tries to run the `default` task, it will first run `backup_oldies` and `backup_newies`.

Aside from rake, there is, of course, Rails. While not a pure, straightforward internal DSL like rake, Rails is full of DSL-like features—bits of code where you can almost forget you are programming in Ruby. Just to take one outstanding example, `ActiveRecord` allows you to specify class relationships in a very DSL-like way:

```ruby
class Manager < ActiveRecord::Base
  belongs_to :department
  has_one :office
  has_many :committees
end
```

Wrapping Up

The Domain-Specific Language pattern is the first pattern that we have examined that is not an original GoF pattern. But don't hold that against it—when paired with Ruby's very flexible syntax, the internal DSL is one of those special techniques in computer science that brings a lot of power and flexibility without requiring a lot of code. The idea behind the internal DSL is really very straightforward: You define your DSL so that it fits within the rules of Ruby syntax; you define the infrastructure required to get a program written in your DSL to do what the DSL program says it should. The punch line comes when you simply use `eval` to execute the DSL program as ordinary Ruby code.

CHAPTER 17

Creating Custom Objects with Meta-programming

In Chapter 13 we looked at the two GoF factory patterns. Both of these patterns try to solve one of the fundamental problems of object-oriented programming: How do you get hold of the right object to solve the problem at hand? How do you get the right parser for your input data? How do you get the right adapter for the database that you need to talk to? Where do you come up with just the security object that you need to deal with *this* version of the specification as opposed to *that* one?

With the factory patterns, the solution was to reduce the problem of getting hold of the right object to the problem of getting hold of the right class; pick the right class and that class will produce the right object for you. This emphasis on picking the right class makes perfect sense when you are dealing with a statically typed language, where the behavior of any given object is completely determined by its class and classes don't change while the application is running. Under those rules, picking the right class is the only game in town.

But as we have already seen, those static rules do not apply in Ruby. Ruby allows you to modify an existing class, modify the behavior of an object independently of its class, and even evaluate strings as Ruby code, right there at runtime. In this chapter, we will look at the Meta-programming pattern, which suggests that we take advantage of these very dynamic behaviors as an alternative way to access the objects that we need. With this pattern, we adopt the perspective that, because in Ruby, classes, methods and the code inside methods are all just programming constructs of one kind or another, a good way to get to the objects that we need is to manipulate those constructs in exactly the same way that we manipulate integers and strings. If this sounds a little scary, it shouldn't: While meta-programming certainly takes a different tack in producing the right object, at its heart this pattern focuses on leveraging the flexibility of Ruby—the same flexibility that I have been going on and on about throughout this book.

Let's start our look at meta-programming[1] by taking yet another run at producing the denizens of our wildlife habitat simulator.

Custom-Tailored Objects, Method by Method

Imagine that we are back in the Chapter 13 jungle, trying to populate it with various plants and animals. The approach we took in Chapter 13 was to use one of the factories to pick the right class for our flora and fauna. But what if we want more flexibility? What if instead of asking for some specific type of organism from a fixed list of possibilities, we want to specify the properties of the organism and get one tailored to our needs? We could, for example, have a method to produce plant life for our habitat, where this method takes some parameters that describe the kind of plant that we are looking for. The punch line is that instead of trying to pick the right class, we could just manufacture the object that we need on the spot:

```ruby
def new_plant(stem_type, leaf_type)
  plant = Object.new

  if stem_type == :fleshy
    def plant.stem
      'fleshy'
    end
  else
    def plant.stem
      'woody'
    end
  end
```

1. You should probably be aware that there is not a tremendous amount of agreement in the Ruby world as to the exact boundaries of the term *meta-programming*. In this chapter, I have tried to cast a reasonably wide net, to try and hit on as many of the meta-programming concepts as possible without worrying too much about the exact definition of the term.

```
    if leaf_type == :broad
      def plant.leaf
        'broad'
      end
    else
      def plant.leaf
        'needle'
      end
    end

    plant
  end
```

The preceding code creates a plain old `Object` instance and then proceeds to tailor this object according to the specifications supplied by the caller. Depending on which options the caller passed it, `new_plant` will add one variant or another of the `leaf` and `stem` methods. The resulting object is more or less unique—most of its functionality does not come from its class (it is just an `Object`, after all) but rather from its singleton methods. In effect, the object that comes out of `new_plant` is made to order.

Using the `new_plant` method is very simple. Just specify the kind of plant you want:

```
plant1 = new_plant(:fleshy, :broad)
plant2 = new_plant(:woody, :needle)

puts "Plant 1's stem: #{plant1.stem} leaf: #{plant1.leaf}"
puts "Plant 2's stem: #{plant2.stem} leaf: #{plant2.leaf}"
```

And that's what you will get:

```
Plant 1's stem: fleshy leaf: broad
Plant 2's stem: woody leaf: needle
```

Of course, there really is no rule that says you need to start your customizations with a plain-vanilla instance of `Object`. In real life, you will likely want to start with an instance of a class that provides some base level of functionality and then tweak the methods from there.

This custom-tailoring technique is particularly useful when you have lots of orthogonal features that you need to assemble into a single object. By simply manufacturing an object to specification, you can avoid creating a whole host of classes with names like `WoodyStemmedNeedleLeafFloweringPlant` and `VinyStemmedBroadLeafNonfloweringPlant`.

Custom Objects, Module by Module

If you would rather not deal with your custom objects method by method, you can always handle this task module by module. Perhaps you have separate modules for plant- and meat-eating animals:

```ruby
module Carnivore
  def diet
    'meat'
  end

  def teeth
    'sharp'
  end
end

module Herbivore
  def diet
    'plant'
  end

  def teeth
    'flat'
  end
end
```

You could also have a second set of modules for animals that are usually up and about during the day like people (well, most people) versus those animals that prowl the night:

```ruby
module Nocturnal
  def sleep_time
    'day'
  end

  def awake_time
    'night'
  end
end
```

```
module Diurnal
  def sleep_time
    'night'
  end

  def awake_time
    'day'
  end
end
```

Because your methods are now bunched up in nice module groupings, the code to manufacture the new objects is a little bit less tedious:

```
def new_animal(diet, awake)
  animal = Object.new

  if diet == :meat
    animal.extend(Carnivore)
  else
    animal.extend(Herbivore)
  end

  if awake == :day
    animal.extend(Diurnal)
  else
    animal.extend(Nocturnal)
  end

  animal
end
```

The `extend` method in this code has exactly the same effect as including the module in the normal way—`extend` is just a bit more convenient when we are modifying an object on the fly.

No matter whether you tailor your objects one method at a time or in module-sized chunks, the ultimate effect is to create a customized object, uniquely made to order for the requirements of the moment.

Conjuring Up Brand-New Methods

Now suppose you receive yet another requirement for your habitat simulator: Your customers would like you to model various populations of plants and animals. For example, they want to be able to group together all of the living things that live in a given area, to group together all of the tigers and trees that share a given section of a jungle or a set of nearby jungles. Oh, and while you are at it, could you please add some code to keep track of the biological classifications of all these creatures, so that we will know that this tiger is of species *P. tigris,* which is part of the genera Panthera, which is part of the family Felidae, and so on up to the kingdom Animalia?

On the surface, what you have here are two separate programming problems: organize the organisms by geographic population on the one hand, and organize them by biological classification on the other hand. The two problems do seem very similar—both have that Composite pattern look to them—but it does seem like you will need to sit down and write some code to handle the population problem and some different code to handle the classification problem. Right? Well, maybe not. Perhaps we can extract out the common aspects of these two problems and implement a single software facility to solve both problems in one go.

Sometimes the best way to approach a task like this one is to imagine what we want the end result to look like and then work backward to an implementation. Ideally, we want to be able to announce in our `Frog` or `Tiger` class[2] that instances of this class are part of a geographic population or part of a biological classification—or both. Something like this:

```
class Tiger < CompositeBase
  member_of(:population)
  member_of(:classification)

  # Lots of code omitted . . .
end

class Tree < CompositeBase
  member_of(:population)
  member_of(:classification)

  # Lots of code omitted . . .
end
```

---

2. I'm going back to the traditional class-based implementations of `Tiger` and `Tree` for this section. It is not that the various meta-programming techniques are incompatible with one another, but rather that trying to explain everything at the same time is incompatible with successfully explaining anything.

What we are trying to say here is that instances of both the `Tiger` and `Tree` classes are the leaf nodes in *two different* composites—one that tracks geographic populations and another that models biological classifications.

We also need to be able to announce that the classes representing species and geographic populations are actually composites:

```
class Jungle < CompositeBase
  composite_of(:population)

  # Lots of code omitted . . .
end

class Species < CompositeBase
  composite_of(:classification)

  # Lots of code omitted . . .
end
```

Ideally, instances of our new tiger, tree, jungle, and species classes would be very easy to use. For example, we should be able to create a tiger and add it to the population of some jungle:

```
tony_tiger = Tiger.new('tony')
se_jungle = Jungle.new('southeastern jungle tigers')
se_jungle.add_sub_population(tony_tiger)
```

Once we have done that, we should be able to get the parent population of our tiger:

```
tony_tiger.parent_population  # Should be the southeastern jungle
```

Finally, we should be able to do exactly the same kind of things with the biological classifications:

```
species = Species.new('P. tigris')
species.add_sub_classification(tony_tiger)

tony_tiger.parent_classification  # Should be P. tigris
```

The `CompositeBase` class, which implements all of this magic, is shown below:

```ruby
class CompositeBase
  attr_reader :name

  def initialize(name)
    @name = name
  end

  def self.member_of(composite_name)
    code = %Q{
      attr_accessor :parent_#{composite_name}
    }
    class_eval(code)
  end

  def self.composite_of(composite_name)
    member_of composite_name

    code = %Q{
      def sub_#{composite_name}s
        @sub_#{composite_name}s = [] unless @sub_#{composite_name}s
        @sub_#{composite_name}s
      end

      def add_sub_#{composite_name}(child)
        return if sub_#{composite_name}s.include?(child)
        sub_#{composite_name}s << child
        child.parent_#{composite_name} = self
      end

      def delete_sub_#{composite_name}(child)
        return unless sub_#{composite_name}s.include?(child)
        sub_#{composite_name}s.delete(child)
        child.parent_#{composite_name} = nil
      end
    }
    class_eval(code)
  end
end
```

Let's analyze this class one bit at a time. `CompositeBase` starts out innocently enough: The first thing that it does is to define a very pedestrian `name` instance variable and an `initialize` method to set it. It's the second method, the `member_of` class method, where things start to get interesting:

```
def self.member_of(composite_name)
  code = %Q{
    attr_accessor :parent_#{composite_name}
  }
  class_eval(code)
end
```

The `member_of` method takes the name of the composite relationship and uses it to cook up a fragment of Ruby code. If you call `member_of` with an argument of `:population` (as our `Tiger` class does), `member_of` will generate a string that looks like this:

```
attr_accessor :parent_population
```

The `member_of` method then uses the `class_eval` method to evaluate the string as Ruby code. The `class_eval` method is similar to the `eval` method that we have seen before, the difference being that `class_eval` evaluates its string in the context of the class instead of the current context.[3] You have probably guessed that the net effect of all of this is to add the getter and setter methods for the `parent_population` instance variable to the class—which is exactly what you need if your class is to be a member of (or, more precisely, a leaf node in) a composite.

The next method in `CompositeBase`, `composite_of`, simply does more of the same—this time adding the methods appropriate for a composite object. Thus, if you call the `composite_of` class method from one of your classes, your class will end up with three new methods: a method to add a subitem to the composite, a method to remove a subitem, and a method to return an array holding all the subitems. Because we construct all of these methods by generating a string and then `class_eval`-ing the string, it is easy to insert the name of the composite into the method names. Thus, when we call `member_of(:population)`, the methods that are actually created are `add_sub_population`, `delete_sub_population`, and `sub_populations`.

---

3. The `class_eval` method is also known as `module_eval`.

The key point to keep in mind about this example is that subclasses of `CompositeBase` *do not* automatically inherit any Composite pattern behavior. Instead, they inherit the `member_of` and `composite_of` class methods, which, if invoked, will add the composite methods to the subclass.

An Object's Gaze Turns Inward

A question that comes up with adding functionality the way we did with the `CompositeBase` class is this: How do you know if any given object is part of a composite or not? More generally, if you are meta-programming new functionality into your classes on the fly, how can you tell what any given instance can do?

You can tell by simply asking the instance. Ruby objects come equipped with a very complete set of reflection features—that is, methods that will tell you all kinds of things about an object, such as the methods that it has and its instance variables. For example, one way to determine whether an object is part of a composite as defined by `CompositeBase` is to look at its list of public methods:

```ruby
def member_of_composite?(object, composite_name)
  public_methods = object.public_methods
  public_methods.include?("parent_#{composite_name}")
end
```

Alternatively, you can just use the `respond_to?` method:

```ruby
def member_of_composite?(object, composite_name)
  object.respond_to?("parent_#{composite_name}")
end
```

Reflection features like `public_methods` and `respond_to?` are handy anytime but become real assets as you dive deeper and deeper into meta-programming, when what your objects can do depends more on their history than on their class.

Using and Abusing Meta-programming

More than any other pattern in this book, the Meta-programming pattern is a very sharp tool that should be taken out of your toolkit only when needed. The key facet of meta-programming is that you are writing programs that augment or change themselves as they run. The more meta-programming that you use, the less your running program will resemble the code sitting there in your source files. This is, of course, the whole point—but it is also the danger. It is hard enough to debug ordinary code, but harder still to debug the ephemeral stuff generated by meta-programming. Thus, while a good set of unit tests is vital in getting garden-variety programs to work, such tests are absolutely mandatory for systems that use a lot of meta-programming.

A key danger with this pattern is the unexpected interaction between features. Think about the chaos that would have ensued in our habitat example if the Species class already had defined a parent_classification method when it called composite_of(:classification):

```ruby
class Species < CompositeBase

  # This method is about to be lost!

  def parent_classification
    #  .  .  .
  end

  # And there it goes  .  .  .

  composite_of(:classification)
end
```

Sometimes you can avoid these unexpected train wrecks by adding a little meta-defensive code to your meta-programming:

```ruby
class CompositeBase

  #  .  .  .

  def self.member_of(composite_name)
    attr_name = "parent_#{composite_name}"

    raise 'Method redefinition' if instance_methods.include?(attr_name)
```

```
      code = %Q{
        attr_accessor :#{attr_name}
      }
      class_eval(code)
    end

    # ...

  end
```

This version of `CompositeBase` will throw an exception if the `parent_<composite_name>` method is already defined. That approach is not ideal but is probably better than just silently obliterating an existing method.

Meta-programming in the Wild

Finding examples of meta-programming in the Ruby code base is a little like trying to find dirty clothes in my son's bedroom—you just have to glance around. Take the ubiquitous `attr_accessor` and its friends `attr_reader` and `attr_writer`. Recall that in Chapter 2, we talked about how all Ruby instance variables are private and that to allow the outside world to get at an instance variable you need to supply getter and setter methods:

```
class BankAccount
  def initialize(opening_balance)
    @balance = opening_balance
  end

  def balance
    @balance
  end

  def balance=(new_balance)
    @balance = new_balance
  end
end
```

Chapter 2 also conveyed the good news that you did not actually need to write all of those silly methods. Instead, you could just insert the appropriate `attr_reader`, `addr_writer`, or the combination punch of `attr_accessor`:

```
class BankAccount
  attr_accessor :balance

  def initialize(opening_balance)
    @balance = opening_balance
  end
end
```

It turns out that `attr_accessor` and its reader and writer friends are not special Ruby language keywords. Rather, they are just ordinary class methods[4] along the lines of the `member_of` and `composite_of` methods that we built in this chapter.

It's actually easy to write our own version of `attr_reader`. Given that the name `attr_reader` is already taken, we will call our method `readable_attribute`:

```
class Object
  def self.readable_attribute(name)
    code = %Q{
      def #{name}
        @#{name}
      end
    }
    class_eval(code)
  end
end
```

Once we have `readable_attribute` in hand, we can use it just like `attr_reader`:

```
class BankAccount
  readable_attribute :balance

  def initialize(balance)
    @balance = balance
  end
end
```

---

4. The `attr_accessor` method and its friends live in the module `Module`, which is included by the Object class. If you go looking for the Ruby code for `attr_accessor`, `attr_reader`, and `attr_writer`, however, you are destined to be disappointed. For the sake of efficiency—but purely for efficiency—these methods are written in C.

We might also recall the `Forwardable` module, which we used to help build decorators. The `Forwardable` module makes creating those boring delegating methods a snap. For example, if we had a `Car` class with a separate `Engine` class, we might say this:

```ruby
class Engine
  def start_engine
    # Start the engine...
  end

  def stop_engine
    # Stop the engine
  end
end

class Car
  extend Forwardable

  def_delegators :@engine, :start_engine, :stop_engine

  def initialize
    @engine = Engine.new
  end
end
```

The line beginning with `def_delegators` creates two methods, `start_engine` and `stop_engine`, each of which delegates to the object referenced by `@engine`. The `Forwardable` module creates these methods using the same `class_eval` technique that we looked at in this chapter.

And then there is Rails. There is so much meta-programming going on in Rails that it is hard to know where to start. Perhaps the most notable example is in the way that you define the relationships between tables in `ActiveRecord`. In `ActiveRecord`, there is one class for each database table. If we were modeling a wildlife habitat in `ActiveRecord`, for example, we might have a table—and therefore a class—for the individual animals. We might also model a complete physical description of each animal in a separate table. Of course, the records in the animal and description tables would bear a one-to-one relationship with each other. `ActiveRecord` lets you express these kinds of relationships very neatly:

```
class  Animal < ActiveRecord::Base
  has_one :description
end

class Description < ActiveRecord::Base
  belongs_to :animal
end
```

You can also express all of the other common database table relationships. For instance, each species includes many individual animals:

```
class Species < ActiveRecord::Base
  has_many :animals
end
```

But each animal belongs to a single species:

```
class  Animal < ActiveRecord::Base
  has_one :description
  belongs_to :species
end
```

The effect of all of this "having many" and "belonging to" kerfuffle is to add the code needed to maintain and support the various database relationships to the `Animal`, `Description`, and `Species` classes. Once we have the relationships that we defined above, we can ask an instance of `Animal` for its corresponding description object simply by saying `animal.description`, or we can get all of the animals that are members of a given species with something like `species.animals`. All of this courtesy of some `ActiveRecord` meta-programming.

Wrapping Up

In this chapter, we took a look at meta-programming, the idea that sometimes the easiest way to get to the code that you need is not to write it at your keyboard but rather to conjure it up programmatically, at runtime. Using the dynamic features of Ruby, we can start with a simple object and add individual methods or even whole modules full of methods to it. Also, using `class_eval`, we can generate completely new methods at runtime.

Finally, we can take advantage of Ruby's reflection facilities, which allow a program to examine its own structure—to look at what is there—before it changes things.

In real life, meta-programming is one of the key underpinnings of the Domain-Specific Language pattern (discussed in Chapter 16). While you can build a DSL with little or no meta-programming—which is pretty much what we did in Chapter 16—meta-programming is frequently a key ingredient in building DSLs that are both powerful and easy to use.

In the next chapter, we will round out our examination of design patterns in Ruby by looking at another pattern that fits well into the meta-programming lifestyle: Convention Over Configuration.

CHAPTER 18

Convention Over Configuration

As the final pattern discussed in this book, we will look at Convention Over Configuration, a pattern that did not originate in *Design Patterns* but comes to us straight from the Rails framework. Convention Over Configuration is arguably one of the keys to the success of Rails. It is a bit different from the other patterns that we have examined in this book in that it is bigger and more ambitious. While the other patterns mostly dealt on the smaller scale of pulling together a number of related classes, Convention Over Configuration is concerned with pulling together whole applications and application frameworks. How do you structure an application or a framework so that it is extensible, so that other engineers can easily add bits to it as the program evolves over time? As we construct ever more ambitious systems, the problem of making them configurable and extensible looms ever larger.

The reaction of the software world to the problem of extensibility reminds me of a quandary I faced when I was in elementary school. You see, I could never decide when to do my homework. Some days I would run home from school, throw open those books, and just *get it over with*. There is nothing like the feeling of just being done with it. But there is also nothing like coming home, chucking the books on the dining room table, jumping on a bike, and heading out for driveways afar. Of course, those stinking books would still be there—and eventually I would have to return, sweaty and tired, and do the homework anyway. Ultimately, I reached a compromise with myself: Do the hated English and boring social studies right after school, and leave the easy math until later in the evening.

Software engineering has gone through an analogous process when it comes to making our systems extensible. Many of us grew up professionally with applications that took pride in their own limitations. These programs supported exactly one protocol, or required that the database schema look just so, or imposed some inflexible interface on hapless users.

The reaction to the heartache produced by this rigidity was to make software systems extensible via configuration. If we pushed the important decisions into a configuration file, we could drive our system to the Utopian ideal of "Hey, just configure me to do what you want." Sadly, we kept right on driving—through downtown Utopia, past the Utopian suburbs, and out into the far side into a new wasteland. We now have configuration-dependent code. We are afflicted with frameworks that are afraid to make the slightest configuration commitment and applications that live in fear that any assumption will inevitably need to be overturned in a hastily arranged patch release.

Java servlets provide a good example of too much configuration. Servlets are a key component of virtually all Java Web applications. A servlet is an elegant little Java class that knows how to handle HTTP requests coming into one or more URLs. But writing a Java class that extends `javax.servlet.HttpServlet` is not enough—not nearly enough. No, you also need to configure the thing, via the `web.xml` configuration file. In its most basic form, a `web.xml` lets you associate a servlet class with an arbitrary name and then associate that arbitrary name with one or more URLs.

And yet, in real life, we rarely need all this flexibility. Mostly—not always, but mostly—we tend to use the class name as the arbitrary name. Mostly—not always, but mostly—we associate the arbitrary name with a URL that bears a startling resemblance to the arbitrary name and, by extension, to the class name. We do so because any name will suffice: best use one that will remind us of the class. And we usually do not care about the exact URL that is fronting our servlet: best use one that reminds us of the class behind the servlet. Programmers (or the good ones, anyway) value simplicity, and the simple thing to do here is to rigorously cancel out all of that flexibility. If you have no use for it, flexibility becomes a danger. All those names and associations become just another way to screw up.

The main motive behind the Convention Over Configuration pattern is to lighten that configuration burden. We want to preserve the essential extensibility of our applications and frameworks, yet get rid of the extraneous configuration. In this chapter we will begin by looking at the principles behind the Convention Over Configuration pattern. Then we will build a hypothetical messaging system showing how you can construct software that, like my final homework strategy, stands in the happy middle ground.

A Good User Interface—for Developers

The problem of writing software that is both flexible and easy to use is a familiar one. Well, it's familiar if you build graphical user interfaces (GUIs) for a living. The folks who build GUIs have evolved a number of design guidelines for creating easy-to-use interfaces:

- *Attempt to anticipate the user's needs.* A good interface tries to make very common tasks nearly effortless—a good interface does the most common case by default. Uncommon or more advanced tasks should still be doable with a bit more effort.

- *Don't make the user repeat himself or herself.* Who among us has not been tempted to put a foot through the CRT when that application asks, for the third time, "Are you sure you want to do this?"

- *Provide a starter template.* Providing your user with a template to build on is another one of those good GUI ideas that we can port to our systems. Don't make your user start with a blank sheet—if he is creating a résumé, give him a résumé template to get him started.

The Convention Over Configuration pattern focuses on applying these same principles to the design of applications and framework APIs. Why save all of the good techniques for the end user? The engineers who are trying to configure your application or program to your API are users, too, and they could use a hand as well. Why not provide a good interface for *all* your users?

Anticipate Needs

No matter whether we are talking about the GUI for an e-mail client or the design of an API, there is one thing that sets a good user interface apart from a bad one: If the user wants to do it (whatever *it* is) a lot, it is the default. Conversely, if the user does not want to do it all that often, it can be a bit harder. This is the reason why moving to the next message in my in-box takes only a press of the down arrow key, whereas doing the configuration for a new e-mail server requires navigating through several menus.

All too often we build APIs that assume every action is exactly as likely as every other action. You can see this assumption in Java servlet configuration—it doesn't matter if I am creating a very commonplace servlet that answers to exactly one URL or a more complex, multipurpose servlet that is hooked up to a number of URLs. It doesn't matter because the more common task takes just about the same amount of work as the less common task. A more considerate interface would make the more common case easy, while requiring somewhat more work for the less common case.

Let Them Say It Once

Another way to drive your technical users crazy is by forcing them to repeat themselves. We know this when it comes to the traditional user interfaces (the kind with menus and icons), but for some reason we tend not to apply the same logic to APIs. How can we avoid making our technical users repeat themselves? We can give them a way to tell us what they want and not ask again. Engineers naturally tend to adopt conventions as a natural part of the way they work. They tend to name files and classes a certain way, to group source files that do similar things in the same directory, and to christen methods with names that follow regular patterns.

The Convention Over Configuration pattern suggests that you define a convention that a sensible engineer might use anyway—put all of the adapters in this directory or name all of the authorization methods this way—and then run with it. Designing a good convention, like designing any good user interface, involves putting yourself in your user's shoes. Try to deduce how your users will behave, what they would call something, and where they would naturally put things; then build your convention around those assumptions. Once you have that convention in hand, get as much mileage out of it as you possibly can—by naming his or her class or putting it in a given directory, the engineer is telling you something. Listen and don't make the engineer tell you again.

Provide a Template

Another thing that you can do is to give your user a kick start by supplying him or her with a model, a template, or an example to follow. Modern word processors no longer expect you to start with a completely blank sheet of electronic paper. Instead, when you create a new document, the program wants to know if it is a résumé, a letter, or a presidential speech. If your document is any one of those or another hundred document types, a good word processor will start you off with the right margins and paragraph styles.

You can do the same for the people who are trying to extend your system: You can give them samples, templates, and working examples to help them get off the ground. If a picture is worth a thousand words, then one or two good examples have got to be worth at least twenty pages of documentation.

A Message Gateway

To see how we can apply these lofty ideals to real code, let's imagine that we have been asked to build a message gateway. Our code will have the job of receiving messages and then sending them on to their final destinations. Messages look like this:

```ruby
require 'uri'

class Message
  attr_accessor :from, :to, :body

  def initialize(from, to, body)
    @from = from
    @to = URI.parse(to)
    @body = body
  end
end
```

The `from` field is a simple string containing something like `'russ.olsen'`, indicating who is sending the message. The `to` field is a URI telling us where we should send the message. The `body` field is a string holding the actual contents of the message. The `Message` class uses the `URI` class, which is a standard part of your Ruby installation, to turn the `to` string into a useful URI object. Initially, the `to` URIs will come to the gateway in three flavors. You will need to send the message out as an e-mail:

```
smtp://fred@russolsen.com
```

Or via an HTTP Post request:

```
http://russolsen.com/some/place
```

Or to a file:

```
file:///home/messages/message84.txt
```

A key requirement of our message gateway is that it should be easy to add new protocols. For example, if we need to send messages via FTP, it should be very easy to extend the gateway to handle the new destinations.

Looking through your favorite book on design patterns,[1] you realize that what you need to handle these different message destinations is an adapter. More precisely, you need three adapters, one for each protocol. In this case, the adapter interface is very simple, consisting of just a single `send_message(message)` method. Here is the adapter that handles forwarding the message as e-mail:

```ruby
require 'net/smtp'

class SmtpAdapter
  MailServerHost = 'localhost'
  MailServerPort = 25

  def send(message)
    from_address = message.from.user + '@' + message.from.host
    to_address = message.to.user + '@' + message.to.host

    email_text  = "From: #{from_address}\n"
    email_text += "To: #{to_address}\n"
    email_text += "Subject: Forwarded message\n"
    email_text += "\n"
    email_text += message.text

    Net::SMTP.start(MailServerHost, MailServerPort) do |smtp|
      smtp.send_message(email_text, from_address, to_address)
    end
  end
end
```

Here is the adapter that uses HTTP to send the message on its way:

```ruby
require 'net/http'

class HttpAdapter
  def send(message)
    Net::HTTP.start(message.to.host, message.to.port) do |http|
      http.post(message.to.path, message.text)
    end
  end
end
```

---

1. This one, of course.

Finally, here is the adapter that "sends" the message by copying it to a file:

```
class FileAdapter
  def send(message)
    #
    # Get the path from the URL
    # and remove the leading '/'
    #
    to_path = message.to.path
    to_path.slice!(0)

    File.open(to_path, 'w') do |f|
      f.write(message.text)
    end
  end
end
```

Picking an Adapter

The next problem that you have is matching up a message with the proper adapter class that will send that message on its way. One solution is to hard-code the adapter selection logic:

```
def adapter_for(message)
  protocol = message.to.scheme
  return FileAdapter.new if protocol == 'file'
  return HttpAdapter.new if protocol == 'http'
  return SmtpAdapter.new if protocol == 'smtp'
  nil
end
```

This hard-coding solution has a problem, however: Anyone adding a new delivery protocol—and therefore a new adapter—would have to dive into the `adapter_for` method to add another adapter. Making someone change existing code does not seem to fall within the bounds of "easily extensible." Perhaps we can do better. Maybe we should have a configuration file that maps protocols to adapter names, something like this:

```
smtp: SmtpAdapter
file: FileAdapter
http: HttpAdapter
```

We could also make this solution work, but with the configuration file we have just traded one form of hard-coding for another. Either way, the person who is adding a new adapter not only needs to write the adapter class, but must also do something else to get the system to recognize the new adapter.

This brings us to the punch line: Why not make writing the adapter class all that is required? If we ask the adapter writer to adhere to the following, very sensible convention, we can reduce the job of adding a new adapter to simply writing the adapter class. Here is the magic convention:

Name your adapter class <protocol>Adapter.

Following this convention, a new adapter to send files via FTP would be called FtpAdapter. If all of the adapters follow this convention, then the system can pick the adapter class based on its name:[2]

```
def adapter_for(message)
  protocol = message.to.scheme.downcase
  adapter_name = "#{protocol.capitalize}Adapter"
  adapter_class = self.class.const_get(adapter_name)
  adapter_class.new
end
```

The adapter_for method pulls the destination protocol off of the message and, using a bit of string legerdemain, transforms a name like 'http' into 'HttpAdapter'. From there it is a matter of a call to const_get to get the class of the same name. With this approach, we have completely lost any hint of a configuration file—to add a new adapter, you simply add the adapter class.

Loading the Classes

Well, almost. We still have to deal with the fact that we need to load the adapter classes into the Ruby interpreter. In terms of code, we need to require in the files that contain the adapter classes:

```
require 'file_adapter'
require 'http_adapter'
require 'smtp_adapter'
```

---

2. You may recall we used this same technique in Chapter 13 to simplify an abstract factory.

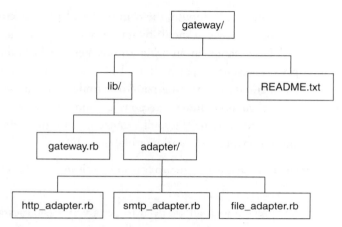

Figure 18-1   Directory structure for the message gateway system

Now we could simply put all of the adapter `require` statements in a file and tell the adapter writer to be sure to add his or her adapter to the list. But once again, we are asking the adapter writer to repeat himself or herself; we are asking the adapter writer to tell us twice that an adapter exists—once by writing and properly naming the adapter class and again by adding it to the list of `include` statements. Besides, we can do better.

Let's start doing better by focusing on directory structures. While we tend to ignore the files and directories that play host to our software, we can actually get a lot of mileage out of conventions based on where various files live. Imagine that we set up a directory structure for our gateway system along the lines of that shown in Figure 18-1.

This directory structure is not particularly original—it is a very common layout for Ruby projects.[3] It is particularly germane to the question of finding adapters because we can use a standard directory structure to solve the problem of loading adapters:

```
def load_adapters
  lib_dir = File.dirname(__FILE__)
  full_pattern = File.join(lib_dir, 'adapter', '*.rb')
  Dir.glob(full_pattern).each {|file| require file }
end
```

3. Perhaps the reason this structure is so common is that you need to lay out a project like this if you want to package it as a gem.

The `load_adapters` method computes the path of the adapter directory by starting with the `__FILE__` constant, which the Ruby interpreter always sets to the path to the current source file. A little manipulation using various methods from the `File` class allows us to come up with a filename pattern for all of our adapters—something like `"adapter/*.rb"`. The method then uses this pattern to find and `require` in all of the adapter classes. This scheme works because `require` is just another method call in Ruby; we can call it from code whenever we need to pull a source file into the Ruby interpreter. We do need to beef up our adapter convention a bit, though:

Name your adapter class `<protocol>Adapter` and put it in the `adapter` directory.

Remarkably, this is pretty much all we need to get a very basic message gateway working. Here is the `MessageGateway` class in full:

```ruby
class MessageGateway
  def initialize
    load_adapters
  end

  def process_message(message)
    adapter = adapter_for(message)
    adapter.send_message(message)
  end

  def adapter_for(message)
    protocol = message.to.scheme
    adapter_class = protocol.capitalize + 'Adapter'
    adapter_class = self.class.const_get(adapter_class)
    adapter_class.new
  end

  def load_adapters
    lib_dir = File.dirname(__FILE__)
    full_pattern = File.join(lib_dir, 'adapter', '*.rb')
    Dir.glob(full_pattern).each {|file| require file }
  end
end
```

Call the `process_message` method and pass in a `Message` object, and in no time your missive will be winging its merry way to its destination.

There are two things to note about our adapter convention. First, the convention focuses squarely on making it easy to add adapters. We did not try to make the whole message gateway easily extensible in every dimension; we just tried to make it easy to add new adapters. Why? Because we anticipate that adding new adapters is what our users (i.e., the future adapter-writing engineers) will need to do. By anticipating that need, we can make life easier for the adapter writer.

Second, while our convention does impose some constraints on the adapter writer—he or she needs to name the adapter just so and put it into the correct directory—these constraints are really quite innocuous. They are, in fact, exactly the kind of thing that a careful engineer would do anyway.

Adding Some Security

Now that we have the basic message gateway working, we need to think about adding some security. Specifically, we want to apply a separate policy to control which users are allowed to send messages to a given host. In addition to the general policy, we need to deal with a variety of special users, who are exceptions to the general policy for a given host.

We can start by deciding to have one authorization class per destination host; this constraint seems acceptable as long as we are dealing with a limited number of hosts. The directory and class name-based convention worked so well for the adapters that we will adopt a similar one for authorization classes:

Name your authorization class <destination_host>Authorizer and put it in the auth directory.

Figure 18-2 shows our updated directory structure.

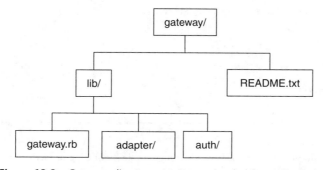

Figure 18-2 Gateway directory structure extended for authorization

Naming the authorization classes after hosts does bring up a problem, however: Host names generally are not valid Ruby class names. What we need is a little string transformation magic. Let's translate a host name like `russolsen.com` to the authorization class `RussolsenDotComAuthorizer`:[4]

```ruby
def camel_case(string)
  tokens = string.split('.')
  tokens.map! {|t| t.capitalize}
  tokens.join('Dot')
end

def authorizer_for(message)
  to_host = message.to.host || 'default'
  authorizer_class = camel_case(to_host) + "Authorizer"
  authorizer_class = self.class.const_get(authorizer_class)
  authorizer_class.new
end
```

But what should the interface for the authorization classes look like? Recall that for any given host, there should be a single set of rules that applies to almost all users. I say "almost" because there may be an exceptional user or two who obey their own rules. For example, we might imagine that anyone is allowed to send short messages to `russolsen.com`, but only `'russ.olsen'` himself is allowed to send really long messages.

One convention we might adopt is that if an authorization class has a method called `<user name>_authorized?`, then we will use that method to authorize the message. Of course, we will have to suitably transform the user name to fit the rules of a method name. If there is no such method, we will fall back to using a generic `authorized?` method. A typical authorizer class might look like this:

```ruby
class RussolsenDotComAuthorizer
  def russ_dot_olsen_authorized?(message)
    true
  end

  def authorized?(message)
    message.body.size < 2048
  end
end
```

---

4. To keep things simple, the `authorizer_for` method does not cope properly with host names that have embedded dashes. Of course, it would not be difficult to cook up some regular expressions to deal with the full range of host names.

The code to implement this policy convention is very straightforward. First, we get an instance of the authorizer for the message that we are processing. Next, we work out the name of the special policy method for the user who sent the message. Finally, we check whether our authorizer object answers to that method. If it does, then that is the method we use. If not, then we use the standard `authorized?` method.

```ruby
def worm_case(string)
  tokens = string.split('.')
  tokens.map! {|t| t.downcase}
  tokens.join('_dot_')
end

def authorized?(message)
  authorizer = authorizer_for(message)
  user_method = worm_case(message.from) + '_authorized?'
  if authorizer.respond_to?(user_method)
    return authorizer.send(user_method, message)
  end
  authorizer.authorized?(message)
end
```

Here is our final authorization convention:

Name your authorization class `<destination_host>Authorizer` and put it in the `auth` directory. Implement the general policy for the host in the `authorize` method. If you have a special policy for a given user, implement that policy in a method called `<user>_authorized?`.

Getting the User Started

There is one other way that we can help the engineer who needs to extend the gateway—we can help him or her get started. Earlier in this chapter, we noted that one of the principles of good interface design is to provide the user with templates and samples to help get started. At one end of the spectrum, we might provide a few examples showing how to create a protocol adapter or an authorizer. At the other end of the spectrum, we could supply a utility to generate the outline or **scaffold** of a class.

For example, we might supply the prospective adapter writer with the following Ruby script, which will generate the bare bones of an adapter class:

```
protocol_name = ARGV[0]
class_name = protocol_name.capitalize + 'Adapter'
file_name = File.join('adapter', protocol_name + '.rb')

scaffolding = %Q{

class #{class_name}

  def send_message(message)
    # Code to send the message
  end

end
}

File.open(file_name, 'w') do |f|
  f.write(scaffolding)
end
```

If we put this code in a file called `adapter_scaffold.rb`, then we can use it to generate a starter adapter for FTP by running

```
ruby adapter_scaffold.rb ftp
```

We end up with a class called `FtpAdapter` in a file called `ftp.rb` in the `adapter` directory.

It is easy to discount the value of this scaffold-generating script. Nevertheless, these kinds of utilities are invaluable to the new user who is overloaded with information about an unfamiliar application or environment, and is struggling just to get started.

Taking Stock of the Message Gateway

We could continue to extend our message gateway, perhaps by adding a transformation step to reformat the message or a flexible auditing facility to log some but not all of the messages. But let's stop here and consider what we have accomplished. We have built a message gateway that is extensible in two different dimensions: You can support new protocols and you can add new authorization policies, complete with exceptions for individual users. We accomplished this with absolutely no configuration files. Instead, the would-be system extender simply needs to write the correct class and drop it into proper directory.

An interesting and unexpected side effect of using conventions is that this approach actually simplifies the main gateway code itself. If we had used configuration files, we would have had to locate and read in the files, perhaps check for errors, and only then begin to set up our adapters and authorization classes. Instead, we simply got on with the task of finding our adapters and authorizers.

Using and Abusing the Convention Over Configuration Pattern

One danger in building convention-based systems is that your convention might be incomplete, thereby limiting the range of things that your system can do. Our message gateway, for example, does not really do a thorough job of transforming host names into Ruby class names. The code in this chapter will work fine with a simple host name like `russolsen.com`, transforming it into `RussOlsenDotCom`. But feed our current system something like `icl-gis.com` and it will go looking for the very illegal `Icl-gisDotComAuthorizer` class. You can usually solve this kind of problem neatly by allowing classes to override the conventions when necessary. In our example, we could allow each authorization class to potentially override the default host name-mapping behavior and specify the hosts to which it applies.

Another potential source of trouble is the possibility that a system that uses a lot of conventions may seem like it is operating by magic to the new user. Configuration files may be a pain in the neck to write and maintain, but they do provide a sort of road map—perhaps a very complicated and hard-to-interpret road map, but a map nevertheless—to the inner workings of the system. A well-done convention-based system, by contrast, needs to supply its operational road map in the form of (gasp!) *documentation*.

Also keep in mind that as the convention magic becomes deeper and more complex, you will need ever more thorough unit tests to ensure that your conventions behave, well, conventionally. There are few things more confusing to users than a system driven by an inconsistent or just plain broken set of conventions.

Convention Over Configuration in the Wild

Rails is still the best example of a system sewn together by conventions. Certainly, our message gateway example lifts many of the Rails convention ideas whole cloth. Indeed, you can trace much of the elegance of Rails to its consistent use of conventions:

- If your Rails application is deployed on `http://russolsen.com`, then a request on `http://russolsen.com/employee/delete/1234` is handled by default by a call to the delete method on the `EmployeeController` class. The `1234` is passed in to the method as a parameter.

- The results of that controller call are, by default, handled by the view defined in the `view/employee/delete.rhtml` file.

- Rails applications typically use `ActiveRecord` to talk the database. By default, a table called `proposals` (note the plural) will be handled by a class called `Proposal` (singular) that lives in a file called `proposal.rb` (note the lowercase) that lives in the `models` directory. A field called `comment` in the `proposals` table shows up unassisted as a field called `comment` in the `Proposal` object.

- Rails comes complete with a whole set of scaffold-generating utilities that help the user create a starter model, views, and controllers.

A typical Rails application is literally sewn together by conventions of one sort or another.

But Rails is not the only example of the wise application of conventions in the Ruby world. RubyGems is the standard software packaging utility used by Ruby applications. It is relatively easy to use, especially if you follow its directory layout conventions—as we did with the message gateway.

Wrapping Up

In this chapter, we looked at the Convention Over Configuration pattern. Convention Over Configuration says that you can sometimes build a friendlier system by binding your code together using conventions based on class names, method names, filenames, and a standard directory layout. By doing so, you can make your programs easily extensible; you can extend your system by simply adding in a properly named file or class or method.

The Convention Over Configuration pattern takes advantage of the same dynamic and flexible Ruby features that make the other two Ruby-specific patterns that we examined in this book possible. Like the Domain-Specific Language pattern, Convention Over Configuration relies heavily on runtime evaluation of code. Like the Meta-programming pattern, it requires a fairly high level of program introspection to function. But these three patterns all share something else: an approach to solving programming problems. Their common message is that you should not just take your language as you find it, but rather mold it into something closer to the tool that you need to solve the problem at hand.

CHAPTER 19

Conclusion

We have come a long way in this book—from our modest beginnings in overriding methods in the Template Method pattern, all the way to dynamically loading classes by convention. During our journey we have seen that the duck-typed, dynamic nature of Ruby changes the way we solve many programming problems. If we need to vary an algorithm that is buried deep in the depths of some class, we might build a Strategy object, but then again we might just pass in a code block. Implementing patterns like Proxy and Decorator—the ones that rely most heavily on delegation—ceases being an exercise in cranking out boilerplate code. The dynamic and reflective features of Ruby let us embrace the idea of a factory while going beyond the inheritance-bound limitations of the classic Abstract Factory and Factory Method patterns. Adapters become less of a problem in a language where we can adjust the interfaces of objects on the fly. External iterators are certainly possible—and occasionally found—in Ruby, but it is the internal iterators that are truly ubiquitous. The internal domain-specific language technique means that we can often use the Ruby interpreter itself as our parser when we build an interpreter.

None of this should really be very surprising. While the appearance of GoF's *Design Patterns* constituted a giant leap forward in the art of writing programs, it has been almost a decade and a half since that book was published. It would be a sad commentary on our profession if, all these years later, we were still solving exactly the same problems in exactly the same ways. Many of the original GoF patterns are truly long-lived solutions, ideas that are likely to be with us for a very long time. But programming has something in common with literature. Translate *Romeo and Juliet* from English into Italian, and you will change the flow of the words, the feeling of the work. Juliet will still be young and beautiful, but Juliet in Italian will somehow be a little different. Translate a design pattern into a different language—into Ruby—and it is still the same, but a little different.

Most of the differences that you will see when you revisit the original *Design Patterns* problems in Ruby stem from the almost unbounded flexibility of the language. When you are programming in Ruby, if you are unhappy with the behavior or interface of some class, you have options. You can certainly wrap instances of the offending class with an adapter. You might decorate or proxy it. You might create a factory to produce those wrapped instances. You might make the factory available as a singleton. And if you are dealing with a complex business object, perhaps one created by some other team in your large organization, all of that might be sensible. However, if you are dealing with some simple object that you understand, you can just modify the object, morphing it to have precisely the behavior that you need. With Ruby, we no longer need to pull out relatively heavyweight design patterns to solve tiny problems. Instead, Ruby allows you to do simple things simply.

One thing that has not changed in the years since *Design Patterns* was published is the need for wisdom. Bruce Tate is fond of pointing out[1] that when a new programming technique or language pops up, there is frequently a wisdom gap. The industry needs time to come to grips with the new technique, to figure out the best way to apply it. How many years had to elapse between the first realization that object-oriented programming was the way to go and the time when we really began to use object-oriented technology effectively? Those years were the object-oriented wisdom gap.

The increasing industry recognition of the value of dynamic and flexible languages such as Ruby has plunged us into yet another wisdom gap. Ruby's powerful features suggest different approaches to the programming problems with which we have wrestled for years. Ruby also gives us the power to do things we have never thought of before. But what things *should* we do? Which shortcuts can we take safely? Which pitfalls must we avoid? With Ruby, we have all of this power at our fingertips, but we need some guidance—some wisdom—to go with it. In this book, I have tried to shed a little light on what to do with the power of Ruby. But as we work our way through the new wisdom gap, we will uncover even more solutions, new design patterns that will fit the dynamic, flexible world of Ruby. I don't know what those new patterns will look like, but I do know that I can't wait to see them. I also know that it is a great time to be a programmer.

---

1. He points it out here, for example:

http://weblogs.java.net/blog/batate/archive/2004/10/time_wisdom_and.html.

APPENDIX A

Getting Hold of Ruby

The good thing about using a popular language is that it is not hard to find. With Ruby, the place to start is the Ruby language home page, located at http://www.ruby-lang.org. What you do from there pretty much depends on what kind of computer you are using.

Installing Ruby on Microsoft Windows

If you are running Microsoft Windows, your best bet is probably the One-Click Ruby Installer, which you can find at http://rubyforge.org/projects/rubyinstaller. This installer will put the basic Ruby environment along with a whole range of useful utilities on your system with only slightly more than one click. Make sure that you enable the RubyGems option to get the standard Ruby third-party code manager.

If you are more of a UNIX-oriented user who happens to use Windows, you might want to look into Cygwin (http://www.cygwin.com), a UNIX-like environment for Windows that comes complete with Ruby.

Installing Ruby on Linux and Other UNIX-Style Systems

If you are using a UNIX-like system such as Linux, you usually have a choice:

- Install a prebuilt package. Chances are that a prebuilt Ruby is available for your system. Make sure that you also install RubyGems to get the standard Ruby third-party code manager. If you use Debian Linux or one of its derivatives (which include the very popular Ubuntu Linux), you should be aware that because of philosophical differences about how software should be packaged, RubyGems is not available as a prebuilt Debian package. If you find yourself in this bind, you might consider building Ruby from source.

- Build Ruby from source. Building your Ruby environment from source is not really very difficult. Simply download the software and follow the instructions in the README file. After you finish with Ruby itself, you will also want to pull down the RubyGems source and build that, too.

Mac OS X

The good news is that OS X Tiger comes with Ruby right out of the box. The bad news is that what comes out of the box is an older version of Ruby. Many—perhaps most—users of Ruby on OS X prefer to build Ruby from source (see the previous section) or to get Ruby from MacPorts (http://www.macports.org/).

As I write this OS X Leopard has been released with much improved Ruby support. So perhaps it is all good news. . . .

APPENDIX B

Digging Deeper

An enormous body of literature has been published on design patterns in the last decade and a half. The literature on Ruby is certainly growing day by day. This appendix points out some of the resources that will be of particular help to the programmer who is interested in both Ruby and design patterns.

Design Patterns

Obviously:

Gamma, E., Helm, R., Johnson, R., and Vlissides, J. *Design Patterns: Elements of Reusable Object-Oriented Software.* Reading, MA: Addison-Wesley, 1995.

I am a big fan of reading the original literature, and if you are interested in design patterns, there is no better source than *Design Patterns.*

Another, less obvious choice, but one that is well worth the time is

Alpert, S., Brown, K., and Woolf, B. *The Design Patterns Smalltalk Companion.* Reading, MA: Addison-Wesley, 1998.

The Smalltalk programming language, as my former small-talking colleagues never tire of reminding me, has all of the good stuff that the rest of us are only now discovering in Ruby, and it had it decades ago. That Smalltalk never really became widely used is perhaps due more to its somewhat strange-looking syntax than to any lack of power or elegance. Language differences aside, *The Design Patterns*

Smalltalk Companion is well worth reading because it is a thoughtful look at applying design patterns to programming in a language that is every bit as dynamic and flexible as Ruby.

A more recent book along the same lines is

Sweat, J. *php\architect's Guide to PHP Design Patterns.* Toronto, ON: Marco Tabini and Associates, 2005.

There is an enormous body of literature on design patterns in various languages, particularly Java. Two Java-oriented books that are worth looking at are

Freeman, E., Freeman, E., Bates B., and Sierra, K. *Head First Design Patterns.* Sebastopol, CA: O'Reilly Media, 2004.

Stelting, S., and Maassen, O. *Applied Java Patterns.,* Palo Alto, CA: Sun Microsystems Press, 2002.

These are two very different books: *Applied Java Patterns* is a very detailed, more traditional treatment, while *Head First Design Patterns* contains a bit less detail but is a lot more fun.

Ruby

By far the most prominent introductory Ruby book is the one by Dave Thomas, Chad Fowler, and Andy Hunt:

Thomas, D., Fowler, C., and Hunt, A. *Programming Ruby: The Pragmatic Programmers' Guide,* second edition. Raleigh, NC: The Pragmatic Bookshelf, 2005.

Programming Ruby is a good all-around introduction to Ruby and its environment and libraries. I have to admit, however, that when I am looking for a truly in-depth discussion of Ruby language issues, the book that I reach for is

Black, D. *Ruby for Rails.* Greenwich, CT: Manning Publications, 2006.

Be aware that despite the name *Ruby for Rails* is about 85 percent Ruby and only 15 percent Rails.

In many ways, Ruby is a language of idioms; there really does seem to be a "Ruby way" of doing things. I have tried to point out the Ruby way of doing things through out this book. If you want to know the Ruby way of doing most anything, look no farther than

Fulton, H. *The Ruby Way,* second edition. Boston: Addison-Wesley, 2006.

The Ruby Way is part cookbook and part introductory text. If you want to know how to do something in Ruby as well as a little bit about why you are doing it that way, this is the book for you. In the same vein is

Carlson, L., and Richardson, L. *Ruby Cookbook.* Sebastopol, CA: O'Reilly Media, 2006.

While books are among my favorite things in the whole world, if you are trying to pick up a new programming language there is a resource that is as important as any book: good programs written in the new language. Anyone who is serious about learning Ruby should spend some time looking at these sources:

- The Ruby standard library. This is all of the code that comes delivered with your Ruby installation. Curious about the `Complex` class? Wondering about `Webrick`? Yearning to know about `URI`? Just have a look, they are sitting right there on your disk.

- Ruby on Rails. Of course, you will also want to look at the Ruby killer application. Be warned, however, that for the most part Rails is pretty advanced Ruby. Don't let that intimidate you—just sharpen your pencil and be prepared to spend some time wondering, "How the heck does that work?" The Rails Web site is http://www.rubyonrails.org.

- Ruby Facets (a huge collection of useful Ruby utilities). Of particular interest for the new Ruby programmer is the fact that many of these utilities are actually extensions to the standard classes that come with Ruby. Worth reading, worth using. You can find the Facets Web site at http://facets.rubyforge.org.

Regular Expressions

I've mentioned regular expressions a number of times in this book. If you haven't already taken the time to learn this incredibly useful tool, it is time to put it at the top of your list. A good place to start is

Friedl, J. *Mastering Regular Expressions.* Sebastopol, CA: O'Reilly Media, 2006.

Blogs and Web Sites

The main Ruby Web site is http://www.ruby-lang.org. Most people who are interested in Ruby will at least be curious about Rails, which can be found at http://www.rubyonrails.org.

There are a number of good Ruby and Rails blogs out there. Here are the ones that I find most useful and interesting:

- Jamis Buck's blog—http://weblog.jamisbuck.org
- Jay Fields's blog—http://blog.jayfields.com
- Ruby Inside—http://www.rubyinside.com (where you will find the collected wisdom of Peter Cooper)

The Web site associated with this book is http://designpatternsinruby.com.

Finally, feel free to see what I am up to at http://www.russolsen.com or e-mail me at russ@russolsen.com.

Index

A

abs method, 26, 169–170
Absolute value, 26, 169–170
Abstract Factory pattern, 16, 239–241
Abstract syntax trees (ASTs) for parsers
  building, 264–267
  complex, 277
  file-finding interpreters, 267–272
  parser-less interpreters, 274–276
  simple, 272–274
  XML and YAML, 276–277
AbstractAdapter class, 173
Account class, 134
Account initialize method, 47
AccountProtectionProxy class
  creating, 178–179
  for delegation, 187–188
AccountProxy class, 186–187
ActiveRecord class
  Adapter pattern, 173
  and DSL, 295
  factory method, 244–245
  magic methods, 260
  migration, 155–156
  observers, 108
  relationships, 310–311
ActiveSupport class
  Decorator pattern, 205
  Singleton pattern, 224–225

adapter_for method, 319–320
Adapter pattern and adapters, 16, 163
  alternatives, 168–170
  in Convention Over Configuration
    example, 316
  examples, 173–174
  file, 319
  FTP, 326
  HTTP, 318–319
  loading, 320–323
  vs. modification, 172
  selecting, 319–320
  single instance modifications, 170–172
  SMTP, 318
  summary, 174
  text rendering, 167–168
  working with, 173
add_child method, 120
add_observer method, 99, 105
add_students method, 48
add_sub_population method, 305
add_sub_task method, 118
AddDryIngredientsTask class, 115–116
AddEmployee class, 158
Addition in Ruby, 24–26
AddLiquidsTask class, 116
addr_writer method, 308
Alexander, Christopher, 4
Algae class, 233, 236
alias keyword, 202

alias_method_chain method, 205
All class, 267–268
all? method, 133
Alternatives
   Adapter pattern, 168–170
   Decorator pattern, 201–203
   Singleton pattern, 215–218
Ampersands (&) in comparisons, 29
And class, 271–272
and operator, 29
Animal class, 311
any? method, 133
Appending array elements, 39
Arguments
   options, 47–49
   parentheses for, 22
Arithmetic operations, 24–26
Array class and arrays
   appending elements to, 39
   as composites, 119
   creating, 38–39
   iterators, 128–133, 135
   methods, 182
   sorting, 39–40, 92
   as strings, 35
   subtraction operator, 270
ArrayIterator class, 128–133, 135
assert method, 72
assert_equal method, 72
assert_not_nil method, 72
Assignments
   shortcuts, 25
   variables, 24, 44
ASTs (Abstract syntax trees) for interpreters
   building, 264–267
   complex, 277
   file-finding interpreters, 267–272
   parser-less interpreters, 274–276
   simple, 272–274
   XML and YAML, 276–277
At signs (@)
   for class variables, 208
   for instance variables, 42
attr_accessor method
   BankAccount, 45, 308–309
   Employee, 96–97
attr_reader method, 45, 308–309

attr_writer method, 45, 308
authorize method, 325
authorized? method, 324–325
authorizer_for method, 324

B

Backslashes (\) for extended statements, 22
Backup class, 287, 291–292
backup method, 285–292
backup_newies task, 295
backup_oldies task, 295
balance method, 44–45
BankAccount
   example class, 41–47
   Proxy pattern, 174–184
Bars (|)
   in comparisons, 29
   Proc objects, 86
basename method, 268
BasicCPU class, 250
Beck, Kent, 4
begin/rescue statement, 52
Berra, Yogi, 14
Big files, finding, 269–270
Bigger class, 269–270
Bignum class, 25–26
Blocks
   as commands, 147–148
   as observers, 104–105
   Strategy pattern, 84–88
Blogs, Ruby, 337
body field in message gateways, 317
Boolean operators, 28–30
break statement, 33
BritishTextObject class, 167–169
BritishTextObjectAdapter class, 168
bto class, 170–172
build utility, 224
builder class, 251–253
Builder pattern, 16, 249
   computers, 250–253
   examples, 259–260
   magic methods, 258–259
   polymorphic, 253–256
   reusable, 257–258
   preventing mistakes, 256–257

summary, 260–261
working with, 259
Button class, 145

C

C programming language, 263–264
C# programming language, 7
  data types, 27
  declarations, 69
  strings, 36–37
  unit tests, 71
call method, 84, 86
camelCase variable names, 23
Car class, 6, 9–10
  delegation, 12–13
  meta-programming, 310
Carnivore module, 300
Case-sensitivity of variables, 23
ChangeAddress class, 159
changed method, 104
ChangeResistantArrayIterator class,
    135–136
Chatty module, 50
check_access method, 179
check_sum method, 199
checksumming_write_line method, 195
CheckSummingWriter class, 199
Checksums, 194–196, 199
Children in composites, 121
class method, 26–27
class_eval method, 305, 310–311
class keyword, 42
class level methods, 210
ClassBasedLogger class, 216–217,
    219–220
Classes
  creating, 41–43
  inheritance, 8
  loading, 320–323
  methods, 209–211
  as singletons, 216–217
  variables, 208–209
ClassVariableTester class, 208–209
clone method, 220
close method, 201
Closure, 84

Code blocks
  and commands, 147–148
  and observers, 104–105
  and strategies, 84–88
Collections. *See* Iterator pattern
Colons (:) for symbols, 37
Command class, 148
Command pattern, 16, 143
  ActiveRecord, 155–156
  for buttons, 145–146
  code blocks, 147–148
  Madeleine implementation, 156–160
  queues, 154
  for recording, 148–151
  subclasses, 144–145
  summary, 160–161
  undo operations, 151–153
  working with, 154–155
Comments, 21
Compilers, 71
Complex parsers, 277
Complex searches, 270–272
Component class, 200
Composite class, 114–115
composite_of method, 305–307, 309
Composite pattern, 15, 111
  arrays, 119
  composites vs. leaf objects, 120
  creating composites, 114–118
  examples, 123–124
  operators, 118–119
  pointers, 120–122
  wholes and parts, 112–114
  working with, 122–123
CompositeBase class
  analyzing, 304–306
  meta-programming, 306–308
CompositeCommand class, 150, 153
CompositeTask class, 117–119, 121–123
Composition and inheritance, 7–12
Computer class, 250–251, 259
computer method, 256–257
ComputerBuilder class, 252–254
Computers, Builder pattern example,
    250–253
Concatenation of strings, 34
ConcreteComponent class, 200

Configuration. *See* Convention Over
        Configuration pattern
Configuration-dependent code, 314
const_get method
    adapters, 320
    IOFactory, 243
Constants, 24, 216
Contexts
    ASTs, 266
    data sharing with strategy, 80–82
Convention Over Configuration pattern, 17,
        313–314
    adapter selection, 319–320
    class loading, 320–323
    examples, 328
    message gateways, 317–319, 326–327
    security, 323–325
    summary, 328–329
    working with, 327
Conventions in GUI development, 316
CopyFile class, 149, 153
Copying files, 149
CPU class, 250
CreateBookTable class, 156
CreateFile class, 148–149, 152
Creators in Factory Method pattern, 232–233
Curly braces ({})
    for code blocks, 85
    for expressions, 35–36
    for hashes, 40
Custom objects. *See* Meta-programming pattern
Cygwin environment, 333

D

Data types, 27
DatabaseConnectionManager class, 222–223
DataPersistence class, 221
DataSource class, 288
<<db_type>>_connection method, 246
Declaring variables, 24, 68–71
Decorator class, 200
Decorator pattern, 16, 193
    components, 200
    delegation, 200–201
    dynamic alternatives, 201–203
    examples, 205

modules, 202–203
overview, 193–199
summary, 206
working with, 204
wrapping methods, 202
def_delegators method, 201
def keyword, 42
Delegation
    Car class, 12–13
    Decorator pattern, 200–201
    for proxies, 187–188
    Strategy pattern, 78–80
delete_observer method, 99
delete_sub_population method, 305
DeleteCommand class, 152
DeleteEmployee class, 158–159
DeleteFile class, 149, 152–153
Deleting
    files, 149
    observers, 99
deposit method
    account, 183
    BankAccount, 43
    missing_method for, 186, 190
describe method, 148
describe_hero method, 49
Description class, 311
DesktopBuilder class, 254–255
DesktopComputer class, 254
<destination_host>Authorizer class, 323, 325
DirectCall class, 190
Directors in builder classes, 253
Distributed Ruby (drb) package, 190–191
Diurnal module, 301
Division, 24–26
do statement, 84–85
Documentation
    Convention Over Configuration pattern,
        327
    rdoc utility, 90–91
doesNotUnderstand method, 184
Dollar signs ($) for global variables, 215
Domain-Specific Language (DSL) pattern, 17,
        283
    examples, 294–295
    file backups, 284–285
    overview, 283–284

PackRat DSL, 284–285
   building, 287–289
   data files, 285–286
   evaluating, 289–290
   improving, 290–293
   summary, 295
   working with, 293–294
Double quotes (") for strings, 22, 34–35
down method in ActiveRecord migrations, 156
downcase method, 34
drb (Distributed Ruby) package, 190–191
Drive class, 251
drive method, 6
DSL. *See* Domain-Specific Language (DSL) pattern
Duck class, 228–229, 233, 236
Duck typing
   safety and flexibility, 69–71
   vs. static typing, 68–69
   Strategy pattern, 82–84
DuckAlgaePond class, 236
DuckPond class, 231
DuckWaterLilyPond class, 234–236
Dynamic alternatives in Decorator pattern, 201–203
Dynamic typing, 24
   with arrays, 39
   safety and flexibility, 69–71
   vs. static typing, 68–69
   Strategy pattern, 82–84

E

each method
   Array, 131
   Hash, 138
   IO, 138
   String, 136
each_byte method
   IO, 139
   String, 136
each_entry method, 139
each_filename method, 139
each_index method, 136
each_key method, 137
each_line method, 139

each_object method, 139–140
each statement, 33
each_value method, 137
Eager instantiation, 214–215
else keyword, 30–31
elsif keyword, 30–31
Email messages
   creating, 259–260
   gateways, 317–319
Employee class, 50–51
   Madeleine implementation, 157
   Observer pattern, 95–105
EmployeeManager class, 157–158
EmployeeObserver class, 108
empty? method, 70–71
EmptyTest class, 71
Encapsulation
   commands, 151
   increasing, 11
   modules for, 49
   preserving, 172
   Proc objects, 147
encrypt method, 164
Encrypter class, 164–166, 173
end statements
   code blocks, 84–85
   loops, 32
Engine class, 10–11, 310
EnhancedIO class, 195
EnhancedWriter class, 194–195
Enumerable module, 133–134
Enumeration interface, 128
eof? method, 165, 173
Equal signs (=)
   for assignments, 44
   with regular expressions, 41
Etc module, 179
eval statement, 286, 289
evaluate method, 265
Exceptions, 52–53
Exclamation points (!)
   for not operator, 29
   with regular expressions, 41
execute method
   AddEmployee, 158
   Command, 150–151
   CompositeCommand, 153

execute method (*continued*)
  CreateFile, 148–149
  Interpreter, 265
  Oracle, 173
execute_command method, 160
Expression class, 267, 275
expression method, 274
Expressions
  regular, 40–41, 274, 278, 337
  in strings, 35–36
extend method, 202–203
Extended statements, 21–22
Extending Factory Method pattern, 237–239
Extensibility. *See* Convention Over
      Configuration pattern
External DSLs, 284
External iterators, 127–133

F

Factory Method pattern, 16, 227–228
  classes, 236–237, 241–242
  examples, 244–246
  extending, 237–239
  names, 242–243
  parameterized methods, 233–236
  pond simulation, 228–230
  summary, 246–247
  template method pattern and, 231–233
  working with, 244
false, 28–30
FalseClass class, 29
__FILE__ constant, 322
File backup DSLs, 284–285
File class, 322
File-finding interpreters, 267–272
FileAdapter class, 319
FileDeleteCommand class, 154–155
FileName class, 268
Files
  copying, 149
  creating, 148
  data, 285–286
  deleting, 149
  finding, 268–270
  sending messages to, 319
  source, 54–55

Find class, 268
find method, 268
Finding files, 268–270
Fixnum class, 25–26
  vandalizing, 169–170
Flexibility in duck typing, 69–71
Floating-point numbers, 25–26
fnmatch method, 268
for_each_element method, 130–131
for loops, 32–33
Formatter class, 78, 81–84
Forward slashes (/) for regular expressions, 40–41
Forwardable module, 200–201, 310
FOX widgets, 124–125
Frame classes, 124
Frog class, 230, 233, 236
FrogAlgaePond class, 234, 236
FrogPond class, 231–232
FrogWaterLilyPond class, 236
from field in message gateway, 317
FtpAdapter class, 320, 326
FXButton class, 124
FXHorizontalFrame class, 124
FXLabel class, 124
FXMainWindow class, 125
FXRuby, 124
FXVerticalFrame class, 124
FXWindow class, 124

G

Gamma, Erich, 4
Gang of Four (GoF), 4
Gateways, message
  extending, 326–327
  overview, 317–319
GenericServer class in WEBrick, 74
Geographical Information System (GIS), 263
get_child method, 120
get_time_required method
  MakeBatterTask, 116
  Task, 115
getc method, 165, 173
getter and setter methods, 45
GetWeatherByZipCode method, 180
GIS (Geographical Information System), 263
Global access, 207–208, 215–216, 220

GoF (Gang of Four), 4
Graphical user interfaces (GUIs), 315
　libraries, 123–124
　needs anticipation, 315–316
　templates, 316
greater than operator (>) for expressions, 28

H

Habitat class, 238–240
Hand waving, 227
Hash class, 137–138
Hashes, 40
Hello World program, 20–22
HelloModule module, 49–50
HelloServer class, 74–75
Helm, Richard, 4
Herbivore module, 300
Hook methods, 66–68
HTML, 277
HTMLFormatter class, 78, 81–83
HTMLReader class, 243
HTMLReport class, 63–65
HTMLWriter class, 243
HTTP Post requests, 317
HttpAdapter class, 318
HttpServlet class, 314

I

if statement, 30–31
Immutable objects
　singleton methods disallowed, 171
　strings, 36–37
include? method, 133
include statement, 49–50
increment method, 209
Indexing
　arrays, 38
　hashes, 40
　strings, 35
Inflections class, 224
Inheritance
　composition over, 7–12
　overview, 46–47
Initialization syntax for hashes, 40

Installing Ruby
　Mac OS X, 334
　Microsoft Windows, 333
　UNIX-style systems, 333–334
instance method, singleton, 212, 214
Instance methods, 42
instance_of method, 27
Instance variables, 42–45
Instances
　modifying, 170–172
　reflection features, 306
Instantiation in Singleton pattern, 214–215
Integers, 25
interactive Ruby (irb) shell, 20–21
InterestBearingAccount class, 46–47
Interfaces, programming to, 5–7
Internal Domain-Specific Language (DSL)
　　　pattern. See Domain-Specific Language
　　　(DSL) pattern
Internal iterators, 130–133
Interpolation, string, 36
interpret method, 265
Interpreter, ruby, 21
Interpreter pattern, 16, 263–264
　AST creation, 272–277
　examples, 278–279
　languages, 264
　parsers
　　building, 264–267
　　complex, 277
　　file-finding interpreters, 267–272
　　parser-less interpreters, 274–276
　　simple, 272–274
　　XML and YAML, 276–277
　process, 264–267
　summary, 279–280
　working with, 277–278
interval method, 285–292
IO class, 138–139
IOFactory class, 243
irb (interactive Ruby) shell, 20–21
isEmpty method, 70
item method, 129
Iterator interface, 128
Iterator pattern, 15, 127
　Enumerable module, 133–134
　examples, 136–140

Iterator pattern (*continued*)
  external iterators, 127–133
  internal iterators, 130–133
  summary, 140–141
  working with, 134–136

J

Java language
  interfaces, 7
  servlets, 314
Johnson, Ralph, 4
join method, 54
Jungle class, 303
JungleOrganismFactory class, 240

K

keys, encryption, 164

L

lambda method, 84
Languages
  DSL. *See* Domain-Specific Language (DSL)
    pattern
  interpreters. *See* Interpreter pattern
LaptopBuilder class, 255, 257–258
LaptopComputer class, 254–255
Lazy instantiation, 214–215
Leaf classes, 114–115, 120
leaf method, 299
Leaf nodes in ASTs, 265
Length and length method
  aggregate classes, 129
  arrays, 38
  strings, 34
Less than signs (<)
  arrays, 39
  Composite pattern, 118–119
  for expressions, 28
Libraries
  GUI, 123–124
  standard, 55
Linux, installing Ruby on, 333–334
Literals, string, 34–35

load method, 286
load_adapters method, 321–322
Loading classes, 320–323
Logging class, 211–215
Loops, 32–34
Lowercase letters for variables, 23

M

Mac OS X, installing Ruby on, 334
Madeleine, 156–160
Magic methods, 258–260
MailFactory builder, 259–260
MakeBatter class, 113
MakeBatterTask class, 113, 116–118
MakeCakeTask class, 117–118
Manager class, 219, 295
Marshal package, 156
math_service proxy, 191–192
MathService class, 191
max method, 133
member_of method, 305–306, 309
member_of_composite? method, 306
merge method, 132
Message class, 317
MessageGateway class, 322
Messages
  creating, 259–260
  gateways, 317–319, 326–327
  passing, 183–184
  sending, 185
Meta-programming pattern, 17, 297–298
  custom-tailored objects
    method by method, 298–300
    module by module, 300–301
    new methods, 301–306
    reflection features, 306
  examples, 308–311
  summary, 311–312
  working with, 306–307
method_missing method
  vs. forwardable, 201
  with magic methods, 258
  Object class, 183–184
  performance, 190
  working with, 184–187

method_name method, 210
MethodMissingCall class, 190
Methods
    class-level, 209–211
    custom-tailored objects, 298–300
    defining, 42
    hook, 66–68
    instance, 208
    magic, 258–260
    new, 301–306
    wrapping, 202
Microsoft Windows, installing Ruby on, 333
min method, 133
Mixins, 51–52
MixTask class, 115–116
Modifying single instances, 170–172
ModuleBasedLogger module, 218, 220
Modules, 49–52
    custom-tailored objects, 300–301
    Decorator pattern, 202–203
    Singleton pattern, 214
    as singletons, 218
Monitor class, 54
Motherboard class, 250
Multiplication, 24–26
Mutable strings, 37
MySQL adapter, 245

N

\n character, 22
Names, variable 23–24
Need for wisdom, 332
Needs anticipation in GUI development, 315
new_animal method
    DuckPond, 231
    DuckWaterLilyPond, 235
    Pond, 232
new_plant method
    DuckWaterLilyPond, 235
    meta-programming, 298–299
NewDocumentButton class, 145
Newline characters, 22
next statement, 33
nil value, 27–28, 30
NilClass class, 28
Nocturnal module, 300

NoMethodError class, 183
Nonterminals in ASTs, 265
Not class, 270–271
not operator
    comparisons, 29
    parsers, 276
notify_observers method
    Employee, 98, 104
    Subject, 102
NumberedWriter class, 203
numbering_write_line method, 195
NumberingWriter module, 197–198, 203
Numbers for strings, 35

O

Object class, 27
    method_missing method, 183–184
    Module module, 309
Object-oriented programming inheritance,
    7–12
Objects
    custom. *See* Meta-programming pattern
    everything is, 26–27
    Factory Method pattern, 236–237, 241–242
ObjectSpace module, 139–140
Observable class, 101
Observable module, 103
Observer pattern, 15, 95
    code blocks, 104–105
    examples, 108–109
    implementing, 100–104
    for information, 95–100
    summary, 109–110
    variations, 105–106
    working with, 106–108
old_write method, 202
old_write_line method, 202
on_button_push method, 144
One-Click Ruby Installer, 333
Operators
    arithmetic, 25–26
    Boolean, 28–30
    Composite pattern, 118–119
Or class, 271
or operator, 29
Oracle adapter, 245

OrganismFactory class, 242
OS X, 334
output_end method, 66
output_line method, 65
output_report method
    HTMLReport and PlainTextReport,
        65, 82
    Report, 80–81
output_start method
    PlainTextReport, 66
    Report, 67

P

PackRat class, 292–293
PackRat DSL, 284–285
    building, 287–289
    data files, 285–286
    evaluating, 289–290
    improving, 290–293
Parameterized factory methods, 233–236
parent_classification method, 307
parent_<composite_name> method, 308
Parentheses () for arguments, 22
Parents in composites, 121
parse method, 274
Parser class, 273–274
Parser-less interpreters, 274–276
Parsers, 265
    complex, 277
    simple, 272–274
    XML and YAML, 276–277
Parts, assembling. *See* Composite pattern
Pass the buck technique, 13
Pathname class, 138–139
Payroll class, 96, 99–100
PDFReader class, 243
PDFWriter class, 243
PlainTextFormatter class, 78, 82–83
PlainTextReport class, 64–66
Plus signs (+) for concatenation, 34
Pointers, 120–122
Polymorphic builders, 253–256
Pond class, 229–232, 234–237
Pond simulation, 228–230
    extending, 237–239
    objects, 236–237

parameterized, 233–236
    templates, 231–233
PondOrganismFactory class, 239
Portfolio class, 54, 134
pos method, 201
Post requests, 317
Pound signs (#)
    for comments, 21
    for string interpolation, 35
PreferenceManager class, 221–223
PrefReader class, 223
Prevayler project, 156
private_class_method call, 213
Proc class
    code blocks, 84–89
    closures, 84
    lambda, 84
process_message method, 322
Products
    builder classes, 253
    Factory Method pattern,
        232–233
Programming to interfaces, 5–7
Protection proxies, 178–179
<protocol>Adapter class, 320, 322
Protocols
    adapters, 319–320
    message gateways, 317–318
Proxy pattern, 16, 175–176
    examples, 190–192
    message passing, 183–184
    message sending, 185
    method_missing method,
        184–185
    protection proxies, 178–179
    purpose, 176–178
    remote proxies, 179–180
    repetitive code, 182–183
    simplifying, 185–189
    summary, 192
    virtual proxies, 180–182
    working with, 189–190
public_class_method method, 219
public_methods method, 306
pull strategy, 106
push strategy, 106
puts method, 21–22

Q

Queries with file-finding interpreters,
    267–272
Queuing up commands, 154

R

Racc parser, 277
Race conditions, 54
raise statement, 52–53
rake utility, 224, 294–295
.rb suffix, 55
rdoc utility, 90–91
readable_attribute method, 309
Recording commands, 148–151
Redoing commands, 151
Regular expressions, 40–41
    information on, 337
    interpreters for, 278
    for parsers, 274
Remote procedure call (RPC) systems, 180
Remote proxies, 179–180
remove_child method, 120
Renderer class, 167
Rendering text, 167–169
Report class
    declarations, 68–69
    hook methods, 66–68
    Strategy pattern, 79–81, 83, 88–89
    Template Method pattern, 59–64, 73–75
require statement, 54–55, 169, 321–322
Resources, 335–337
respond_to? method, 306
ResultSet, 128
return statement, 44
Reusable builders, 257–258
reverse method, 39
reverse! method, 39
reverse_each method, 136
Reversing array elements, 39, 136
rewind method, 201
REXML package, 108
ri command, 91
RIGenerator class, 91
round method, 26
RPC (remote procedure call) systems, 180

Ruby language overview
    arguments, 47–49
    arithmetic operations, 24–26
    arrays, 38–40
    benefits, 17, 19–20
    Boolean operations, 28–30
    classes, 41–43
    current object, 46
    decision statements, 30–32
    exceptions, 52–53
    hashes, 40
    Hello World program, 20–22
    inheritance, 46–47
    instance variables, 43–45
    interactive, 20
    interpreter, 21
    loops, 32–34
    modules, 49–52
    nil value, 27–28
    objects, 26–27
    regular expressions, 40–41
    source Files, 54–55
    strings, 34–37
    summary, 55–56
    symbols, 37
    threads, 53–54
    variables, 23–24
RubyGems packaging system, 55, 333
run method
    Backup, 287
    HelloServer, 75
run_it method, 87
run_it_with_parameters method, 87–88
Runt library, 55, 278
RuntimeException class, 53
RussolsenDotComAuthorizer class, 324

S

Safety
    in duck typing, 69–71
    Singleton pattern, 219–220
SaveButton class, 144
SaveCommand class, 146–147
SAX2Parser class, 108–109
scaffolding, 325
scan method, 274

Searches by file-finding interpreters, 267–272

Security in Convention Over Configuration example, 323–325

select_all method, 173–174

self keyword, 46, 210

SelfCentered class, 46

Semicolons (;) in statements, 21

send method, 185

send_message method, 318

Sending messages, 185

Separating changes from stable code, 5, 61–64

Servlets, 314

set_balance method, 44

setup method, 72

Sharing data between context and strategy, 80–82

Shortcuts, assignment, 25

Simple parsers, 272–274

SimpleLogger class, 211–215, 224

SimpleWriter class, 197–199

Single instance modifications, 170–172

Single quotes (') for strings, 22, 34–35

singleton class, 171

singleton_methods method, 172

Singleton pattern, 16, 207
   alternatives, 215–218
   classes, 216–217
   counts, 221
   examples, 224–225
   global access, 207–208
   lazy and eager, 214–215
   logging class, 211–213
   methods, 209–211
   modules, 214, 218
   safety features, 219–220
   scattered uses, 221–223
   summary, 225
   testing, 223–224
   variables, 208–209, 215–216, 220

size method, 38

Skeletal methods. *See* Template Method pattern

SlickButton class, 144–145, 147

Smalltalk programming language, 184, 335–336

SmtpAdapter class, 318

SOAP, 180

Software adapters, 164–167

sort method
   arrays, 39, 92
   Enumerable, 133

sort! method, 39

Sorting arrays, 39–40, 92

Source files, 54–55

Special characters for delimiting strings, 36

Species class, 303, 307, 311

SQL language, 277

sql method, 173

Square braces ([]) for arrays, 38

start_engine method
   Car, 12–13
   Engine, 310

Statements, 21–22

Static typing, 68–71

stem method, 299

stop_engine method
   Car, 12–13
   Engine, 310

Strategy pattern, 15, 77
   delegation, 78–80
   duck typing, 82–84
   examples, 90–92
   procs and blocks, 84–88
   quick-and-dirty strategies, 88–90
   sharing data between context and strategy, 80–82
   summary, 92–93
   working with, 90

String class and strings, 22
   with ArrayIterator, 130
   iterators in, 136
   methods, 182
   object representation as, 27
   regular expression pattern matching, 40–41
   scan method, 274
   working with, 34–37

String interpolation, 36

StringIO class, 174

StringIOAdapter class, 165–167, 173–174

StringTokenizer interface, 128

sub_populations method, 305

Subclasses, 8, 46–47, 144–145

Subject class, 100–101

subject method, 181–182

Subject module, 102–104
Subjects in proxies, 176
Subtasks, 113
Subtraction, 24–26, 270
succ method, 26
super method, 103
Superclasses, 8, 46–47
Symbols
  for hash keys, 40
  as immutable identifiers, 37

T

\t character, 22
Tab characters, 22
Task class, 113, 115, 121–123
Tate, Bruce, 332
TaxMan class, 99–100
teardown method in tests, 72
Template Method pattern, 15, 59–61
  drawbacks, 77
  examples, 74–75
  hook methods, 66–68
  overview, 65
  for separation of code, 61–64
  unit tests, 71–72
  working with, 73–74
Temporal expressions, 278
Terminals in ASTs, 265
TestMethodMissing class, 184–185
Tests
  Singleton pattern, 223–224
  unit, 71–72
Text rendering, 167–169
TextObject class, 167–168
Thread class, 53–54
Thread safe code, 54
Threads, 53–54
Tiger class, 238, 302–303
Tildes (~) with regular expressions, 41
timestamping_write_line method, 195
TimeStampingWriter class, 199
TimeStampingWriter module, 203
to field in message gateways, 317
to method, 285–292
to_s method, 27
total_num_of_tasks method, 122

Tree class, 238, 302–303
true, 28
TrueClass class, 28–29
truncate method, 26
TurboCPU class, 250
Types, 68–71

U

Underscores (_) for variables, 23
Undo operations, 151–153
unexecute method
  Command, 151
  CopyFile, 153
  CreateFile, 152
Unit tests, 71–72
UNIX-style systems, installing Ruby on,
  333–334
unless statement, 31–32
until loops, 32
up method, ActiveRecord migrations, 156
upcase method, 34
update method, 98, 106
Uppercase letters for constants, 24
URI class, 317
<user name>_authorized? method, 324–325

V

Variables, 23–24
  classes, 208–209
  instance, 42–45
Vehicle class, 9–11
Vertical bars (|)
  in comparisons, 29
  Proc objects, 86
Virtual proxies, 180–182
VirtualAccountProxy class, 181–182
VirtualProxy class, 188–189
Vlissides, John, 4

W

WaterLily class, 233, 236
Web sites, information from, 337
web.xml file, 314

WEBrick library
  singletons in, 207
  Template pattern, 74
while loops, 32
Wisdom gap, 332
withdraw method, 43, 190
Wrapping methods, 202
Writable class, 270
Writable files, finding, 269–270
write method
  wrapping, 202
  WriterDecorator, 201
write_line method, 195, 205
write_line_with_numbering method, 205
write_line_with_timestamp method, 205
write_line_without_timestamp method, 205
Writer class, 203
WriterDecorator class, 197–198, 200–201

X

XML parsing
  Factory Method pattern, 244
  Limitations in Interpreter pattern, 276–277
  package, 108
XMLRPC implementation, 244
XOR encryption, 164

Y

YAGNI (You Ain't Gonna Need It) principle,
    13–14, 244
YAML (YAML Ain't Markup Language) parsers,
    276–277
yield keyword
  Backup, 292
  internal iterators, 130

SHORT CUTS are succinct, to the point, quick-reads on new and existing technologies. They're digital, delivered in Adobe Reader PDF. They're quick to publish. They're a quick-to knowledge. Short cuts will show you how to solve a specific problem and introduce you to a new topic. Written by industry experts and bestselling authors, short cuts are published with you in mind—getting you the technical information that you need now.

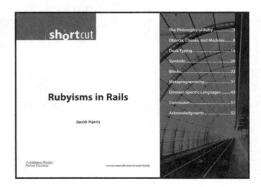

RUBYISMS IN RAILS

JACOB HARRIS | ISBN: 0-321-47407-4

A look at how the grace and philosophy of the Ruby language are reflected in the design of Ruby on Rails. The main goal is simply aesthetic appreciation. But if you are a beginning programmer in Rails who is stymied in your understanding of Ruby—or an intermediate Rails developer still writing code that looks like Ruby-tinged PHP or Java—this short cut will enlighten and inspire you about the Ruby way of programming. It also reveals how the revolutionary design of the Rails framework can only be built upon the beauty of Ruby.

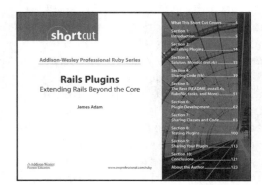

RAILS PLUGINS
Extending Rails Beyond the Core
JAMES ADAM | ISBN: 0-321-48351-0

This short cut introduces Rails plugins and considers each aspect of their behavior and development. You'll learn what plugins are, how they work, and why they're useful. Discover how to find and install plugins using the provided script, then explore the world of plugin development, including common plugin idioms, testing, and version control. Finally, learn how to share your own plugins with the rest of the world.

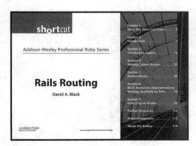